"*Contemporary Advances in Food Tourism Management and Marketing* provides an excellent overview of challenging issues in the field of food tourism. Gastronomy is such an intriguing ingredient in tourism, and the contributions in this book convincingly demonstrate this. It also points to areas to be studied in greater detail in the future, by scholars and by perceptive students and innovative practitioners."

Anne–Mette Hjalager, *Editor-in-Chief of* Journal of Gastronomy and Tourism

"Food tourism is an emerging arena of experiential consumption and co-creation for modern prosumers. The present volume is a welcome addition to enrich the contemporary and future trends of the global food tourism industry. The authors have curated sixteen conceptual and empirical chapters from globally acknowledged experts, making the title increasingly relevant for both food connoisseurs and tourists."

Prof. Saurabh Kumar Dixit, *PhD, North-Eastern Hill University (Shillong, India)*

"This book is an invaluable road map to understand and navigate this fast growing, complex, and exhilarating field of travel. It's the first volume to address such a wide scope of the Food Tourism industry's major components. This book is one of the industry's seminal texts because it weaves empirical research and case studies into a holistic view that inspires thoughtful discussion, fosters greater understanding and nurtures impactful action, for researchers and practitioners alike."

Philip Ruskin, *Owner, Ruskin Consulting, and External Lecturer, ESSEC Business School (Paris, France)*

Contemporary Advances in Food Tourism Management and Marketing

This comprehensive, multidisciplinary and expert-led book provides insight into the most current and insightful topics within food and beverage tourism practice and research, elaborated by leading researchers and practitioners in the field.

The relationships between food and tourism have not only been at the core of recent tourism experiences, but they are expected to be crucial in the transformation of tourism futures. International in approach, this book analyzes the food tourism phenomenon from supply and demand perspectives, from health and politics to high-touch and high-tech, and brings together the relevant issues that inform these contemporary advances in food tourism research and practice. Providing a holistic approach to recent and future trends, the book is divided into 16 carefully selected and specially commissioned chapters that discuss the significance of food tourism research, the management and marketing of contemporary food and beverage experiences, the role of responsibility in the production and consumption of food tourism and the anticipation of future trends in food and beverage tourism. This volume combines academic research with practitioner experience, allowing the authors to explore, debate and analyze our industry's future challenges and solutions.

This book is essential reading for students and researchers with an interest in food tourism, as well as practitioners.

Francesc Fusté-Forné is a professor and researcher at the Department of Business, University of Girona. He holds a PhD in Tourism (University of Girona) and a PhD in Communication (Ramon Llull University). His research is focused on food and rural marketing and tourism. Particularly, he has studied the connections between authenticity, food heritages and identities, landscapes and landscapers, regional development, rural activities, street food and tourist experiences. He also conducts applied research on the role of gastronomy in relation to mass media and as a driver of social change. He has extensively published about these topics.

Erik Wolf is the founder of the culinary travel trade industry and Executive Director of the World Food Travel Association, the world's leading authority on food and beverage tourism. He is the publisher of *Have Fork Will Travel* (a practical handbook for our industry), author of *Culinary Tourism: The Hidden Harvest* and is also a highly sought strategist and speaker around the world on gastronomy tourism. He has been featured in *The New York Times*, *Newsweek*, *Forbes*, and on CNN, Sky TV, the BBC, the Australian Broadcasting Corporation, PeterGreenberg.com and other leading media outlets.

Contemporary Geographies of Leisure, Tourism and Mobility

Series Editor: C. Michael Hall, *Professor at the Department of Management, College of Business and Economics, University of Canterbury, Christchurch, New Zealand*

The aim of this series is to explore and communicate the intersections and relationships between leisure, tourism and human mobility within the social sciences.

It will incorporate both traditional and new perspectives on leisure and tourism from contemporary geography, e.g. notions of identity, representation and culture, while also providing for perspectives from cognate areas such as anthropology, cultural studies, gastronomy and food studies, marketing, policy studies and political economy, regional and urban planning, and sociology, within the development of an integrated field of leisure and tourism studies.

Also, increasingly, tourism and leisure are regarded as steps in a continuum of human mobility. Inclusion of mobility in the series offers the prospect to examine the relationship between tourism and migration, the sojourner, educational travel, and second home and retirement travel phenomena.

The series comprises two strands:

Contemporary Geographies of Leisure, Tourism and Mobility aims to address the needs of students and academics, and the titles will be published simultaneously in hardback and paperback. Titles include:

Resilient Destinations
Governance Strategies in the Transition towards Sustainability in Tourism
Edited by Jarkko Saarinen and Alison M. Gill

Tourism and Innovation, 2nd Edition
C. Michael Hall and Allan M. Williams

Routledge Studies in Contemporary Geographies of Leisure, Tourism and Mobility is a forum for innovative new research intended for research students and academics, and the titles will initially be available in hardback only. Titles include:

Contemporary Muslim Travel Cultures
Practices, Complexities and Emerging Issues
C. Michael Hall, Siamak Seyfi and S. Mostafa Rasoolimanesh

Contemporary Advances in Food Tourism Management and Marketing
Edited by Francesc Fusté-Forné and Erik Wolf

For more information about this series, please visit: www.routledge.com/Contemporary-Geographies-of-Leisure-Tourism-and-Mobility/book-series/SE0522

Contemporary Advances in Food Tourism Management and Marketing

Edited by Francesc Fusté-Forné
and Erik Wolf

LONDON AND NEW YORK

First published 2023
by Routledge
4 Park Square, Milton Park, Abingdon, Oxon OX14 4RN

and by Routledge
605 Third Avenue, New York, NY 10158

Routledge is an imprint of the Taylor & Francis Group, an informa business

© 2023 selection and editorial matter, Francesc Fusté-Forné and Erik Wolf;
individual chapters, the contributors

The right of Francesc Fusté-Forné and Erik Wolf to be identified as the authors of the
editorial material, and of the authors for their individual chapters, has been asserted in
accordance with sections 77 and 78 of the Copyright, Designs and Patents Act 1988.

All rights reserved. No part of this book may be reprinted or reproduced or utilised
in any form or by any electronic, mechanical, or other means, now known or
hereafter invented, including photocopying and recording, or in any information
storage or retrieval system, without permission in writing from the publishers.

Trademark notice: Product or corporate names may be trademarks or registered trademarks,
and are used only for identification and explanation without intent to infringe.

British Library Cataloguing-in-Publication Data
A catalogue record for this book is available from the British Library

Library of Congress Cataloging-in-Publication Data
Names: Fusté-Forné, Francesc, editor. | Wolf, Erik, editor.
Title: Contemporary advances in food tourism management and
marketing / edited by Francesc Fusté-Forné and Erik Wolf.
Description: Abingdon, Oxon ; New York, NY : Routledge, 2023. |
Series: Contemporary geographies of leisure, tourism and mobility |
Includes bibliographical references and index. |
Identifiers: LCCN 2022042189 (print) | LCCN 2022042190 (ebook) |
ISBN 9781032252841 (hbk) | ISBN 9781032252889 (pbk) |
ISBN 9781003282532 (ebk)
Subjects: LCSH: Food tourism. | Tourism–Marketing.
Classification: LCC TX631 .C665 2023 (print) |
LCC TX631 (ebook) | DDC 641.01/3–dc23/eng/20221117
LC record available at https://lccn.loc.gov/2022042189

ISBN: 978-1-032-25284-1 (hbk)
ISBN: 978-1-032-25288-9 (pbk)
ISBN: 978-1-003-28253-2 (ebk)

DOI: 10.4324/9781003282532

Typeset in Bembo
by Newgen Publishing UK

Contents

List of Figures	x
List of Tables	xi
Acknowledgements	xii
List of Contributors	xiii

Introduction	1
FRANCESC FUSTÉ-FORNÉ AND ERIK WOLF	

PART I
Setting the Stage   5

1	Cuisine: A Manifestation of Culture	7
	TRACY BERNO	
2	The Role of Creators, Makers and Other Entrepreneurs	20
	STEVEN SHOMLER	
3	Changing Consumer Culinary Expectations	35
	SUSANA RACHÃO, VERONIKA JOUKES AND CARLOS FERNANDES	
4	Challenging Consumer Culinary Expectations	49
	AMANDA KATILI NIODE	

PART II
From Home to Media   65

5	Food as High Touch	67
	F. XAVIER MEDINA	

viii   *Contents*

6 Food as High Tech   81
ROBERTA GARIBALDI AND ANDREA POZZI

7 The Influence of Media on Food Travel   94
JONATAN LEER

8 The Role of Digital Marketing in the Future of
Food Tourism   108
ANDREA WINTERGERST

PART III
Important Old and New Influences   123

9 Sustainability Issues at the Local Level   125
ISABEL COLL-BARNETO AND FRANCESC FUSTÉ-FORNÉ

10 Responsibility and Sustainability: Everything Has Changed   138
DIVYA VAGHELA AND ULPA CHAUHAN

11 Culinary Culture, Co-Creation and the Sharing Economy   149
ELISABETH KASTENHOLZ, MARIANA CARVALHO AND LUÍS SOUZA

12 Health and Safety Issues in Food and Beverage Tourism   164
ALICIA OREA-GINER

PART IV
Looking towards the Future   181

13 The Changing Face of Gourmet Tourism   183
MATTHEW J. STONE

14 Elevating Gastrodiplomacy's Role in Marketing Identity   197
JOHANNA MENDELSON FORMAN AND KATHIANA LEJEUNE

15 The Double-Edged Role of Cuisine in Both Research
and Practice   212
HENNIE FISHER AND GERRIE DU RAND

16 What's in Store for Food Tourism in the Coming
   10 Years? 228
   BENDEGUL OKUMUS

Conclusion 240
FRANCESC FUSTÉ-FORNÉ AND ERIK WOLF

Index 242

Figures

1.1	Rice with *kap khao* as prepared by the author in Chiang Mai	13
1.2	The author learning to harvest rice in Northern Thailand as part of 'rice tourism'	15
2.1	Lobster roll from LDI Lobster on Little Deer Isle, Maine, America looking out toward the Deer Isle-Sedgwick Bridge which is spanning the Eggemoggin Reach	23
2.2	Bougatsa from the Artos bakery in Goumenissa, Kilkis, Greece	24
2.3	Belizean rice and beans prepared by Executive Chef Enrique Awe, Sirenian Bay Resort Placencia, Belize	25
2.4	A Pork and Chestnut dish prepared by Chef Savas Misirkos. Photo taken at the Chatzivariti Winery Κτήμα Χατζηβαρύτη Goumenissa, Kilkis, Greece	31
3.1	Conceptual model of the food tourism future trends	38
6.1	Summary of the technological applications by the travel stages, the (main) tourist needs, the function(s) of the technology	87
7.1	The NOMA burger	100
7.2	Global Brooklyn in Copenhagen	104
9.1	A Catalan ecological accommodation philosophy	131
9.2	A Catalan ecological accommodation integrated to the environment	133
11.1	Dimensions of co-creation in meal-sharing experiences	156
12.1	COVID-19 infection risk nodes at restaurants considering the level of coverage with the application of COVID-19 protocols	170
12.2	A model of COVID-19, allergen and cross-contamination avoidance protocols in food tourism services	175
15.1	Beef stew with Venda Kale dombolo	220
15.2	Wrap with Venda Kale leaves	221
15.3	Caesar salad with Venda Kale	221
15.4	Carob macaroon with melktert filling and marula ice cream	223

Tables

3.1	Sociodemographic profile of the expert panel members	40
3.2	Results of the Delphi round ($n = 23$)	41
13.1	Attributes of travelers related to gourmet food tourism	185
13.2	Percentage of American travelers in each category	188
13.3	Participation in food/beverage/culinary activities on recent trips. Percentage of respondents who have participated in the following activities while traveling in the past two years	189
16.1	Policy-related food production and supply chain issues that may affect the future of food tourism	231

Acknowledgements

Today we live in a world that none of us could have predicted even 10 years ago. Yet here we are. We would like to thank all the culinary artisans and entrepreneurs in our industry, and in every country, who give tirelessly, time and time again. And despite adverse current affairs, they keep getting back up to start again. To revise again. To create again. To triumph again. Without you and your passion, we would have little impetus to preserve in our culinary cultures. Without you, we would not have been tempted by your tasty creations that have inspired us to continue to enjoy life, and which have inspired others to add value and create again. Food has the power to change, and we have the power to change our cuisine as well. Continue to put your love into everything you create. May you never lose your passion. Thank you for all you do.

The editors would also like to thank all the authors who have contributed to this book, who accepted to participate in this journey and who generously offered their expertise. We appreciate their commitment to the project. We also thank the Routledge editorial support received along the book stages, especially from Emma and Harriet.

Contributors

Tracy Berno is Professor and Associate Dean Postgraduate at AUT University in Auckland, New Zealand. Her interests include the relationship between agriculture, tourism and cuisine, sustainable food systems and food politics. She has researched and published widely on agriculture, culture, cuisine and tourism development in the South Pacific and Asia, and has co-authored three international award-winning books in this area.

Mariana Carvalho is Invited Adjunct Professor at the Coimbra Higher Education School, Polytechnic Institute of Coimbra, Portugal. Her main research areas of interest are experience co-creation, food and wine tourism, the tourist experience, rural tourism, cultural tourism and creative tourism.

Ulpa Chauhan is Director of Genius Concepts B2B at Beyond Bamboo Global, working with organisations to help move them towards becoming a more planet conscious business. She is also the founder of Travel Kind Connect, a non-profit organisation encouraging business and leisure travellers to help rejuvenate environments and communities whilst travelling. Ulpa also facilitates empowerment programmes with RoundTable Global and works on the Global Youth Awards project, championing and awarding young people making a change in the world. She is a TEDx speaker and regularly contributes to blogs, panel talks and webinars around travel, hospitality, sustainability and innovative solutions.

Isabel Coll-Barneto is a recent graduate of the double degree in Business Administration and Management and Economics at the University of Girona. She has started the research in the field of regenerative, conscious and transformative tourism through her final degree projects. She will start her career in the field of auditing and wants to complement it with research into the development of new tourism systems that are in line with the regenerative tourism's principles.

Gerrie du Rand is Associate Professor in the Department of Consumer and Food Sciences at the University of Pretoria, South Africa, now in a post-retirement position. She is recognised academically as a researcher and expert in the field of Food and Hospitality-related consumer behaviour.

xiv *List of Contributors*

Her specialty area of interest is Food Tourism and the use of Local foods in culinary mapping. Her current involvement with postgraduate students focuses on consumer food practices and behaviour, culinary practices, innovative culinary product and recipe development and food tourism. She is also affiliated with WFTA as the Academy director.

Carlos Fernandes is Associate Professor in Tourism Studies at the Polytechnic of Viana do Castelo, Portugal. His research interests include tourism innovation, tourism as a development strategy, gastronomy, religious tourism and diaspora tourism. He co-ordinates the ATLAS Gastronomy and Tourism Research Group; an external expert at IGCAT-International Institute of Gastronomy, Culture, Arts and Tourism; member of the Scientific Commission for the Observatory on Gastronomy Tourism in Italy; external expert for the Platform European Regions of Gastronomy. Researcher at the Centre for Transdisciplinary Development Studies at the University of Trás-os-Montes e Alto Douro and the Centre for Research, Development, and Innovation in Tourism, Portugal.

Hennie Fisher is a culinary arts lecturer in the Department of Consumer and Food Sciences. He holds a PhD in Food Management for which he developed and validated a Food Literacy Measurement Instrument using Rasch Modelling. Other research involves Cultural Food such as the Chikanda of Zambia, Sensory Research regarding Mogodu (a local tripe dish) as well as collaborative work in areas of Food Waste, and modernizing Culinary Training through Flipped Learning and on-line submission of practical preparation documents. Hennie co-authored a book chapter titled 'Eating and Drinking in Southern Africa', edited by Professor Herbert Meiselman. Hennie holds an advanced diploma from the Cordon Bleu School as well as a two-year Diploma from the Cape Wine Academy. Hennie writes about food and wine for the *Pretoria News* and the *Sunday Times*, writes monthly reviews for the Eat Out Restaurant Guide website and contributes to the annual *Eat Out Top 500 Restaurant* print guide. Hennie has contributed regularly to television cooking shows.

Francesc Fusté-Forné is Professor and Researcher at the Department of Business, University of Girona. He holds a PhD in Tourism (University of Girona) and a PhD in Communication (Ramon Llull University). His research is focused on food and rural marketing and tourism. Particularly, he has studied the connections between authenticity, food heritages and identities, landscapes and landscapers, regional development, rural activities, street food and tourist experiences. He also conducts applied research on the role of gastronomy in relation to mass media and as a driver of social changes. He has extensively published about these topics over the recent years.

Roberta Garibaldi is the CEO of the Italian National Tourism Board – ENIT and professor of Tourism Management at the University of Bergamo, Italy. She holds different positions at national and international level, including Advisory Board member at World Gastronomy Institute and President's Council member of the Italian Society of Tourism Science – SISTUR. She is both the author and editor of many books and has written different scientific publications in peer-reviewed journals and books. She has been invited as keynote speaker at major international tourism conferences, including the UNWTO and the World Economic forums.

Veronika Joukes is a researcher at CETRAD. She has a leading role in the Erasmus+ projects SILVHER and CultRural+. Her areas of interest are sustainable/responsible tourism, health and wellness tourism, history of tourism, e−/b-learning in tourism and interactive teaching methods.

Elisabeth Kastenholz is Associate Professor at the Department of Economics, Management, Industrial Engineering and Tourism at the University of Aveiro, where she teaches Tourism and Marketing-related subjects since 1994, also integrating the University's Research Unit Governance, Competitiveness and Public Policies. Her main research interests are rural tourism and related fields (food and wine, nature-based, slow tourism), consumer behaviour in tourism, destination marketing, sustainable destination development, the tourist experience, cultural and accessible tourism.

Amanda Katili Niode is the co-founder and chairperson of Omar Niode Foundation, a nonprofit organization in Indonesia working to foster awareness on local agriculture, food and culinary arts. She is a certified "Food and Climate Shaper" in a program by the UN Food and Agriculture Organization, and the Future Food Institute. She contributed to and edited several books, including *Trailing the Taste of Gorontalo*, listed in the "Gourmand World Cook Book Awards Best of the Best 1995–2020." Her last book is *Choosing Climate Friendly Food and 39 Gorontalo Recipes* (in Bahasa Indonesia). She writes a weekly column on food, environment and climate change at an online news portal. Amanda is a climate reality leader trained by former US Vice President Al Gore, and a certified executive coach specializing in climate and sustainability actions. She holds a PhD from the School of Environment and Sustainability, University of Michigan.

Jonatan Leer is Assistant Professor in Culture and Consumption at Aalborg University. He has published extensively on food culture, including the new Nordic movement, the gendering of food culture, food design and digital food cultures. He has edited *Food and Media* (Routledge, 2016) and *Research Methods in Digital Food Studies* (2021).

Kathiana LeJeune is the author of *The Power of the Palate: Through the Great Exchange*. She currently works as Diversity, Equity and Inclusion Consultant in the Washington, DC metro area. Kathiana is passionate about peace-building policy, women's rights, human rights, women's access to global higher education, diversity and belonging and global public relations. She was inspired to write her book because she realized how food drives our relationships, connections and society. She hopes to harness the power of gastrodiplomacy to pursue its application in conflict resolution and diplomacy.

xvi   *List of Contributors*

F. Xavier Medina holds a PhD in social anthropology. He is the co-director, research director and full professor at the Department of Food and Nutrition, Faculty of Health Sciences, Universitat Oberta de Catalunya, Barcelona, Spain. Director of the UNESCO Chair on Food, Culture and Development. He is the current World Chair of the International Commission on the Anthropology of Food and Nutrition. Director (PI) of the FoodLab Research group on Food, Nutrition, Society and Health.

Johanna Mendelson Forman is a premier expert on gastrodiplomacy, social gastronomy and how food is central to survival and resilience in the world's most active conflict zones. Her lifelong career working with some of the leading organizations in this space led her to create Conflict Cuisine®: An Introduction to War and Peace Around the Dinner Table – a course and curriculum designed to educate about food security, culinary and gastrodiplomacy. Johanna Mendelson Forman is a highly regarded expert in international relations and peacebuilding. She has focused on specific regions of Latin America and the Caribbean, with extensive field experience in Haiti, the Dominican Republic, Central America, Colombia and Brazil. Her extensive list of professional credentials includes her ongoing roles as an adjunct professor at American University's School of International Service and Distinguished Fellow at the Stimson Center, where she also heads the Food Security Program. She is a founding member of the Social Gastronomy Movement, a global organization that uses the power of food to create social change. She is a member of the Council on Foreign Relations, Les Dames d'Escoffier and also serves on the Smithsonian Museum Food Program's Kitchen Cabinet. She is a board member of Creative Learning and Earthspark International.

Bendegul Okumus is Associate Professor at the University of Central Florida's Rosen College of Hospitality Management. She has work experience at theme parks and hotels in Orlando, particularly in food preparation, food services, restaurant management and event management. She also worked at Florida's Orange County Health Department in the Women, Infants, and Children Division as a nutritionist. Her main research areas include food/culinary tourism, healthy eating, eating behaviour in different age groups (school children, Millennials and seniors), food safety in restaurants and food trucks, health and wellness in hospitality, and tourism, mental health and food waste (Google Scholar). Her multidisciplinary and multicultural experiences have emboldened her to develop and teach numerous courses such as Nutrition Concepts and Issues in Food Services, Wellness Management in Hospitality and Tourism, International Cuisine and Culture, Sanitation in the Food Service Industry, Food Sanitation, Event Industry, Marketing in Hospitality and Tourism and Principles of Management and Leadership in Hospitality and Tourism.

Alicia Orea-Giner is Associate Professor in Tourism (tenure track) at the Department of Business Economics (Universidad Rey Juan Carlos) and

Social Technologist for Sustainable Tourism ((*ST*)2). She is Associate Editor at *Tourism Management Perspectives* (JCR Q1) and part of the Editorial Board of the *Journal of Sustainability and Resilience*. In addition, she is a member of the Openinnova research group and collaborates with CETUR. She is an associated researcher at the Équipe Interdisciplinaire de Recherches sur le Tourisme and supervisor of master's theses at Université Paris 1 Panthéon-Sorbonne. She actively participates in international conferences and serves as a reviewer of JCR-indexed journals.

Andrea Pozzi is Research Fellow and Lecturer in Marketing and Tourism Industry at the University of Bergamo, Italy. His main fields of research are food and creative tourism. He is a member of the Italian Society of Tourism Science (SISTUR). He is also a PhD student at the University of the Balearic Islands. Previously he worked as a project manager in European Union co-funded projects in regional bodies.

Susana Rachão is Adjunct Professor at ISAG – European Business School, Portugal. She is a research member at the Centre of Transdisciplinary Studies for Development, UTAD and at CICET – FCVC. Her areas of interest are creative and food-and-wine tourism, innovation and product development and tourism market analysis.

Steven Shomler is a passionate storyteller and life change champion. He has created multiple platforms to celebrate great places, great food and the people who create them. These include the Culinary Treasure Network www.CulinaryTreasureNetwork.com, and the Culinary Treasure Podcast www.culinarytreasurepodcast.com. He inspires and helps people realize their dreams via his own brand of life story alchemy at Spark to Bonfire www.SparkToBonfire.com. You can follow Steven's adventures at www.StevenShomler.com as well as on Facebook, Twitter and Instagram @StevenShomler.

Luís Souza is Adjunct Professor at the Department of Hospitality and Tourism at the Federal University of Pernambuco, Brazil. He focuses his research on 'tourist experience', 'sharing economy in tourism', 'consumer behaviour in tourism', 'tourism and sustainability', 'urban tourism', 'authenticity in tourism'. He is a member of the research unit on Competitiveness, Governance and Public Policies of the University of Aveiro, Portugal, working within the group of Tourism and Development.

Matthew J. Stone is Associate Professor of Marketing at California State University, Chico. His research focuses on consumer behaviour in tourism with a specialization in food tourism research, and he serves as lead research advisor for the World Food Travel Association.

Divya Vaghela is a political science, psychology and master of environment and sustainability graduate from the University of Western Ontario in Canada. Divya specialized in international relations and global climate xviii *List of Contributors*

politics before completing her masters where she gained further insight into how businesses and the planet could work in tandem for a better future. Divya is passionate about creating circular economies and learning about new ways to sequester carbon and swap out components of products to create more sustainable goods.

Andrea Wintergerst is Project Manager at the World Food Travel Association. She holds a bachelor's degree in tourism management (Universidad Anáhuac/ Le Cordon Bleu) as well as a master's in food tourism (Basque Culinary Center). She developed a love for diverse cultures from a young age and has worked in many areas of the tourism and hospitality industry. Andrea moves often, most recently living in San Sebastián, Spain, allowing her to experience and learn from the culinary cultures around her. She writes about this and other tourism-related subjects in her blog, Two Forks and a Passport.

Erik Wolf is the founder of the culinary travel trade industry, and Executive Director of the World Food Travel Association, the world's leading authority on food and beverage tourism. He is the publisher of *Have Fork Will Travel* (a practical handbook for our industry), author of *Culinary Tourism: The Hidden Harvest*, and is also a highly sought strategist and speaker around the world on gastronomy tourism. He has been featured in *The New York Times*, *Newsweek* and *Forbes*, and on CNN, Sky TV, the BBC, the Australian Broadcasting Corporation, PeterGreenberg.com and other leading media outlets.

Introduction

Francesc Fusté-Forné and Erik Wolf

This book delves into the understanding of food and beverage tourism (hereafter, "food tourism") as a consolidated field of research and serves as the ultimate holistic approach to understanding and applying recent and future trends to our industry. The book is divided into 18 chapters (including introduction and conclusion) that discuss the significance of food tourism research, the management and marketing of contemporary food experiences, the role of responsibility in the production and consumption of food tourism, and the anticipation of future trends in food tourism. The book includes a mixture of conceptual and empirical chapters which make it a robust volume, not only in terms of topics, but also regarding the methodological approaches adopted. A group of 26 academics and practitioners from all over the world, representing the five continents, Africa, Asia, Europe, Oceania, and both North and South America, have provided a heterogenous picture of the contemporary advances in food tourism management and marketing.

Food tourism, also referred to as culinary tourism or gastronomy tourism, is a type of tourism which provides the opportunity to gain knowledge about a place, its cultural and natural landscapes, and its people. Also, the relationships between food and tourism have not only been at the core centre of recent tourism experiences, but they are also anticipated to be crucial in the transformation of tourism futures. Often terms like gourmet, wine tourism, agritourism, and beer tourism are used as part of the conversation around the same topic, namely discovering a place through its culinary culture. This book delves into the understanding of food tourism from a multidisciplinary and thought-provoking approach, and it analyzes the food tourism phenomenon from supply and demand perspectives, from health and politics, and from high-touch and high-tech in order to bring together the relevant issues that inform the contemporary advances in food tourism research and practice, positioning the book as a unique work within food and beverage tourism studies that allows the understanding of the current situation of the field and its role in the coming years.

The book is divided into four parts, which help to offer cohesion and coherence to the volume, and highlight the contributions of the book, from the understanding of food as culture, to food as a future driver of tourism systems.

DOI: 10.4324/9781003282532-1

2 *Francesc Fusté-Forné and Erik Wolf*

The first part of the book is entitled *Setting the Stage*. Chapter 1 presents the relationship between cuisine and culture through the ways in which food shapes our individual and collective identities, and it explores how food, culture cuisine and place work in synergy to create deeper and more meaningful experiences for tourists. Chapter 2 acknowledges the role of artisans and designers in the creation and promotion of the food and beverage tourism experience, which is key to offering an authentic product rooted in the territory. Chapters 3 and 4 take a consumer approach, and analyze the changing and challenging culinary expectations of food tourists to identify the trends that drive global food tourism consumption (Chapter 3) and critically discuss the complexity of food systems (Chapter 4).

The second part of the book, *From Home to Media*, takes a holistic approach to the relationships between food and tourism from their internal and external influences. Chapter 5 discusses food as a pathway to show the values that people and places give to gastronomy. Food is a sign of a close relationship between people – the person who serves and the person who consumes are sharing the food moment. This encounter may also happen in a technological environment. Chapter 6 discusses how the increasing adoption of technology in food tourism is revolutionizing the food experience. Chapter 7 delves into the influences of media on food travel and highlights the current omnipresence of media in eating, drinking and travelling. In line with this, Chapter 8 contributes to the understanding of the significance of digital marketing and social media platforms and how they contribute to the development of gastronomy as an essential element in the portfolio of destinations.

The third part of the book is entitled *Important Old and New Influences*. Chapter 9 studies how changes in sustainable practices may result in a transformation of the food and beverage tourism experiences and Chapter 10 is a call to action in relation to the development of a circular model of consumption. Later, Chapter 11 discusses the sharing economy platforms, which facilitate tourists' immersion in local culture and engagement with the genuine features of a territory, through the opportunity of close interaction with local hosts, in daily life contexts. Finally, Chapter 12 delves into the process of change that food service providers have gone through because of the COVID-19 pandemic, as well as the impact of safety standards, allergies and cross-contamination control protocols on the experience of food and beverage tourism.

The fourth part of the book, *Looking Towards the Future*, anticipates crucial drivers of food tourism futures. Chapter 13 explores the changing meaning of gourmet in food tourism and demonstrates how a destination can branch out from gourmet dining to culinary diversity to build a food travel brand that attracts more visitors. Chapter 14 critically discusses the role of gastrodiplomacy in marketing identity, and how citizens can incorporate gastrodiplomacy into their daily food experiences, offering practical examples of different approaches to citizen food diplomacy. Also, countries have the opportunity to promote gastrodiplomacy to forge new connections across both the public and private sectors worldwide, expanding our understanding of the diversity of global

Introduction 3

cuisine. Chapter 15 addresses the contemporary relevance of food offerings and analyzes the bridges between academia and the tourist industry. Chapter 16 discusses future trends and issues in food tourism and proposes possible solutions for its development over the next decade from the perspectives of supply and demand in anticipation of the role of food in tourism futures.

At the end of the book, the editors provide a short concluding chapter where they summarize the main contributions of the book, the importance for theory and practice, and the projection of the book as a source of updated knowledge about food and beverage tourism from the perspectives of management and marketing.

Part I
Setting the Stage

1 Cuisine

A Manifestation of Culture

Tracy Berno

Introduction

Several years ago, I was invited to be a speaker at a gastronomy tourism forum in Bangkok. I was to be part of an expert panel discussing the "four pillars of gastronomy tourism" (Berno, Dodd & Wisansing, 2019) in Thailand: (1) farming systems; (2) the story of food; (3) the creative industries; and (4) sustainable tourism. I had been asked to speak on the topic "what is gastronomy tourism?" It was very important to me to convey the essence of the relationship between food, culture and identity within gastronomy tourism and how important this is to experiencing a destination in a deep and meaningful way. As I sat on the stage listening to the other panellists, I realised that what I had so carefully prepared in anticipation of the event was not going to do justice to what I really wanted to share. As I started to re-construct my presentation in my mind, a single grain of rice on the floor by my chair caught my eye. It had been left behind after a traditional rice folk dance performance earlier in the day. Suddenly, I realized what it was that I wanted to say. When my time came to speak, I leaned over and quietly picked up the single grain of rice and placed it in the palm of my hand. As I took my place at the podium, I held out my hand with the single grain of rice, scanned the faces in the audience and said "This is gastronomy tourism in Thailand".

The chapter commences with a discussion of the relationship between food and identity. This relationship is further developed to consider the relationship between food, culture, cuisine and place. Following this, the role of food and cuisine in tourism in terms of placemaking is discussed. The story of rice in Thailand provides an example of the importance of how food offers a gateway for tourists to engage in local culture in a meaningful and authentic way.

Food and Identity

Food, foodways and food traditions are among the most fundamental elements of culture. Every living organism eats. Or as Timothy (2015: 1) rightly points out, "[h]umans have a habit of eating". Food, however, is not just an edible product that provides nutritional sustenance; food is central to our sense of

DOI: 10.4324/9781003282532-3

8 *Tracy Berno*

individual and collective cultural identity. For humans, food is "the sense of identity which is at the core of human autonomy. The biological need for food and the social act of eating combine to give … a particular meaning, a kind of cultural power" (Simpson, 1996: 6).

The choices that we make about food, whether it is as a group or as an individual, reveal a great deal of information about us. As Lawrence and Tushman (2020:34) suggest, "Food choices tell stories of communities, tribes, families, the adaptation, resistance, changes over times, and personal and peer identity. By closely examining the reasons for our food choices, we come closer to understanding ourselves and the society". The way in which a particular group of people eats asserts its diversity, hierarchy and organization. Food reflects the cultural norms and values of people, places and times. It reveals the realities of geography and place. It tells a story of humankind's struggle to control and subdue nature (Timothy, 2015). Timothy (2007) suggests that cuisine and foodways provide insight into the history of humankind in ways that other elements of human culture cannot, making gastronomic traditions among the most pervasive and obvious elements of cultural heritage and identity (Di Giovine & Brulotte, 2016).

Food helps us define belongingness and otherness by shaping our collective identity in three separate, but related ways: (1) common characteristics uniting a given community (sameness); (2) unique characteristics that reinforce the distinctiveness of a community (singularity); and, (3) other food practices — elements that reinforce differences in reference to other communities that do not share the same characteristics or tastes (difference) (Ruiz, 2018). On an individual level, we are all constructed biologically, psychologically and socially by the food that we consume. Food not only nourishes us, but it also signifies us (Fischler, 1988). We are, indeed, what we eat.

Food, in a similar way to language, is also a powerful vehicle for expressing culture (Lawrence & Tushman, 2020). As Barthes (1979: 167) suggested when asking "For what is food? It is not only a collection of products that can be used for statistical or nutritional studies. It is also, and at the same time, a system of communication, a body of images, a protocol of usages, situations, and behavior." Kittler, Sucher and Nelms (2017: 4) further suggest that "[e]ating is a daily reaffirmation of [one's] cultural identity". Indeed, food is increasingly regarded as a multidimensional, commonplace artifact which incorporates the very identity of a place or individual (Kunwar, 2017).

This expression of cultural identity through food is what we refer to as cuisine. Cuisine, by definition, is a particular style of rules, ingredients and food preparations characteristic of a region. Cuisine, as opposed to food, is a key characteristic that differentiates us from animals and is one of the things that makes us human. Its meaning and significance, however, is much deeper than this simplistic definition suggests. Cuisine is the outcome of a region's unique history, its products/ingredients (and their terroir, discussed further below), and the social norms and customs of the group that dictate the way in which food is prepared and consumed. The ways in which we transform ingredients into cuisine, the cultural classifications and rules that dictate, is one of the ways that we as humans bring order and meaning to our world (Fischler, 1988). Cuisine is imbued with social and cultural capital and is a significant marker of intangible cultural heritage (Berno, 2017a). Timothy (2015) goes as far as to suggest that all components of culture, whether it be communication, cognition, material objects or behaviour, are all connected to food in some way. As such, cuisine is about more than just the sum of its (food) parts; cuisine, like other art forms, is a powerful communicator of history, tradition, custom, ritual, culture, sociality, organization, uniqueness and celebration (Berno, 2017b; Ruiz, 2018).

Food, Culture, Cuisine and Place

A key activity that can create synergies between culture, history and nature is an exploration of cuisine, place and people (Berno, Rajalingam, Miranda & Ximenes, 2022). Place, in this sense, is not exclusively geographic, it is a product of the intersection of social relations, expressions of identity and the practice of culture (Appadurai, 1996). Food is an important component of sense of place. Geography has a large influence on the taste of food and the range of products produced. This reflects important place-specific "geographies of taste" (Montanari, 2002, 2009). Place-based consumption provides a platform through which a visitor can be engaged more deeply with a destination through its food. A tourist who eats local cuisine that originated in a particular locale is not only incorporating the nutritional characteristics of the food, but is also 'tasting' its symbolic features: nature, culture and the identity of the area (Berno, Wisansing & Dentice, 2020). Consuming regional specialities at their point of origin,

> is an act of complicity with the place, a way of becoming a part of the intimacy of that place and of the other, a symbolic consumption of a land, a region, a province, its climate, its history, its scenery ... embodying it in a real sense.
>
> (Bessière, 2001: 117)

One of the main ways in which this territorial uniqueness is communicated is through the concept of terroir. Although the term terroir is normally associated with the wine growing regions of France it is now applied internationally to both food and wine products. The concept of terroir is complex and does not just include environmental aspects such as climate, water, sunshine exposure, soil and topography but also integrates the agronomic, social and cultural dimensions of the place, with each of the individual components of terroir interacting in a dynamic way to influence flavor and other inherent characteristics (Harrington, 2005; Trubek, 2008). As such, terroir is not only the place itself, but also the relationship that exists between the land and the people that work it (Deloire, Prévost & Kelly, 2008; Fusté-Forné & Berno, 2016). Similar to Adema's (2007) suggestion that a foodscape has both a tangible manifestation (one that can be heard, smelled, tasted, and touched) and an intangible element (one that evokes an affective response), when a person consumes a product with terroir association, they consume both the physical product and the emotional and psychological representations of the terroir. In essence, along with the landscapes and foodscapes, they consume the intangible aspects of the place itself (Deloire et al., 2008; Fusté-Forné & Berno, 2016). In this way, food and place are inseparably intertwined (Feagan, 2007).

Related to the concept of terroir, McNeill (1974) talked about the natural relationship between the land, its climate and the qualities of the food produced on it. It is this geographical diversity which contributes to the distinctiveness of regional culinary traditions and the evolution of their cultural heritage. The authenticity of the cuisine is reflected in both natural and cultural components (Fusté-Forné, 2015; Hashimoto & Telfer, 2008; Kim & Ellis, 2015; Sims, 2009). On the one hand, the unique physical environment of a region lends itself to the development of a distinctive cuisine; on the other hand, the cultural component represents the values, ethos and beliefs shared by the local community (Alonso, 2013; Bèssiere, 2013; Cohen & Avieli, 2004; Gyimóthy & Mykletun, 2009; Staiff & Bushell, 2013). Both components contribute to food being a material part of cultural identity, ensuring its continuity and providing evidence of its commitment to the region (Fusté-Forné & Berno, 2016; Hillel, Belhassen & Shani, 2013).

Similarly, the connection between food and people is not static; it is a dynamic and continuously changing relationship (Abarca & Colby, 2016; Harrington, 2005; Santich, 2009). Food and its cultural expression (cuisine) are a function of place and time. In this way, the connections between food, history and memory "produce narratives of personal and collective cultural and social identity … by which people's emotional, psychological, social, economic, political, historical, and cultural realities are embodied social and cultural realities" (Abarca & Colby, 2016: 4). It is not our food that defines social and cultural subjectivities, rather it is the narratives, the food stories that we tell that do so (Berno et al., 2022; Abarca & Colby, 2016).

Culture and cuisine have a symbiotic relationship: culture can be represented in cuisine and cuisine can be an expression of individual and collective cultural identity (Berno, Dentice & Wisansing, 2019; Santich, 2009). Concomitantly, culture shapes cuisine and cuisine shapes culture. Culture enshrines and perpetuates eating habits. Progressively, these eating habits become respected, and, ultimately, transform into traditions. Culture and tradition shape the way these foods are viewed and used, and these tastes become part of a place or region's identity, "the mainstay of its gastronomic character" (Santich, 2009: 58). Over time, particular dishes and/or ingredients come to be associated with a specific place. As Santich (2009: 125) points out:

> While cuisine is both practice and product, a medium of cultural expression and a consumable artifact produced by culture, it is the latter aspect that tends to dominate, such that a national or regional cuisine is usually described in terms of characteristic and customary dishes which in

turn come to epitomise the culture. Alin Laubreaux had such an interpretation in mind when he wrote in *The Happy Glutton* (1931) that a 'cookery book will tell you more about the soul of a country than a whole row of Baedeckers'.

(Santich, 2009: 125)

Food, Culture and Tourism

Considering these realities of place and culture, particular ingredients and dishes have become intrinsically connected with specific regions, thus "forming a gastronomy-driven heritage identity that often translates into tourism potential" (Timothy & Ron, 2013: 281). Tourists are some of the most pervasive consumers of cultural heritage (Timothy 2015). For years, many countries have used cuisine as cultural heritage as a platform to differentiate and promote themselves as destinations by inviting tourists to literally consume and 'taste' local culture (Berno, Dentice & Wisansing, 2019). It is this relationship between food and culture that encourages many tourists to seek out local cuisines when they travel, in the belief that it will allow them to explore, appreciate and understand local culture in a deeper, more meaningful and authentic way.

Food is one of the most important resources of any tourist destination and is integral to a sense of authenticity and place. The UN World Tourism Organization (UNWTO)(2012) suggests that gastronomy, as part of the tourist experience, allows visitors to experience the cultural and historical heritage of a destination, making it possible for them to approach culture in a more authentic, experiential and participatory way (Berno, Dentice & Wisansing, 2019; Fusté-Forné & Berno, 2016). Consuming local cuisine *in situ* in tourism is an effective form of placemaking and is an important avenue though which a place is experienced and made meaningful (Sthapit, 2017). Local foods function as powerful cultural commodities for placemaking in tourism (Di Giovine, 2016; Kim & Iwashita, 2016; Park, Muangasame & Kim, 2021) and have an innate ability to symbolise place and culture (Sims, 2009). In this way, tourists consume food to experience place (Farrelly & Makkar, 2022).

Of Rice, Culture and Tourism

As I stood on the stage with the grain of rice in the palm of my hand, the story of how that single grain represented Thai culture unfolded. For me to visit Thailand and not consume rice was inconceivable. After many years working in Thailand, I knew that rice is synonymous with life for the Thai people. It is an irrefutable part of all that is Thai-ness. For a tourist to experience Thai culture in a deep and meaningful way, the starting point must be to eat Thai rice. Such is the importance of rice that one cannot understand Thai culture without appreciating the role and significance of rice.

12   Tracy Berno

Rice for Life

In terms of sense of place and placemaking, rice dominates the Thai agricultural landscape. To travel through Thailand is to travel a landscape of rice. More than 60 percent of Thailand's population are farmers, most of them dependent on rice as their main crop (Poonyarat, 2003). This connection to the land is reflected in a well-known Thai saying: *nai nam mee pla nai na mee kao* ('there are plenty of fish in the river and plenty of rice in the paddy field'). In Thai culture 'rice' and 'fish' symbolize strength, representing the prosperity and abundance of the land, as well as the staple foundation of the Thai diet (Wongcha-Um, 2010). For centuries, rice has held a central role not just in Thai cuisine, but in all of Thai culture. In Thai culture, beliefs and values are inextricably intertwined with rice. Rice is an intrinsic part of Thai heritage, plays an important role in cultural rituals and religion, is an important part of the economy and even influences the roles and responsibilities of government leaders (Gomez, 2001). Similar to other countries in Southeast Asia, Thais greet each other by saying, "*Kin kao laew reu young?*" ('Have you eaten rice yet?'). In asking, "Why is rice very important in the context of Thai society?" Siriwan (n.d.: 2) asserts that "Rice is not just the main food of [Thailand] … rice represents the notion of self as it belongs to the country and signifies the nationality of its people". Rice is fundamental not just to Thai cuisine, but to every aspect of Thai culture. "Rice is the essence of [Thai] life" (Gomez, 2001: 1) and for a Thai, life without rice is unthinkable.

In Thailand, rice is more than just food; rice is intimately linked with the life cycle of Thai people in terms of landscape, consumption, religious belief and ritual practice (Siriwan, n.d.). For Thais, rice is a sacred food, divinely given, and fundamentally associated with human life. With its seasons of birth, death and rebirth, the life cycle of rice is associated with that of humanity. Rice also becomes pregnant, gives birth, and dies (Barnes, 2003). Thais believe that rice has its own soul, which manifests through Mae Posop, the goddess and mother of rice. To demonstrate their deep respect and gratitude to Mae Posop, Thai farmers bless their rice at every stage of its life cycle, starting with the planting and finishing with the harvesting. Rice is essential to the Thai economy, and it is the foundation for Thai festivals, rituals and customs. Rice has shaped the country's very landscape. "[Rice] has created a society, culture and cuisine that are uniquely Thai … Rice has made the Thai Thai" (Thompson, 2002: 98–99). Rice is at the very heart of Thainess.

Rice is so central to Thai culture that the most common term for 'eat' is *kin khao* (meaning to consume rice) and, as discussed earlier, one of the most common Thai greetings is 'have you eaten rice yet?'. Rice is commonly eaten at all meals, and to not eat rice with a meal is tantamount to not having eaten at all (Barnes, 2003). Although many tourists and foreigners believe that rice is an accompaniment to a Thai meal, rice is central to a Thai meal with the other dishes seen as complementary. These dishes are called *kap khao*, literally 'rice add-ons' (Seubsman, Suttinan, Dixon & Banwell, 2009) or 'that which is to be eaten with rice' (Punyaratabandhu, 2011). "The concept that rice is the main

Figure 1.1 Rice with *kap khao* as prepared by the author in Chiang Mai

dish and everything in the *samrap* (full meal) is there to accompany it cannot be overstated" (Punyaratabandhu, 2014: 33). *Kap khao* are prepared, seasoned and presented with the expectation that they are always eaten with two to three tablespoons of rice (Figure 1.1). To eat *kap khao* without rice risks them being perceived as too spicy, too salty or over-seasoned; rice is integral to the correct balance of sweet, sour, spicy, salty that comprises the flavour profile of Thai cuisine. Although rice is an essential part of Thai cuisine and Thai culture, for many tourists it is simply a side dish, its cultural and culinary significance not appreciated or understood.

Rice Is Everywhere

The gastronomy tourism forum itself reflected the myriad of ways that rice is connected to Thai culture. For example, presentations at the forum were interspersed with expressions of rice through art. I took inspiration from a dance troupe that depicted the life cycle of rice (and dropped the single grain that inspired my presentation), a pop-up art gallery of works that expressed the linkages between agriculture/rice, food and tourism and even a couture outfit worn by a delegate that symbolized the rice harvest. Everywhere I looked at the forum, there was rice.

14   *Tracy Berno*

As I held the grain of rice in my palm I spoke of the spiritual nature of rice, the intrinsic links with Thai history and culture, how rice shapes the landscape, how it unites people and communities through shared understandings and the sharing of food. I spoke of how rice is represented through Thai culture not just as food but in song, dance, poetry, legends and stories. I also spoke of terroir — how even if I planted the rice back at home in New Zealand and it grew, it would never be Thai rice because it would come from a different soil, with different water and a different climate. It is only Thai rice, grown and consumed in Thailand, that would allow me to experience Thai culture in such a meaningful way. I held the grain of rice in my hand respectfully, cognizant that it is a unique symbol of the connection between land, people, culture and food in Thailand.

My narrative on rice as symbolic of Thai gastronomy tourism reflected Wisansing and Vongvisitsin's (2017) suggestion that discovering Thainess within the context of tourism comprises three pillars: nature (landscapes); life (society and culture); and art (the culinary arts/gastronomy). However, Wisansing and Vongvisitsin (2017) went beyond these three pillars to consider how the linkages between tourism and Thainess can be expressed specifically through the "art of food" (p. 2). They defined the art of food as including not only the culinary arts, but also the "aesthetic presentation of food through forms of visual art … food can be viewed as the new art incorporating a holistic experience, such as tastes and smells, food design and decoration, cooking simulation or performing arts" (p. 5). Wisansing and Vongvisitsin (2017) explored "the links between agriculture, senses of place and how to create a pairing of food and local performing arts" (p. 1) in which pairing art with gastronomy created a platform for "Tourism with Thainess" (p. 13). They concluded that Thai food, with its origins in local agriculture, can increase the value of a destination, as well as increase the value of local identity as expressed through the art of food. Building on the concepts introduced by Wisansing and Vongvisitsin (2017), Berno, Dodd and Wisansing (2019) suggested that there are four pillars of food tourism in Thailand. These pillars comprise: (1) farming systems; (2) food stories; (3) the creative industries; and (4) sustainable tourism. These four pillars are experienced as a 'journey' co-created by the tourist and the host community in which they come together in a place-based approach that reflects local culture. Specifically, agriculture underpins the food system; it is the source of cuisine. Cuisine, however, is more than just food, it is an expression of culture and identity. Through partaking of local food and cuisine, tourists gain a deeper and more meaningful experience. In the Thai gastronomy tourism context, I argued that it is rice that provides this gateway to culture through the unique combination of the four pillars: agricultural products (farming), story (heritage), the creative industries (including culinary arts), and taste of place (tourism).

Rice in Tourism in Thailand

The role of rice in providing a gateway for a deeper and more meaningful engagement with Thai culture and life is also reflected in the 'Amazing Thai

Taste' tourism campaign launched in 2017 which has a focus on the role that rice plays in Thai culture. Like my narrative to the forum audience, the campaign focuses on more than just rice as cuisine (see for example Figure 1.2). The campaign invites tourists to participate in rice-centric activities that include co-created activities across the four pillars of Thai gastronomy tourism. As part of this campaign, two YouTube video clips promoting 'Amazing Thai Rice' were produced. In the first of these videos, *Amazing Thai Rice Introduction*, two tourists are seen with local Thais in a range of rice-related activities including a cooking class, eating rice and visiting a rice paddy where they plant and harvest rice. The relationship between agriculture, rice and society is emphasised throughout the video (Amazing Thailand, 2017a). The second video, *Amazing Thai Rice Route*, extends the idea of rice as more than

Figure 1.2 The author learning to harvest rice in Northern Thailand as part of 'rice tourism'

just a side dish by describing it as being expressive of "life and Thainess". The video invites tourists to "Discover each region of Thailand through the enchanting culture of Thai rice" and to "Enjoy the unique experience of [the] Thai way of life and way of rice" (Amazing Thailand, 2017b). As with the first of the videos, tourists are depicted participating in rice-centric activities. In this video, activities are presented by region and are themed: rice and art, where "rice stimulates creativity to create an artwork" (Northern); rice and festivals (North Eastern); rice and cycling (Central); rice and learning (Eastern); and rice and happiness (Southern). A strong emphasis on the relationship between agritourism, culture and rice as part of the Thai experience is evident throughout the video.

Concluding Thoughts on Cuisine as a Manifestation of Culture

In recalling my presentation on the panel at the gastronomy tourism forum, I was able to demonstrate how a single grain of rice is a powerful signifier of cultural identity. I was also able to articulate how this relationship between food and identity is a vehicle for tourists to experience a deeper and more meaningful 'taste' of culture. That single grain of rice gave me license to speak of how cultural, historical, and social values shape food culture, and in turn how culture shapes food. Rice, in the Thai context, is a badge of Thai identity and represents Thai people and the land from which they come. Rice is what makes the Thai Thai. Through this discussion, I was also able to demonstrate how Thailand is taking advantage of the culinary tradition of rice and using it as a visitor attraction.

For tourists seeking rich and authentic cultural experiences, food and cuisine is an ideal gateway. Everybody eats, but by exploring how others eat, we gain knowledge of their culture; part of their culture literally and figuratively becomes part of us. But equally, we learn more about our own culture through consuming the otherness of the place in which we find ourselves in tourism. Experiencing this sense of place through food creates deep and meaningful experiences and salient memories. We truly become what we eat.

Food for Thought

- What food or dish best represents your cultural identity? Why?
- Is there a particular food or dish that you have eaten as a tourist that causes you to recall the specific place you were when you ate it? Why is this so?
- Explain why terroir is an important concept for understanding the relationship between land, culture and people and placemaking.

Cuisine: A Manifestation of Culture 17

References

Abarca. M. & Colby, J. (2016) Food memories seasoning the narratives of our lives. *Food and Foodways*, *24*(1–2), 1–8.

Adema, P. (2007). Foodscapes: An emulsion of food and landscape. *Gastronomica: The Journal of Food and Culture*, *7*(1), 3.

Alonso, A. D. (2013). Tannat: The positioning of a wine grape as symbol and "referent" of a nation's gastronomic heritage. *Journal of Heritage Tourism*, *8*(2–3), 105–119.

Amazing Thailand. (2017a). *Amazing Thai rice introduction* [video file]. Available: www.youtube.com/watch?v=_TvladWPjlE

Amazing Thailand. (2017b). *Amazing Thai rice route* [video file]. Available: www.youtube.com/watch?v=F__xJW6aKfk.

Appadurai, A. (1996). *Modernity al large: Cultural dimensions of globalization*. Minneapolis, MN: University of Minnesota Press.

Barnes, C. (2003). The art of rice. *Humanities, 25*(5). Available: www.neh.gov/humanities/2003/septemberoctober/feature/the-art-rice

Barthes, R. (1979). Towards a psycho-sociology of contemporary food consumption. In R. Forster & O. Ranum (Eds.) *Food and drink in history* (pp. 166–174). Baltimore, MD: John Hopkins University Press.

Berno, T. (2017a). Building the New Zealand advantage: Putting the 'Culture' back into agriculture. In C. Massey (Ed.), *The New Zealand land and food annual* (pp. 181–192). Palmerston North: Massey University Press.

Berno, T. (2017b). Will the real Pasifika cuisine please stand up. *Kai and culture: Food stories from Aotearoa* (pp. 110–114). Christchurch: Freerange Press.

Berno, T., Dentice, G., & Wisansing, J. (2019). Kin kao laew reu young ('have you eaten rice yet')? A new perspective on food and tourism in Thailand. In *Food tourism in Asia* (pp. 17–30). Singapore: Springer.

Berno, T., Dodd, D., & Wisansing, J. (2019). *The development of ASEAN gastronomy network and region of gastronomy master plan*. Bangkok: Ministry of Sport and Tourism, Thailand.

Berno, T., Rajalingam, G., Miranda, A. I., & Ximenes, J. (2022). Promoting sustainable tourism futures in Timor-Leste by creating synergies between food, place and people. *Journal of Sustainable Tourism*, *30*(2–3), 500–514.

Berno, T., Wisansing, J. J., & Dentice, G. (2020). Creative agritourism for development: Putting the 'culture' into agriculture in Thailand. In *Tourism and Development in Southeast Asia* (pp. 197–213). Routledge.

Bessière, J. (2001). The role of rural gastronomy in tourism. In L. Roberts & D. Hall (Eds.), *Rural tourism and recreation: Principles to practice* (pp. 115–118). Wallingford: CABI International.

Cohen, E. & Avieli, N. (2004). Food in tourism: Attraction and impediment. *Annals of Tourism Research*, *31*(4), 755–778.

Deloire, A., Prévost, P. & Kelly, M. (2008). Unravelling the terroir mystique—An agro-socioeconomic perspective. *Perspectives in Agriculture, Veterinary Science, Nutrition and Natural Resources, 3* (32), 1–9.

Di Giovine, M. A. (2016). The everyday as extraordinary: Revitalization, religion, and the elevation of Cucina Casareccia to heritage cuisine in Pietrelcina, Italy. In R. L. Brulotte & M. A. Di Giovine (Eds.), *Edible identities: Food as cultural heritage* (pp. 77–92). Routledge.

18   *Tracy Berno*

Di Giovine, M. A. & Brulotte, R. L. (2016) Introduction: food and foodways as cultural heritage. In R.L. Brulotte & M.A. Di Giovine (Eds.), *Edible Identities: Food as Cultural Heritage*, pp. 1–27. Farnham: Ashgate

Farrelly, F., & Makkar, M. (2022). Augmenting the food experience through the projection of place: the case of Tasmania. *Current Issues in Tourism*, 1–18.

Feagan, R. (2007). The place of food: mapping out the 'local'in local food systems. *Progress in human geography*, *31*(1), 23–42.

Fischler, C. (1988). Food, self and identity. *Social science information*, *27*(2), 275–292.

Fusté-Forné, F. (2015). El turisme gastronòmic: Autenticitat i desenvolupament local en zones rurals. *Documents d'Anàlisi Geogràfica*, *61*(2), 289–304

Fusté-Forné, F., & Berno, T. (2016). Food tourism in New Zealand: Canterbury's foodscapes. *Journal of Gastronomy and Tourism*, *2*(2).

Gomez, K. (2001, September 20). *Rice the grain of culture*. Paper presented at the Siam Lecture Series, Bangkok: The Siam Society.

Gyimóthy, S., & Mykletun, R. J. (2009). Scary food: Commodifying culinary heritage as meal adventures in tourism. *Journal of Vacation Marketing*, *15*(3), 259–273.

Harrington, R. J. (2005). Defining gastronomic identity: The impact of environment and culture on prevailing components, texture and flavors in wine and food. *Journal of Culinary Science & Technology*, *4*(2–3), 129–152.

Hashimoto, A. & Telfer, D. J. (2008). From sake to sea urchin: Food and drink festivals and regional identity in Japan. In C. M. Hall & L. Sharples (Eds.), *Food and wine festivals and events around the world: Development, management and markets* (pp. 249–278). Oxford: Elsevier.

Hillel, D., Belhassen, Y., & Shani, A. (2013). What makes a gastronomic destination attractive? Evidence from the Israeli Negev. *Tourism Management*, *36*, 200–209.

Kim, S., & Ellis, A. (2015). Noodle production and consumption: From agriculture to food tourism in Japan. *Tourism Geographies*, *17*(1), 151–167.

Kim, S., & Iwashita, C. (2016). Cooking identity and food tourism: The case of Japanese udon noodles. *Tourism Recreation Research*, *41*(1), 89–100.

Kittler, P. G., Sucher, K. P., & Nelms, M. (2017). *Food and culture*. Cengage Learning.

Kunwar, R. R. (2017). Food tourism revisited. *Journal of Tourism and Hospitality Education*, *7*, 83–124.

Lawrence, B., & Tushman, M. (2020). Food traditions and its national identity. *Journal of Biochemistry, Biotechnology and Allied Fields*, *5*(1), 34–38.

McNeill, F. M. (1974). *The Scots kitchen: Its lore and recipes*. St. Albans, NY: Mayflower Book.

Montanari, A. (2002). *Food and environment: Geographies of taste*. Rome: SGI-Home of Geography.

Montanari, A. (2009) Geography of taste and local development in Abruzzo (Italy): Project to establish a training and research centre for the promotion of enogastronomic culture and tourism. *Journal of Heritage Tourism*, *4*(2): 91–103.

Park, E., Muangasame, K., & Kim, S. (2021). 'We and our stories': constructing food experiences in a UNESCO gastronomy city. *Tourism Geographies*, 1–22.

Poonyarat, C. (2003). Development-Thailand: Rice culture withering away, warn experts. Available: www.ipsnews.net/2003/01/development-thailand-rice-culture-withering-away-warn-experts/

Punyaratabandhu, L. (2011). Thai food for low-carbers. Available: http://shesimmers.com/2011/08/thai-food-for-low-carbers.html

Punyaratabandhu, L. (2014). *Simple Thai food: Classic recipes from the Thai home kitchen*. Berkley, CA: 10 Speed Press.

Ruiz, M. N. (2018). Part I introduction: Taste identity and authenticity. In N. Namaste & M. Nadales (Ed.) *Who decides?: Competing narratives in constructing tastes, consumption and choice* (pp. 3–5). BRILL.

Santich, B. (2009). *Looking for flavour.* Wakefield Press.

Seubsman, S. A., Suttinan, P., Dixon, J., & Banwell, C. (2009). Thai meals. In H. L. Meiselman (Ed.), *Meals in science and practice* (pp. 413–451). New York, NY: CRC Press.

Simpson, T. (1996). *A distant feast: The origins of New Zealand's cuisine.* Random House New Zealand.

Sims, R. (2009). Food, place and authenticity: Local food and the sustainable tourism experience. *Journal of Sustainable Tourism, 17*(3), 321–336.

Siriwan, S. (n.d.). *Rice, ritual and performance: Thai identity in the green field. Unpublished manuscript.* Available: www.academia.edu/8876327/Rice_Ritual_and_Performance_Thai_Identity_in_the_Green_Field

Staiff, R. & Bushell, R. (2013). The rhetoric of Lao/French fusion: Beyond the representation of the Western tourist experience of cuisine in the world heritage city of Luang Prabang, Laos. *Journal of Heritage Tourism, 8*(2–3), 133–144.

Sthapit, E. (2017). Exploring tourists' memorable food experiences: A study of visitors to Santa's official hometown. *Anatolia, 28*(3), 404–421.

Thompson, D. (2002). *Thai food.* Berkley, CA: Ten Speed Press.

Timothy, D. J. (2007) *Let them eat Moussaka: cuisine and foodways as cultural heritage. Invited keynote address at the Philoxenia International Symposium on Gastronomy and Wine Tourism,* 1–4 November, Thessaloniki, Greece.

Timothy, D. J. (2015). Introduction: Heritage cuisines, foodways and culinary traditions, in Dallen J. Timothy (Ed.) *Traditions, identities and tourism* (pp. 1–24). Taylor-Francis.

Timothy, D. J., & Ron, A. S. (2013). Heritage cuisines, regional identity and sustainable tourism. In *Sustainable Culinary Systems* (pp. 275–290). Routledge.

Trubek, A. B. (2008) *The Taste of Place: A Cultural Journey into Terroir.* Berkeley, CA: University of California Press.

UNWTO (2012). Global Report on Food Tourism. UNWTO.

Wisansing, J., & Vongvisitsin, T. (2017). *Mechanisms for the art of food: Tourism with Thainess and multi-stakeholder participation approach.* Barcelona: International Institute of Gastronomy, Culture, Arts, and Tourism. Available: https://igcat.org/wp-content/uploads/2017/03/MECHANISMS-FOR-THE-ART-OF-FOOD-TOURISM-WITH-THAINESS-AND-MULTI-STAKEHOLDER.pdf

Wongcha-Um, P. (2010). *Thai culinary identity construction: From the rise of the Bangkok dynasty to its revival (Unpublished master's thesis).* Singapore: National University of Singapore.

2 The Role of Creators, Makers and Other Entrepreneurs

Steven Shomler

Introduction

The Artisan Is the Hero

A comprehensive understanding of culinary tourism has to include this incredibly salient point: the local artisan creating food and beverage delights is the hero. Period. Full stop. It is sadly easy to overlook this reality. When it comes to culinary tourism, the local artisan – the baker, the chef, the bartender, the distiller, the chocolatier, the farmer, the winemaker, the cheesemaker – these craftspeople are the real heroes! Here is why: *people love to read stories about heroes* and *given the chance, people love to meet real-life heroes*. If you are one of these real-life artisans, understand that culinary tourists see you as a star. They want to learn more about you, and, if possible, meet you! If you have one of these roles, you are likely putting in long in hours at your craft and you may not feel like a hero at all. Trust me – you are. The implications of this important reality will be unpacked throughout this chapter.

Before we move on, let me cover one more culinary tourism hero – the entrepreneur. During my culinary tourism adventures, I have encountered wonderful business owners who are not local artisans themselves, yet they are still vital to food tourism (Wolf, 2014). Entrepreneurs who own tour companies, wineries, restaurants, etc. are often unsung heroes. Entrepreneurs make it possible for culinary tourists to have wonderful adventures and we thank them for it. The challenge comes when an entrepreneur fails to recognize or respect that culinary tourists *also* see the local artisan as a hero. Case in point –restaurants are often owned by the chef. However, many times a restaurant is owned by an entrepreneur, who is not the chef. I have encountered entrepreneurs who were quite certain that they were a hero because they operated a successful restaurant. This is true; however, problems arise when the entrepreneur who owns the restaurant fails to accept that the chefs cooking in their restaurant are also heroes. This type of situation is incredibly off-putting to culinary tourists who believe in giving credit where credit is due.

I am a food & travel professional and the majority of what I am sharing in this chapter comes from my own experiences traveling the globe as a business

DOI: 10.4324/9781003282532-4

The Role of Creators, Makers and Other Entrepreneurs   21

consultant, writer, author, podcaster, and content creator. Above all though, I consider myself a culinary tourist. I have had the good fortune to enjoy many magnificent culinary experiences while connecting with local people, savoring & sharing their stories. In this chapter I am covering topics that I have found to be very helpful to nurturing the symbiotic relationship that exists amongst culinary artisans, culinary entrepreneurs, and culinary tourists: 'Local is How You Win with Culinary Tourists', 'The Elements of an Effective Culinary Story', 'People Want to Have Options for a Deeper Experience', 'From Passive Fans to Passionate Fans', 'Use Special Events to Grow and Deepen Your Fan Base', and 'The Power of Promoting Local Treasures.

Local Is How You Win with Culinary Tourists

I was recently in Hawaii, on the island of Oahu in the city of Honolulu. I walked into the Paniolo Bar and took a seat. I started chatting with Yulia, the fantastic bartender there, and shared that I love gin. I told her that whenever possible, I like to have local gin. Yulia wasted no time in giving me a taste of Fid St Gin, distilled by Hamaille Distillery on the island of Maui (Hali'imaile Distillery, 2022).

It was wonderful! Yulia went on to make me a special cocktail utilizing this local version of my favorite spirit and I was a happy man (Shomler, 2022). Don't miss the importance of this anecdote: Because my desire to enjoy local gin was immediately and enthusiastically honored – Yulia, the Paniolo Bar, Fid St Gin, and Hamaille Distillery ALL gained me as a *passionate fan* who now tells others about them. Businesses win when they use local ingredients, local produce, local meat, local fish, local flour, local wine, local spirits, local bread, I could go on – hopefully you get the picture. Culinary tourists go mad for this stuff. They want to taste the region where they are (Stanley & Stanley, 2015).

Local Ingredients

So, what is "local" when it comes to culinary tourism? As long as you are up front and transparent about the details, the meaning of "local" can have some flexibility. "Local" produce can come from a farm 2 kilometers away, "local" meat can come from your region, "local" wine might be from the next region over. The trick is to tell us the details – let us in on the story behind the origins of your produce, meat, or wine and who produces them. This gets us more invested in consuming them!

Local Growers and Producers

Many businesses underestimate the importance of communicating the fact that they are a local producer. It can be easy to overlook the fact that people may find it interesting or appealing that your operation is based in the area. Sharing this information can be very helpful to your business. Your hummus might be tasty, even tastier than all of the others on offer in the grocery. But add that your hummus is made in Oregon from garbanzo beans local to the Pacific Northwest and you will catch the eye of consumers who find those details important and attractive. You have to say important parts like these out loud, or people won't find you. Get in the habit of regularly "saying" these details on your website and social media accounts as well. Another example: The Oregon coast is one of the most beautiful regions of the United States. Highway 101 runs along the Oregon coast and if you were to drive the entire Oregon coast from Brookings to Astoria, it would take you about 7 hours. Along that route are many charming towns with a wealth of culinary artisans therein. Between the relatively large towns of Lincoln City and Tillamook is the very small, blink-and-you-will-miss-it town of Cloverdale where you will find a little shop selling wonderful cheese (Nestucca Bay Creamery, 2022).

This business may think of themselves as simply a cheese shop that happens to be in Cloverdale. It is true that they are located in Cloverdale; however, there is so much more that is interesting to potential culinary tourists. For example: This cheese shop sells cheese that they make at their very own creamery less than a mile away. Plus, the milk for their cheese comes from their very own 5th generation dairy that is so close, if you look carefully, you can see the cows from the parking lot of the cheese shop. Talk about local!

And don't miss this – not only is this producer located in the town of Cloverdale, they are also part of the larger Oregon coast community. I mentioned how beautiful the Oregon coast is and it is a special place of significance to many people. But don't just take my word for it: According to Travel Oregon, the Oregon coast gets more than 15 million overnight visitors each year (Oregon Coast Visitors Association, 2018). Not all of those tourists are *culinary tourists*, but many of them are. Or could be. The fact that this little cheese shop sells cheese made on the Oregon coast is a detail that matters. It adds instant appeal. Details like these are often overlooked, but they are precious and important and are like catnip to culinary tourists. So, for practice, let's tie this together. This is how I would tell a story about this little cheese shop that would be compelling to culinary tourists seeking local delights: "We are a creamery located in Cloverdale, Oregon, a charming, very small town on highway 101 that has a population of 177. We also own a 5th generation dairy that supplies the milk to make our cheese. Both the creamery and the farm are less than one mile from our cheese shop. We sell more than 8 kinds of cheese including Camembert, Feta, Havarti, Gouda, and more. Some of the best cheese made on the Oregon coast is made right here."

Whether you are a culinary producer in Cloverdale, Oregon or Burriana, Spain on the Costa del Azahar – the Orange Blossom Coast, the same storytelling wisdom applies to you (Ochyra, 2021; TurEspaña, 2022). Share your story about what makes you, your area, and your product special. Culinary tourists want to experience a sense of place while they are enjoying your food and beverage creations.

Local Dishes

Culinary tourists love to "eat local". They want to experience dishes from the area while they are in the area. Another example from my recent trip to Hawaii: "Loco Moco" is a "Hawaiian" dish that is very important to people who live in Hawaii. Loco Moco was purportedly created around 1949 in the town of Hilo on the Big Island of Hawaii. Legend has it that it was created at either Café 100 or at the Lincoln Grill, the lack of consensus adds to the mystery and fun of it all (Onolicious Hawai'i, 2021). For those not in the know, Loco Moco is a hamburger patty atop a mound of white rice, covered in brown gravy and topped with an egg. It is a great dish! If you ever get to the American state of Hawaii, get yourself some Loco Moco! I myself have had Loco Moco at many places in Hawaii, including Café 100 in Hilo, as well as places outside of Hawaii. Hands down, I always enjoy Loco Moco more in Hawaii. It is not that is it objectively better, but more that when I eat it in Hawaii, I enjoy its history and its flavors at the origin. Just like eating pizza in Italy, there is an added layer of enjoyment having a local dish prepared at the source.

I love seeking out local delicacies, no matter where I am. I enjoy Maine lobster rolls when I am in Maine (Figure 2.1). I have Dungeness Crab Mac & Cheese

Figure 2.1 Lobster roll from LDI Lobster on Little Deer Isle, Maine, America looking out toward the Deer Isle-Sedgwick Bridge which is spanning the Eggemoggin Reach

Figure 2.2 Bougatsa from the Artos bakery in Goumenissa, Kilkis, Greece

when I am on the Oregon coast. When I am in Thessaloniki Greece, I enjoy Trigono Panoramatos and Bougatsa (Figure 2.2). When I am in Goumenissa, Greece I enjoy Xinomavro Chocolate Cake. When I am in Bilbao Spain, I enjoy Bacalao Pil-pil, Pintxos and Txakoli. In Georgia I want Khinkali, Khachapuri and, of course, lots of Georgian wine! When I am in Belize, I make sure to have Fry Jacks, Rice & Beans, Marie Sharp's, and a Belikin. I was recently in Belize, and local people were often surprised that I wanted to enjoy rice and beans (Belize, 2022) on my visit instead of the fancier international cuisine that was on offer.

I was delighted to find rice and beans on the menu at an upscale resort in Placencia, Belize (Figure 2.3). You can bet your bippy that I ordered that dish! Now this was the fanciest version of Belizean rice and beans I have ever encountered, mind you, but it was still Belizean rice and beans, in Belize, and I loved it. This is the difference between a tourist and a culinary tourist. Culinary tourists love local dishes experienced at the source. I made sure to compliment the Executive Chef, Enrique Awe, for featuring such a brilliant rendition of the national dish.

Figure 2.3 Belizean rice and beans prepared by Executive Chef Enrique Awe, Sirenian Bay Resort Placencia, Belize

Hear This as Well – if You Don't Tell Us – We Don't Know

If you make or serve a local, regional, or national dish or beverage and you don't tell us culinary tourists about it, you run the risk of missing out on our business (Getz et al., 2014). This is just the kind of stuff we want and you can create the demand for it! Tell us about Loco Moco and why we should eat it at your place while we are in Hilo. Or please educate us that Khachapuri is a beloved traditional dish made all over the country of Georgia. If you sell more than one variety of Khachapuri at your restaurant in Georgia – let us know that fact as well. Culinary tourists want to know details like this. On a side note – if you have never had Khachapuri – you have got to enjoy it at least once in your life. If you love melted cheese and baked savory pastry dishes – you will love Khachapuri! (Dzagnidze, 2017; Taste Atlas, 2022).

You Have to Tell Your Story and You Have to Promote Your Endeavor!

All around the world one single radio station is the most popular one. Its call sign is Wii-FM, also known as What's in it For Me. Here is what is in it for you as a culinary provider when you properly tell your story and promote your business. You increase your odds of attracting not just tourists, but culinary tourists. Not all tourists are created equal. Culinary tourists are gold – they are often kinder, pleasant to serve and interested in more than capturing the perfect Instagram photo (Getz et al., 2014; Wolf, 2014). They actually care about your story, your culinary endeavor, and they tend to spend more money when they have an enjoyable experience interacting with you.

If you are a culinary artisan or producer or entrepreneur, you have to tell your story (Bowles et al., 2022; Wolf, 2014). This enables people to find you and become interested in you. The best place for you to tell your story and attract potential culinary tourists is on your website and social media accounts. Let me illustrate why. I previously mentioned Burriana, Spain. If you wanted to travel there and you did a cursory search online for info about this lovely place, you would learn that Burriana is home to an orange museum, a few churches, and a great beach. You would also find a handful of restaurants. That's the extent of information you can find on travel and tourism websites about Burriana. Burriana, Spain is on the on the Costa del Azahar (the Orange Blossom Coast) and it has a population of about 34,000 people (City Population, 2021). It must have interesting culinary destinations beyond a few restaurants!

If you are a culinary tourist, you want to know about Burriana's culinary artisans. Where do you find the interesting cheese shops, cocktail bars, notable cafes / coffee houses, wineries, chocolate shops, bakeries, distilleries, breweries, and farms open to visitors? Unfortunately, travel and tourism websites often don't list helpful content like this – content that attracts culinary tourists.

I did my own search online via Google (love the translation feature!) using a variety of terms that did not turn up any wineries or distilleries or cocktail bars in Burriana. They may exist, but I could not find them anywhere online. That's a problem. If I were there in Spain, on the ground, I could probably sniff out these places, but on the internet they just don't exist. Here is what I did find though: A notable café / coffeehouse, two great looking bakeries, a wine shop, a charcuterie shop, and a business selling locally made bonbons and chocolates. Six potentially wonderful destinations that seem perfect for culinary tourists, none of them listed on traditional tourism websites. I found these places because they had their own websites.

Don't miss this – regular tourists may not put in extra effort to find your business, pre-trip or while abroad. However, *culinary tourists absolutely will*. Part of the joy for culinary tourists is planning their trip ahead of time, from their computer and armchair at home. If you own a culinary endeavor and you can get yourself listed on one of the local tourism websites, great, do it for the publicity. However, it would be a mistake to rely on the local tourism board or travel guides to do your promotion for you. They are not all-inclusive. You still need to market yourself effectively via your own website and social media to reach culinary tourists who want to find YOU. Make it easy for them to add you to their itinerary by becoming searchable online and telling your story!

The Elements of an Effective Culinary Story

There is wisdom in telling your story on your website and social media accounts to attract culinary tourists. But how do you actually do this? Here are the elements I have found that make for an effective culinary story:

When. When did your culinary endeavor begin? People find that fact to be interesting and give a frame of reference for your story. Whether you've been doing your thing for 5 years, 50 years, or 5 minutes, it helps set the stage (Jiwa, 2018).

Who. Tell us about "Who" makes the magic happen at your place (Storr, 2020). You can tell us about more than one person, but you need to tell us about at least one person who is integral to the endeavor. Say you are a 4th generation bakery. You don't need to tell us about each generation – tell us about Great Grandpa Felix who started the bakery and Alfredo who is your current head baker. This nicely bookends your story and people begin to build an emotional connection with your culinary endeavor when they hear about who is involved.

Why. What is your why, your purpose in starting this business? This also grabs people emotionally. And don't be afraid to sell us on your product: tell us why we should purchase the vegetables you grow on your farm, or why we should visit your bakery and buy your bread. Don't be shy!

What. Don't overlook this important detail. It is easy to assume that people will know – "the word 'bakery' is in our name, so duh, we bake stuff". That may be true; however, do you bake bread? Cookies? Cakes? Do you have a specialty? Get specific, but also keep it simple. Here's an example using an award-winning winery located in the state of Maine in the US (Cellardoor Winery, 2022). If I worked at this winery and I was writing about it, this is what I would say: "At our winery we make 20 different varietals of wine using grapes grown in Washington State, New York, and California. Of special note is our 3 sparkling wines made with grapes grown right here in Maine, on the same property as our winery." Maine is not known for either wineries or for having a grape growing region. This example answers questions that wine lovers might typically have about a winery located in Maine and creates intrigue that is irresistible; what on Earth does Maine sparkling wine taste like?!

Where. Tell us where you are located and tell us *about* where you are located, including your region (Fallon & Senn, 2006). Out of town visitors who are considering traveling to Poggibonzi may not immediately realize that this charming, small Italian hamlet is in the heart of Tuscany, within striking distance of many other cute little towns, and has tons of interesting history. This makes it a more appealing destination and helps potential visitors visualize it.

People Want to Have Options for a Deeper Experience

Keep in mind that if you have an attractive culinary endeavor, culinary tourists love the opportunity to have a deeper experience with it. You can leverage this desire to strengthen and grow your enterprise. Here is how you can do this:

Visitors and Tours

Regardless of what kind of culinary endeavor you have, culinary tourists are eager for a deeper experience and an opportunity for further interaction with you. This is easily accomplished with a visit or a tour. These onsite visits will likely lead to sales, an increase in your fanbase and word of mouth spreading the news about you. These tours don't have to be complicated or time consuming.

Say you are a smaller farm and don't have the capacity to offer tours daily; you can start with weekly or by appointment. For instance, you could offer a one hour experience every Saturday at 10 AM that includes a guided walking tour with time for questions and photo ops. Pictures are very important to people these days and a means of communication with their loved ones; "Look at me, see what I did!". If possible, have a tasting of what you grow. This encourages people to buy your stuff at the end of the tour. You would be surprised how much people treasure an experience like this. Why? Read on:

The Backstage Pass

Have you ever been to a concert? Live music is awesome and for me, any seat in the building is good. That being said, the closer my seat is to the front row, the better my experience. You know what's even better than a front row seat? Having a front row seat and a Backstage Pass. By offering tours you can provide your fans this same kind of Backstage Pass experience.

It can feel normal, boring even for YOU to walk to the area when the brewing tanks are, or to see the cows being milked, or be in the room where the cheese is made, or where the donuts are proofed and cut. Don't miss this though: For your fans, getting to see these things is a cherished glimpse into the place where the magic happens. *You are giving them their very own Backstage Pass experience.*

I had the fantastic opportunity a few years ago to be part of a startup brewery. We have a taproom in the front, and onsite, in the back, was/is the brewery. People loved it when I gave them a behind the scenes tour of one of the best breweries in Portland – these were visitors who loved craft beer and many of them had never been in a real-life brewery amongst the tanks and other equipment. They were being given a glimpse of the inner sanctum from a fellow fan (me) who understood the sacredness of that experience.

I gave so many people tours of the brewery when we were first starting out and it was an easy and wonderful marketing tool. I knew just enough about the brewing equipment and the brewing process to offer a halfway decent tour.

The Role of Creators, Makers and Other Entrepreneurs 29

Even though my technical knowledge was limited, my commitment to the brewery and the fact that I knew our story so well made for a great experience that delighted existing fans of the brewery and created new ones.

From Passive Fans to Passionate Fans

One of the goals you need to have if you want your culinary endeavor to succeed is to grow your fan base. In the early stages of your business development, most of your fans will be passive fans. They are true fans for sure, they just aren't passionate fans. A passive fan watches and really enjoys *Star Trek Discovery & Star Trek Strange New Worlds*. A passionate fan buys the memorabilia and goes to the conventions. #CaptainBurnham #LetsFly #CaptainPike #HitIt

Every time I gave a tour at that brewery, some of our passive fans became passionate fans. A passionate fan not only buys your stuff they help you tell your story. Passionate fans become evangelists for your culinary endeavor. They tell everyone they know about how cool you and your product are. Be creative and come up with ways to help your passive fans become passionate fans.

Use Special Events to Grow and Deepen Your Fan Base

If you have a culinary endeavor, special events are a great way to promote and grow your business. An easy special event that you can do is to celebrate your anniversary each year. If you are a donut shop or a bakery, make a special, limited-edition donut or a special pastry and sell it the entire week of your anniversary. When you promote your anniversary event on social media, you allow fans near and far to feel like they are part of the festivities. Remember this – your fans want you to win and love seeing you make it through another year.

You can also come up with other random special events and do them whenever the mood strikes. Maybe a chili cook-off featuring your hot sauce or a grilled cheese party featuring your chutneys. A quarterly special dinner at your restaurant with the Executive Chef in attendance. I have found that if your time and resources are limited, three or four special events that you do every year are plenty.

Seasonal Events

When your fans get a sense that you will be doing a certain event the same time of year on an annual basis, they will start to plan for it. If you have been doing an annual one-day event and it gets too popular (a nice problem to have), consider breaking it up into a two-day event instead. You want to make sure that the actual event is a good experience for your fans and too crowded is no fun, for anyone.

I know of one craft brewery that does an annual event that had become very popular. Tickets would sell out each year within an hour of being released. Unfortunately, this event had grown too large for the space with too many people, very long lines, and very long waits for 3 oz pours of beer. If I were in charge of this event, I would limit the tickets sold to a reasonable number. Better to disappoint fans because they could not get a ticket than to disappoint fans because they paid good money to attend an oversold and overcrowded event. Don't be greedy, keep it classy.

Festivals – a Rising Tide That Lifts All of the Boats

Culinary themed festivals are common is many parts of the world. Google the phrase "best food festivals" and check out the slew of articles that come up (Kruchten, 2016; Oluwafemi, 2022). A well administered food festival can bring lots of people to your town and to your region.

When an established, well-run annual food festival happens in a town and lots of people come to it, many of the businesses in the area benefit (Everett, 2016). If you live somewhere that does not currently have a food festival, consider starting one. Really. Here is an example of what could be done: Let me preface this story by saying that chestnuts hold a nostalgic place in my heart. I gleefully eat them whenever and wherever I can find them, including yearly at a popular Portland Oregon winter craft beer festival (Holiday Ale, 2022).

Now for the story; early in 2020 I attended a media trip to Greece. One of our stops was in the charming town of Goumenissa located in the regional unit of Kilis. Goumenissa is about 70 kilometers northwest of Thessaloniki. There are many wonderful wineries in the Kilkis region. We were the first group of wine and food writers to ever be hosted on a tour of this regional unit of Greece. I fell in love with this little town and with the whole region itself. My imagination began working overtime to come up with ways to help the wonderful local people promote this terrific place – kind people, great wine, excellent food, beautiful scenery – what more could a culinary tourist want?

On my first day in Goumenissa I perked up at the mention of chestnuts being grown nearby. I already knew this region was fantastic, but to find out they have chestnuts too?! I desperately wanted to head up to those hills and see the groves of chestnut trees … but that was not part of our busy itinerary. Later that same day, I met a local chef who told me about a special pork dish he made that had chestnuts in it. Chestnuts again! I love this place! The chef was shocked and delighted that I knew about chestnuts and that I had eaten them before. It was a fun discussion, but we were soon off to the next stop on the tour.

The next day, we were scheduled for a late lunch at one of the many incredible local wineries that they have there (Chatzivaritis Estate, 2022). That afternoon, I was standing with a few of the food and wine writers I was traveling with following a delightful tour of the winery and their vineyard. We were happily chatting and enjoying wine as our meal was being prepared. One of the winery staff people came over to our little group and asked for me by name. I was reflexively wondering if I was in some kind of trouble. Once I cautiously identified myself, I was told that "a chef has come here to see you". The chef

Figure 2.4 A Pork and Chestnut dish prepared by Chef Savas Misirkos. Photo taken at the Chatzivariti Winery Κτήμα Χατζηβαρύτη Goumenissa, Kilkis, Greece

I had visited with the day before had prepared that local pork chestnut dish (Figure 2.4) for me and brought it to the winery for us all to enjoy. I was so touched by this and yes, it was absolutely amazing!

This is when it hit me – Kilkis and the surrounding area should put on a fall food festival celebrating the locally grown chestnuts! Many local civic leaders and people from the local tourism board were conveniently there at the winery that day. I gathered them up, had them all taste this pork dish and then told them about my vision for the *Kilkis Chestnut Festival*. At first, they thought I was some crazy American who had too much wine.

Slowly, some of them started to warm to the idea. COVID derailed the progress of this plan and many others like it, but we've stayed in touch and the last I heard, they may yet start a chestnut festival. I am certain that if they did this, they would get people from as far away as Thessaloniki and beyond to attend. It could be the kind of festival that would greatly benefit many of the businesses in that area. Plus – chestnuts – c'mon!

The Power of Promoting Local Treasures

You may not think of your local community as having valuable treasures, it may all seem quite ordinary to you. However, to culinary tourists there are enticing offerings all around you. Promoting these local treasures will help your culinary endeavor flourish. Back to our little Greek town of Goumenissa, population about 3600. I arrived in this charming town and stayed for just over 24 hours. Even though my time was cut short due to the onset of the COVID-19 pandemic, I came across a number of stellar local finds. The area around Goumenissa has at least 7 great wineries you can visit. In addition, within the tiny little town of Goumenissa itself there is:

- A great guesthouse (hotel) that serves a scrumptious breakfast, and upon request, will procure you a cake made with chocolate and xinomavro wine – *local treasure number 1* (Everett, 2016).
- A terrific bar that highlights live music and has a fun last-call tradition – *local treasure number 2.*
- A noteworthy bakery that sells both sweet and savory bugatsa (an amazingly good pastry) – *local treasure number 3.*
- A stunningly beautiful church – *local treasure number 4.*
- A very lovely park with a number of trails that take you along a very pretty river and this park also has some really cool foot bridges you can see, photograph, and cross over – *local treasure number 5.*
- Had I been there even one more day, I am certain that I would have come across even more local treasures!

If I were to put together a marketing plan for this region, I would urge people to come visit this really cool traditional Greek town 70 kilometers northwest of Thessaloniki, surrounded by amazing wineries, and check out all five of these local treasures. Even while marketing heavily to wine lovers/wine tourists, remember that people who travel for wine don't just visit wineries when they travel.

Conclusion

If you are a culinary artisan, there is a whole community of culinary tourists that want to know you and your story and sample your wares. Make it easy for culinary tourists to find you. Utilize the internet to help. Promote your business on your website and via your social media accounts. Make sure that you also promote the other local treasures in your community and in your region. Culinary tourists love local stuff. Use this to your advantage.

You may not realize it, but you absolutely do have local treasures in your community. Your local park or your local bakery or your local bar might be a place that a culinary tourist would appreciate. And so are your local foods, beverages, and festivals. If you promote both yourself and the other local treasures in your region to culinary tourists, everyone will reap a tremendous harvest.

Food for Thought

- Do you have an online presence, and does it tell your story and where you are located?
- What deeper experiences could your culinary endeavor offer?
- What local treasures are you overlooking or dismissing?

References

Belize (2022). Belize Cuisine – Savor Belize ~ Belize Rice and Beans. Retrieved from https://belize.com/belize-cuisine/

Bowles, M., Burns, C., Hixson, J., Jenness, S. A. & Tellers, K. (2022). *How to Tell a Story: The Essential Guide to Memorable Storytelling from The Moth*. Crown Publishing Group.

Cellardoor Winery (2022). Cellardoor. Retrieved from https://mainewine.com/

Chatzivaritis Estate (2022). *Κτήμα Χατζηβαρύτη - Chatzivariti Winery*. Retrieved from https://chatzivaritis.gr/

City Population (2021). Burriana, Spain. Retrieved from www.citypopulation.de/en/spain/comunitatvalenciana/castell%C3%B3n/12032__borriana/

Dzagnidze, B. (2017). A Regional Guide to Georgian Khachapuri. Retrieved from https://theculturetrip.com/europe/georgia/articles/a-regional-guide-to-georgian-khachapuri/

Everett, S. (2016). *Food and Drink Tourism: Principles and Practices*. SAGE Publications Ltd.

Fallon, P. & Senn, F. (2006). *Juicing the Orange: How to Turn Creativity into a Powerful Business Advantage*. Harvard Business School Press.

Getz, D., Robinson, R., Andersson, T. & Vujicic, S. (2014). *Foodies and Food Tourism*. Goodfellow Publishers Ltd.

Hali'imaile Distillery (2022). Hali'imaile Distilling Company. Retrieved from https://haliimailedistilling.com/

Holiday Ale (2022). Holiday Ale Festival. Retrieved from http://holidayale.com/

Jiwa, B. (2018). *Story Driven: You don't need to compete when you know who you are*. Perceptive Press.

Kruchten, L. (2016). The 24 Food Festivals Around the World You Need to Experience Before You Die. Retrieved from https://spoonuniversity.com/place/the-24-food-festivals-around-the-world-you-need-to-experience-before-you-die

Nestucca Bay Creamery (2022). Handmade Farmstead Cheese. Retrieved from https://nestuccabaycreamery.com/

Ochyra, H. (2021). The Orange Blossom Coast: the Spanish costa you've never heard of. Retrieved from www.roughguides.com/article/costa-del-azahar/

Oluwafemi, E. (2022). 27 Food Festivals Around the World. Retrieved from https://asoothingliving.com/food-festivals/

Onolicious Hawai'i (2021). Loco Moco. Retrieved from https://onolicioushawaii.com/loco-moco/

Oregon Coast Visitors Association (2018). *Regional Cooperative Tourism Program (RCTP) 2019–2021*. Travel Oregon.

Shomler, S. (2022). The Lanikai Passion – a Fantastic Cocktail Featuring Fid Street Gin! Retrieved from www.culinarytreasure.com/the-lanikai-passion-a-fantastic-cocktail-featuring-fid-street-gin/

Stanley, J. & Stanley, L. (2015). *Food Tourism: A Practical Marketing Guide*. CABI.

Storr, W. (2020). *Science of Storytelling*. Abrams Press.

Taste Atlas (2022). Khachapuri. Retrieved from www.tasteatlas.com/khachapuri

TurEspaña (2022). Coast of Castellon. Retrieved from www.spain.info/en/region/costa-castellon/

Wolf, E. (2014). *Have Fork Will Travel: A Practical Handbook for Food & Drink Tourism Professionals*. World Food Travel Association.

3 Changing Consumer Culinary Expectations

Susana Rachão, Veronika Joukes and Carlos Fernandes

Introduction

During the past few decades, society has been changing dramatically. This rapid and often unpredictable change affects cultural expressions and practices. Insights in the of quality of life have been shifting and people increasingly question their surroundings, preferences and values. Changes in social structures, perceptions and consumption require that contemporary society learns from the past, rethinks the present and adapts itself to the current and emerging tastes and preferences of consumers.

This shift in consumer habits is questioning the traditional definitions of heritage, as increased emphasis is placed on immaterial heritage whereas in the past mainly the material heritage was of interest. Immaterial heritage in the form of human values in a cross-cultural perspective is alluring to the new travellers and their exploring inclinations (Knollenberg et al., 2021).

For the contemporary traveller, traditional, static destinations have little appeal. Travellers are seeking lasting memories through physical connection, different types of experiences and personal emotional development for overcoming their expectations during a holiday (Rachão et al., 2021a). A growing number of people travel not to escape but to connect.

Thus, there is a need for destinations to develop a new range of skills which go beyond the traditional management of tourism services, and which move into the arena of experience development, creativity and innovation (OECD, 2012). Gastronomy plays a key role in trendsetting, image building and establishing quality standards demanded by today´s resilient tourists (Richards, 2021). It engages tourists in a taste of place creating new stories, new emotions rooted in sensory driven experiences about food and wine through storytelling (Frost et al., 2020). Tourists reveal a need to learn who is behind the food, where the food comes from and how it is processed, and perceive local food nostalgically as healthy food. It is not just about consuming good food, but about consuming culture. Such consumer behaviour suggests a more sustainable approach towards food production (Rachão et al., 2021b). The trend is to foster a close relationship between a territory and its products in terms of quality and uniqueness, in the sense of "food is landscape in a pot". Visitors are pushed to

DOI: 10.4324/9781003282532-5

connected with artisanal food producers by focusing more on the market and less on the supermarket. An unelaborate cuisine with emphasis on local fresh seasonal ingredients and more transparency around the preparation of the food is preferred. Increasingly restaurants are opting for "open kitchens" where their customers can learn, discover, and be inspired through gastronomy.

To understand some of the new challenges posed on food tourism after two years of lockdown due to COVID-19, the main goal of this chapter is to ascertain international trends in food consumption in the face of changes in tourist behaviour as perceived by gastronomy experts in different parts of the world. The chapter is organized as follows: i) introductory section; ii) literature review; iii) methodology; iv) results and discussion, whereas the last section, v), presents the main conclusions.

Literature Review

The all-inclusive term 'food tourism' considers tourism activities related with food and beverages and is regularly substituted by terms like gastronomy/gastronomic tourism, culinary tourism, gourmet tourism (Ellis et al., 2019; Horng & Tsai, 2012; Rachão et al., 2019). According to one of the main definitions, food tourism means "visitation to primary and secondary food producers, food festivals, restaurants and specific locations for which food tasting and/or experiencing the attributes of specialist food production region are the primary motivating factor for travel" (Hall & Sharples, 2003: 10). Food tourists appreciate discovering authentic local tastes, flavours, textures, cultures, heritage, and customs (World Food Travel Association, 2019).

For some decades now, food tourism has been popular worldwide as a research area and as a management tool and, moreover, its progress has accelerated in the new millennium for different reasons: it is a means to "grow community awareness of, and pride in, local culinary cultures", to "attract more sustainable, respectful, and educated visitors" (World Food Travel Association, n.d.), to promote the uniqueness of destinations, to preserve local heritage and to stimulate local economies (Okumus, 2021; Robinson et al., 2018).

As the global food tourism market is expected to increase until 2027 and as Europe is one of the largest markets and is expected to count for 35% of the market by then (CBI, n.d.), it makes sense that a Portuguese research team analyses food trends that take the effects of the COVID-19 pandemic into account.

When destinations design specific products or define marketing strategies for "foodies", such as food-oriented events, tours, and packages, as well as tasting sessions, agritourism and farmers' markets (Kim et al., 2022; Smith & Xiao, 2008), they should do so intelligently, accentuating locally produced ingredients, sustainable food systems or traditional culinary styles and thus contribute to the destination's competitive advantage (Getz et al., 2014; Kline et al., 2014; Knollenberg et al., 2021).

Developing marketing strategies, a food tourist stands in the middle of attention. It is essential to understand that he/she doesn't belong to a homogeneous group with standardized demographics, psychographic values, or lifestyles.

He/she belongs to a segment, determined by a singular variable such as levels of motivation or food involvement, or a combination of both, possibly enriched with attitudes or behavioural intentions (Levitt et al., 2019). He/she is usually categorized via three perspectives: conceptualization, demographic profiling and motivations-based profiling (Robinson et al., 2018). Recently ten foodie traveller activity profiles have been defined that can be used to refine marketing strategies: Cooking Foodie, Thirsty Foodie, Gardner Foodie, Cultural Foodie, Political Foodie, Social Media Foodie, Social Foodie, Trendy Foodie, Curious Foodie and Obsessed Foodie (Knollenberg et al., 2021). Through the literature review it was found that foodies might be especially sensitive to the following ten trends, which can be described as follows.

1. Culinary storytelling is gaining more importance on the side of the provider through telling stories about where some dishes/ingredients/processes come from, and through sharing compelling stories about, for example, family achievements. But visitors, on the other hand, are also urged to participate in the process, filling out narrative gaps and sharing their own experiences (co-creation) (Batat, 2019; Batat et al., 2019).
2. Sensory experiences, with their visual, olfactory, tactile or aural dimensions continue to play a central role (Batat & Addis, 2021; Batat et al., 2019; Hiamey et al., 2021).
3. The personalization of tourism experiences implies that visitors may choose their preferred menu from the recipe book (or in a cooking class) or that the instructor (or chef) adapts the menu to the visitors' dietary needs or religious belief. Customize food-themed tours is another possibility (Okumus, 2021).
4. Today there is a general interest in healthy foods. Also, in a tourism context, a larger choice can be offered to please health-conscious clients, varying from vegetarian dishes, vegan dishes, grilled food and vegetables, or wild foods (Fusté-Forné, 2019; Pardo-De-Santayana et al., 2005). Applying the principles of the slow food movement in one's restaurant might be another appreciated teaser.
5. COVID-19 seems to have accentuated the desire of people to eat in outdoor food spaces, be it in an urban or rural environment.
6. The trend of co-creation is also present in the food tourism context, as shopping in a traditional market or cooking in the kitchen of a resident can be considered as examples of co-production. The fact that visitors are ever more willing to participate in creating and designing a culinary product, is another example (Batat & Addis, 2021).
7. In the eye of the consumer authenticity is crucial. Therefore, it must be guaranteed that he/she perceives this authenticity, highlighting the use of local vegetables, meat and fish or maintaining the traditional way of preparation. Other options of the provider are to adhere to the Ugly Food Movement or to put his client in contact with native residents (Craig, 2020).
8. Social interaction is another factor which seems to be valued by tourists, regardless the type of contact: with professional or volunteer staff, with natives of the place, or with residents.

38 *Susana Rachão, Veronika Joukes and Carlos Fernandes*

Figure 3.1 Conceptual model of the food tourism future trends

Changing Consumer Culinary Expectations 39

9. Digitalization is one of those obligations that our changing society imposes to keep up with. This might be done through virtual tours, digital bookings, online orders, apps and digital platforms for promotion/information, social media (Instagram) or even through the creation of user-generated content on social media (Fountain, 2021).

10. The last hot topic that was detected is sustainability. Some aspects that fit under this umbrella are the use of (certified) biological/organic products, guaranteeing the traceable origin of ingredients/products, weighing ethical concerns around food production practices, preferring short food chains, retaining a local food identity, and avoiding food waste (Kuang & Bhat, 2017; Stalmirska, 2021).

The ten disclosed food tourism future trends have been summarized in Figure 3.1.

By researching travel preferences, expectations, and types of experiences that foodies prefer, destinations management can adjust their offerings for making their destinations more appealing for food tourism-seeking travellers. This argument was the basis for pursuing this research on how food tourism experts perceive the future of this sector.

Methodology

The main objective of the present study is to identify the potential international trends in food tourism, considering the changes in consumer behaviour on food and wine products. To achieve the study's aim, a Delphi technique was employed as it is commonly used in forecasting future events in tourism (Lin & Song, 2015). As this research is about forecasting future trends in food tourism expectations, the Delphi technique was considered appropriate. The Delphi technique is a qualitative forecasting method composed by an expert panel (Rowe & Wright, 2001) and a set of anonymous rounds of inquiries aiming at converging the responses (Lopes et al., 2022).

The panel selection is of the utmost importance to verify the feasibility of the trends. Bearing in mind this requirement, a snowball technique was employed to find the experts. To be included in the international panel of experts you needed to have professional and/or academic experience in the tourism industry. Despite the lack of consensus regarding the panel size, Rowe and Wright (2001) stated that the panel may comprise 5 to 20 experts with different expertise.

Frequently, statistical measures such as the variance of the experts' answers is the most used parameter to assess the level of consensus (Hanafin, 2004), and it is assumed that the smaller the variance, the greater the consensus observed (Rowe & Wright, 1999). It was pre-defined that the coefficient of variation (CV) could be up to 30% as it expresses the statistical dispersion of the responses and if it exceeded 30%, the item would be re-assessed in the subsequent round or excluded from the analysis, following other studies (Lopes et al., 2022). The data analysis used descriptive statistics based on measures of central tendency, namely mean and measures of dispersion, particularly standard deviation (SD) and coefficient of variation (CV).

40   *Susana Rachão, Veronika Joukes and Carlos Fernandes*

The first and only round was developed through an online survey sent by email to 75 worldwide experts who were given a 12-day window to respond. The questionnaire was written in English. A total of 23 responses were received. Considering the timeframe restrictions and given the consensus level gathered in the first round, the authors decided not to proceed with a subsequent round. The panel included experts from Argentina, Canada, Italy, Malta, Portugal, Romania and Spain. The Delphi round occurred in May 2022.

The online survey included ten trends disclosed by the literature review which involved scientific research as well as travel and tourism reports from different international organizations. The ten collected trends were: culinary storytelling, sensory experiences, personalization, healthy foods, outdoor food spaces, co-production, perceived authenticity, social interaction, digitalization and sustainability. The trends were ranked in a Likert-scale ranging from 1 – least important and 5 – most important. Table 3.1 displays the sociodemographic and professional characteristics of the experts included in the study.

Table 3.1 Sociodemographic profile of the expert panel members

Expert number	Gender	Age	Experience in the tourism industry (years)	Position in the tourism industry/academic world
1	Prefers not to say	Prefers not to say	40	University
2	Female	38	5	Researcher
3	Male	60	–	Academic researcher
4	Female	34	11	Teacher
5	Female	51	22	Associate professor
6	Female	63	Management 5/ lecturing 30	Lecturer
7	Male	67	45	Lecturer and researcher
8	Female	60	> 40	Educator
9	Male	47	24	Academic
10	Female	42	25	Academic
11	Male	64	35	Professor
12	Male	64	30	Professor/tourist guide/ event organizer
13	Male	60	30	Senior lecturer
14	Male	58	40	Director
15	Female	43	20	Teacher
16	Female	59	–	Professor
17	Male	39	10	Contracted professor
18	Male	60	30	Academic
19	Male	65	50	Professor
20	Female	32	1	PhD student
21	Female	42	10	High school teacher
22	Female	27	1	PhD student
23	Female	Prefers not to say	>20	Professor

The sample included 12 female and 10 male experts and 1 preferred not to specify his/her gender, with an average age of 50 years old. Concerning the years of experience in the tourism industry, it is possible to attest that it is a well-experienced panel, particularly in academic research, teaching and doctoral studies. The next section will present the main results of the study and the discussion of the main topics.

Results and Discussion

Table 3.2 illustrates the results of the panel of experts on the ten dimensions identified in the literature review. It is possible to determine that the sustainability trend has the highest rank ($\overline{x}$ = 4.33). This trend included six items, in which the item 'retention of a local food identity' ($\overline{x}$ = 4.65; SD = 0.56)

Table 3.2 Results of the Delphi round ($n = 23$)

Trend/dimensions and items	Mean	SD	CV (%)	Result (to include)
Culinary storytelling	**4.04**	**0.94**		
To tell historical stories	4.30	0.80	0.19	To be included
To communicate compelling stories	4.22	1.06	0.25	To be included
Visitors fill narrative gaps, share their own experiences (co-creation)	3.78	0.98	0.26	To be included
To tell about culinary making process	4.09	0.78	0.19	To be included
Visitors are encouraged to share their personal stories and experiences	3.83	1.09	0.28	To be included
Sensory experiences	**4.03**	**0.91**		
Visual dimensions	4.22	0.78	0.18	To be included
Olfactory dimensions	4.30	0.86	0.20	To be included
Tactile dimensions	3.87	1.03	0.27	To be included
Aural dimensions	3.74	0.99	0.26	To be included
Personalization	**3.84**	**0.83**		
Visitors may choose their preferred menu from the recipe book (cooking class)	3.39	0.71	0.21	To be included
Instructor (*chef*) adapts to visitors' dietary needs, belief, and restrictions	4.09	0.97	0.24	To be included
Customized food-themed tours	4.04	0.81	0.20	To be included
Healthy foods	**3.75**	**0.89**		
Vegetarian dishes	4.17	0.92	0.22	To be included
Vegan dishes	3.83	0.92	0.24	To be included
Grilled food and vegetables	3.48	0.93	0.27	To be included
Wild foods	3.30	0.91	0.27	To be included
Slow food	3.96	0.81	0.20	To be included
Outdoor food spaces	**4.17**	**0.85**		
In urban environment	4.00	0.93	0.23	To be included
In rural environment	4.35	0.76	0.17	To be included

(continued)

42   Susana Rachão, Veronika Joukes and Carlos Fernandes

Table 3.2 Cont.

Trend/dimensions and items	Mean	SD	CV (%)	Result (to include)
Co-production	**3.90**	**0.89**		
Shopping in the traditional market	4.26	0.79	0.19	To be included
Cooking in someone's kitchen	3.65	0.91	0.25	To be included
Visitors participate in creating and designing a culinary product	3.78	0.98	0.26	To be included
Perceived authenticity	**4.23**	**0.88**		
Local vegetables	4.57	0.71	0.16	To be included
Local meat and fish	4.57	0.71	0.16	To be included
Ugly Food Movement	3.35	1.20	0.36	**Not to be included**
Traditional way of preparation	4.43	0.82	0.19	To be included
Native residents	4.22	0.93	0.22	To be included
Social interaction	**4.09**	**0.84**		
With professional staff	4.00	0.72	0.18	To be included
With staff (not professionals)	3.83	0.87	0.23	To be included
With natives of the place	4.35	0.87	0.20	To be included
With residents	4.17	0.92	0.22	To be included
Digitalization	**3.99**	**0.92**		
Virtual tours	3.26	1.19	0.36	**Not to be included**
Digital bookings	4.22	0.88	0.21	To be included
Online orders	4.04	0.95	0.24	To be included
Apps and digital platforms for promotion/information	4.26	0.94	0.22	To be included
Social media (Instagram)	4.13	0.68	0.16	To be included
Creating user-generated content on social media	4.04	0.86	0.21	To be included
Sustainability	**4.33**	**0.82**		
Biological products (certified)	4.00	0.93	0.23	To be included
Traceable origin of ingredients/products	4.22	0.83	0.20	To be included
Ethical concerns around food production practices	4.39	0.82	0.19	To be included
Short food chains	4.22	0.93	0.22	To be included
Retention of a local food identity	4.65	0.56	0.12	To be included
Not wasting food	4.52	0.83	0.18	To be included

Note: SD – standard deviation; CV – coefficient of variation

and 'not wasting food' gathered the highest scores ($\bar{x}$ = 4.52; SD = 0.83). Regarding the last item, past research (e.g. Gretzel et al., 2019) had already claimed that food waste reduction is the most important issue for the next 75 years in the hospitality industry. Yet, more critical insights and academic research are needed on food waste in particular market segments such as food tourists.

The second trend most ranked by the experts was the 'perceived authenticity' ($\bar{x}$ = 4.23). This trend included five items, in which 'local vegetables' and 'local meat and fish' ($\bar{x}$ = 4.57; SD = 0.71) obtained the best ranks. However, the 'Ugly Food Movement' item was excluded since it did not gather the consensus of the experts (the coefficient of variation exceeded 30%). Using local ingredients such as endogenous vegetables, fish and meat will emphasize the local food identity, which will, according to the experts of the panel, impact the consumer culinary expectations positively. These findings reflect what is argued by Okumus (2021), Robinson et al. (2018) and Knollenberg et al. (2021) who consider authenticity as one of the main drivers for food tourists.

The 'healthy foods' trend obtained the lowest score ($\bar{x}$ = 3.75) followed by the 'personalization' trend ($\bar{x}$ = 3.84). Unlike what previous studies suggest about the increase of healthy lifestyles, particularly in vegetarianism and veganism (Rachão et al., 2021b), the experts considered this trend as the least important.

The trend with the second and last item that should be removed, integrates the 'Digitalization' trend. The item with the lowest score was 'Virtual tours' ($\bar{x}$ = 3.26), illustrating that food tourists will continue to prefer experiencing local cuisine on the spot.

Main Conclusions in a Wider Context

The aim of this chapter being to comment on changing consumer culinary expectations, it is convenient to return to before the COVID-19 pandemic struck. Then restaurants were accustomed to customers seeking authentic gastronomic experiences, particularly at regions where food became synonymous with a region's way of life and its intangible heritage. People identified specific foods with certain places and in doing so learned more about local culinary icons and food traditions. It was not just about the food. Indeed, significant emphasis was placed on the meal experience: it was not so much about providing a service, but rather about offering memorable and unique experiences, with a focus on conviviality and increasingly also on the provenance of the ingredients. Customers were really into everything having to do with food including the storytelling: what is the origin of the recipe, what is the cooking process, what is the customary gathering around the table, how do they pair off food and beverages, etc.? Simply serving a local meal was no longer enough.

By highlighting the essence of food and heritage, food providers play crucial roles in the design of gastronomic experiences. Not only do customers seek authenticity related to tradition, but increasingly also place importance on regional and fresh food, and the importance of production and sustainable agriculture. From the farm to the table; from the sea to the table; "0" kilometres; etc. This approach has been very effective for the preservation of food traditions. Also, it played an important role in providing a pre-emptive means for regions slowly losing their food cultures, as tastes are changing.

However, the conditions of uncertainty caused by the COVID-19 pandemic have inflicted behavioural changes in consumers. This chapter explores emerging trends and identifies prospects for food providers to adapt to the changing circumstances.

The comfortable association of certain foods with particular regions is being challenged by the growing mobility of food, the modification in culinary tastes, the increasing de-differentiation of local food and the expectations of what constitutes a gastronomic experience with less focus on the conviviality. Concerns arise as to whether "old" ways of life offer "new" experiences for today's ever apprehensive, yet demanding customers, and whether local gastronomic practices can be sustained in increasingly complex and more globalized agro-food supply chains.

Due to COVID-19 not only tourists, but people in general, have been changing their behaviour. They are less likely to gather in large groups, affecting the conviviality factor inherent to the gastronomy experience. They may reduce their visits to urban areas to avoid large crowds causing urban spaces, restaurants for example, to be experienced and consumed differently. People may change their preference for open air environments and less visited areas and "off-the-beaten track" experiences. In such a situation, there may potentially emerge a new demand for the *re-ruralization* of gastronomy – or a going back to the roots movement. Generally, people still hold a dear place in their hearts for home-cooked meals served in restaurants in the countryside. Such a change could be positive for the development of rural areas.

The changes that are taking place will require ongoing joint efforts by regional food providers and other stakeholders to work out solutions that would make it possible to anticipate such food consumption changes in the future or at least partly counteract them or mitigate their effects. Strong linkages between gastronomy, local food production, fisheries and agricultural activities need to be sufficiently explored for creating added value for the taste palates of the diverse customer base. Moreover, it is important to recognize that the sustainability of gastronomy needs to consider more than just preserving the past, but also being more creative in the future. Having food providers look for inspiration in the region's humble cooking traditions may well become a key influencing factor for culinary innovation.

However, modern tastes and preferences require that this generation of *chefs* take on a new attitude for rejuvenating regional gastronomy. It is true that cooking is a continuous process of learning about what the ingredients can achieve. But regional gastronomy should be modified using good sense. Another way of innovating is through the (partial) digitalization of selling and marketing practices. Therefore, the delicate question "how much innovation is adequate?" will remain.

The transformation of the food and beverage tourism industry happened hand in hand with changes in dining and cooking: for example, the growing interest in the consumption of foods that are unprocessed or the increasing influence of trends such as street food and vegetarian/vegan dishes. Changes in consumer demands and their heterogeneity urge providers of gastronomic services to pay attention to the relationships between visitor expectations and satisfaction, to personalize their offer to individual needs of customers, to create opportunities for socializing with residents, to include sensory experiences. They also must be able to innovate when crisis hits. In other words, should destinations jump into innovation as a form of meeting contemporary consumer preferences or opt for incremental adjustments for safeguarding the cultural heritage of regional food?

Indeed, the occurrence of the COVID-19 pandemic may contribute to people hesitating to interact with food for social reasons and/or in social occasions. Providing a genuinely authentic product or experience is no longer the priority. Customers are now prioritizing on sanitary safety and cleanliness. As conviviality might endanger one's safety, people socialize less. Certainly, this trend resulted in changes on the part of food providers who improved their safety performance. And with this trend that hasn't been integrated in our list, we end this chapter to alert to the fact that trends are always changing and surprising and that the food tourism providers will have to show repeatedly that they are capable of adapting to a context in continuous evolution.

Food for Thought

- Which of the tendencies that were listed in this chapter apply to your region and which don't? In the positive case, can you give concrete examples? In the negative case, can you explain why? Is this positive or negative for tourism destinations in general and food tourism destinations in particular?
- Which are the three trends you foresee will have a longer lasting effect? Please justify.
- Which changing culinary expectation and corresponding consequences was/were omitted in this chapter? For each case, please describe the phenomenon and its consequences.

Acknowledgments

The writing of this chapter has been supported with funds of the research centre CETRAD (FCT project UIDB/04011/2020). We would like to thank those who participated in the Delphi questionnaire.

References

Batat, W. (2019). *Food and Experiential Marketing: Pleasure, Wellbeing and Consumption.* Routledge.

Batat, W., & Addis, M. (2021). Designing food experiences for wellbeing: A framework advancing design thinking research from a customer experience perspective. *European Journal of Marketing, 55*(9), 2392–2413. https://doi.org/10.1108/EJM-12-2020-0893

Batat, W., Peter, P.C., Moscato, E. M., Castro, I. A., Chan, S., Chugani, S., & Muldrow, A. F. (2019). The experiential pleasure of food: A savoring journey to food well-being. *Journal of Business Research, 100*, 392–399. https://doi.org/10.1016/j.jbusres.2018.12.024

CBI. (n.d.). Entering the European market for food tourism products. www.cbi.eu/market-information/tourism/food-tourism/market-entry

Craig, L. (2020). *Ugly Food for Thought: Ripple Effects from a New Food Movement*. Senior Capstone Projects.

Ellis, A., Park, E., Kim, S., & Yeoman, I. (2019). What is food tourism?. *Tourism Management, 68*, 250–263.

Fountain, J. (2021). The future of food tourism in a post-COVID-19 world: Insights from New Zealand. *Journal of Tourism Futures*, ahead-of-print. https://doi.org/10.1108/JTF-04-2021-0100

Frost, W., Frost, J., Strickland, P., & Smith Maguire, J. (2020). Seeking a competitive advantage in wine tourism: Heritage and storytelling at the cellar-door. *International Journal of Hospitality Management, 87*(March 2019), 102460. https://doi.org/10.1016/j.ijhm.2020.102460

Fusté-Forné, F. (2019). Seasonality in food tourism: Wild foods in peripheral areas. *Tourism Geographies*, ahead-of-print, 1–21. https://doi.org/10.1080/14616688.2018.1558453

Getz, D., Robinson, R., Andersson, T., & Vujicic, S. (2014). *Foodies and food tourism*. Goodfellow Publishers Ltd.

Gretzel, U., Murphy, J., Pesonen, J., & Blanton, C. (2019). Food waste in tourist households: a perspective article. *Tourism Review, 75*(1), 235–238. https://doi.org/10.1108/TR-05-2019-0170

Hall, C. M., & Sharples, L. (2003). The consumption of experiences or the experience of consumption? An introduction to the tourism of taste, in M. Hall, L. Sharples, R. Mitchell, N. Macionis & B. Cambourne (Eds.), *Food Tourism Around the World*. Oxford: Butterworth-Heinemann.

Hanafin, S. (2004). *Review of literature on the Delphi Technique*. Dublin: National Children's Office.

Hiamey, S. E., Amenumey, E. K., & Mensah, I. (2021). Critical success factors for food tourism destinations: A socio-cultural perspective. *International Journal of Tourism Research. 23*(2), 192–205. https://doi.org/10.1002/jtr.2402

Horng, J. S., & Tsai, C. T. (2012). Culinary tourism strategic development: An Asia-Pacific perspective. *International Journal of Tourism Research, 14* (1), 40–55.

Kim, S. (S.), Choe, J.Y. (J.), King, B., Oh, M. (M.), & Otoo, F. E. (2022). Tourist perceptions of local food: A mapping of cultural values. *International Journal of Tourism Research, 24*(1), 1–17. https://doi.org/10.1002/jtr.2475

Kline, C., Knollenberg, W., & Deale, C. S. (2014). Tourism's relationship with ethical food systems. In C. Weeden, & B. Boluk (Eds.), *Managing ethical consumption in tourism* (pp. 104–121). Abingdon: Routledge.

Knollenberg, W., Duffy, L. N., Kline, C., & Kim, G. (2021). Creating competitive advantage for food tourism destinations through food and beverage experiences. *Tourism Planning and Development, 18*(4), 379–397. https://doi.org/10.1080/21568316.2020.1798687

Kuang, Y. T., & Bhat, R. (2017). Sustainability challenges in food tourism. In R. Bhat (Ed.), *Sustainability Challenges in the Agrofood Sector.* https://doi.org/10.1002/978111 9072737.ch19

Levitt, J. A., Zhang, P., Dipietro, R. B., & Meng, F. (2019). Food tourist segmentation: Attitude, behavioral intentions and travel planning behavior based on food involvement and motivation. *International Journal of Hospitality & Tourism Administration, 20*(2), 129–155. https://doi.org/10.1080/15256480.2017.1359731

Lin, V. S., & Song, H. (2015). A review of Delphi forecasting research in tourism. *Current Issues in Tourism, 18*(12), 1099–1131. https://doi.org/10.1080/13683 500.2014.967187

Lopes, H. S., Remoaldo, P. C., Ribeiro, V., & Martín-Vide, J. (2022). Pathways for adapting tourism to climate change in an urban destination – Evidences based on thermal conditions for the Porto Metropolitan Area (Portugal). *Journal of Environmental Management, 315* (December 2021), 115161. https://doi.org/10.1016/j.jenvman.2022.115161

OECD (2012), Food and the Tourism Experience. OECD.

Okumus, B. (2021). Food tourism research: A perspective article. *Tourism Review, 76*(1), 38–42. https://doi.org/10.1108/TR-11-2019-0450

Pardo-De-Santayana, M., Tardío, J., & Morales, R. (2005). The gathering and consumption of wild edible plants in the Campoo (Cantabria, Spain). *International Journal of Food Sciences and Nutrition, 56*, 529–542. https://doi.org/10.1080/09637480500490731

Rachão, S., Breda, Z., Fernandes, C., & Joukes, V. (2019). Food tourism and regional development: A systematic literature review. *European Journal of Tourism Research, 21*, 33–49.

Rachão, S., Breda, Z., Fernandes, C., & Joukes, V. (2021a). Drivers of experience co-creation in food-and-wine tourism: An exploratory quantitative analysis. *Tourism Management Perspectives, 37* (December 2020), 1000783. https://doi.org/10.1016/j.tmp.2020.100783

Rachão, S., Breda, Z., Fernandes, C., & Joukes, V. (2021b). Food-and-wine experiences towards co-creation in tourism. *Tourism Review, 76*(5), 1050–1066. https://doi.org/10.1108/TR-01-2019-0026

Richards, G. (2021). Evolving research perspectives on food and gastronomic experiences in tourism. *International Journal of Contemporary Hospitality Management, 33*(3), 1037–1058. https://doi.org/10.1108/IJCHM-10-2020-1217

Robinson, R. N. S., Getz, D., & Dolnicar, S. (2018). Food tourism subsegments: A data-driven analysis. *International Journal of Tourism Research, 20*, 367–377. https://doi.org/10.1002/jtr.2188

Rowe, G., & Wright, G. (1999). The Delphi technique as a forecasting tool: issues and analysis. *International Journal of Forecasting, 15*(4), 353–375.

Rowe, G., & Wright, G. (2001). Expert opinions in forecasting: The role of the Delphi technique. In J. S. Armstrong (Ed.), *Principles of forecasting* (pp. 125–144). Springer. (International Series in Operations Research & Management Science).

Smith, S. L. J., & Xiao, H. G. (2008). Culinary tourism supply chains: A preliminary examination. *Journal of Travel Research, 46*, 289–299. http://dx.doi.org/10.1177/0047287506303981

Stalmirska, A. M. (2021). Local food in tourism destination development: The supply-side perspectives. *Tourism Planning & Development*, ahead-of-print, 1–18. https://doi.org/10.1080/21568316.2021.1928739

World Food Travel Association (2019). State of the food tourism industry 2019 Annual Report. World Food Travel Association, available at: https://worldfoodtravel.org/food-tourism-research/

World Food Travel Association. (n.d.). *What is food tourism.* https://worldfoodtravel.org/what-is-food-tourism/

4 Challenging Consumer Culinary Expectations

Amanda Katili Niode

Introduction: Taste and Story

Strange foods may encourage travelers to visit a destination for a number of reasons. One is where the food comes from, whether it is from the ocean, the forest, the farm, the plantation, or the garden. Other reasons are the food's ingredients, tastes, cooking methods, and locations. Human aspects such as the people who prepared the dishes, the stories behind them, and the experiences of those who consumed them may also change consumers' expectations.

As a country with more than 17,500 islands and 1,330 ethnic groups, Indonesia is an ideal destination for food tourism, which is defined as "the act of traveling for a taste of place in order to get a sense of place" (World Food Travel Association, n.d., para. 1). Hendijani (2016) found that, in relation to food experiences in Indonesia, tourists' overall satisfaction considerably depends on the aspects of heritage and ingredients. Wijaya et al. (2017) went further by identifying factors related to travelers' preconceptions in consuming local food. Consuming novel local food, according to the author, might cause some assumptions, especially for first-time visitors. Apparently, factors underlying visitors' expectations may be categorized into human aspects and food aspects. They include staff quality, local servicescapes, sensory attributes, food uniqueness, food authenticity, food familiarity, and food variety.

Klosse (2019) explained why people choose certain foods over others by mentioning "convenient, affordable, and tasty". Convenient refers to the ability of using the food. Affordable means consumers can purchase the food. Tasty indicates enjoyment for those who eat the food. In other words, travelers may not enjoy certain foods if they are troublesome, expensive, and unpalatable. Food acceptability depends on customer characteristics, sensory characteristics of the food, and the "feel-good" factor (Maina, 2018). Consumers in this case have knowledge, attitudes, and beliefs. Their sense of innovation and perception of particular food products influence acceptability. Food's appearance, taste, texture, and aroma are some of its sensory characteristics, while the "feel-good" factor means food that is enjoyable rather than insipid.

Food is a universal language that touches every aspect of human life. Sara Roversi, the founder and president of Future Food Institute, says: "Food is life,

DOI: 10.4324/9781003282532-6

energy, and nourishment. It is the vehicle of values, culture, and identity. Food is sociality. Eating is an essential activity for human beings, but today it requires consciousness and awareness." (Future Food Institute, 2022, para. 3). Hence, the stories behind foods, even strange foods, will lead to awareness that eventually leads to acceptability.

This chapter will use Indonesia as a location to explore strange foods from the food systems perspective and investigate how they may enhance the experience of travelers to increase the number of visitors to the country.

> Food systems embrace the entire range of actors and their interlinked value-adding activities involved in the production, aggregation, processing, distribution, consumption, and disposal (loss or waste) of food products that originate from agriculture (incl. livestock), forestry, fisheries, and food industries, and the broader economic, societal, and natural environments in which they are embedded.
>
> (von Braun et al., 2021: 8)

Archipelago Destinations

As the largest archipelago in the world, Indonesia is known as the emerald of the equator, having 81,000 km of coastline. It consists of small and large tropical islands, the largest being Java, Sumatra, Borneo, Sulawesi, and Papua. With 500 volcanoes, 127 of which are active, Indonesia is an ideal place for those seeking scenic views and adventures. The country is located between two continents and two oceans: Asia and Australia and the Pacific and Indian Oceans. The distance between its west and east coasts is similar to that between San Francisco and New York or London and Moscow. The latest census shows that Indonesia currently has 34 provinces and a total population of more than 270 million with Bahasa Indonesia as their national language, in addition to 650 regional languages.

Historically, Indonesia's vibrant culture has undergone many changes. In the prehistoric era, many cultural traditions centered on the locals' animistic beliefs, involving supernatural beings and forces. Eventually, the Hindus began to influence Indonesia in the first century, followed by cultural influences from China, the Middle East, Portugal, and the Netherlands (Indonesia Travel, n.d.-a). The spread of Islam in Indonesia began in the 13th century, although some believe it started in the 7th century, through Arab Muslim traders. It was adopted by local rulers, and the influence of Sufism. With Muslims as the majority, the use of pork products in many areas is quite limited. As one of the megadiverse countries, Indonesia shows a diversity of life and interactions at the genetic, species, and ecosystem levels. This jurisdiction of over 5 million square kilometers, 84% water and 16% land, is home to 11% of the world's flowering plants, 13% of its mammals, 6% of its amphibians, 7% of its reptiles, 16% of its birds, and 14% of its freshwater and saltwater fish (Fauna & Flora International, 2019).

Indonesia's biodiversity for food and agriculture includes food resources that encompass 800 species of food plants, over 1,000 species of medicinal plants, thousands of varieties of microalgae, 77 kinds of carbohydrate sources, 75 types of fats and oils, 26 types of nuts, 389 kinds of fruit, 228 sorts of vegetables, 40 beverage ingredients, and 110 different herbs and spices (Khudori, 2010). Such biogeodiversity and cultural diversity creates a wealth of travel destinations in Indonesia. Seven places were described as popular by CNN Indonesia (2021): Bali, the Island of the Gods; Labuan Bajo, the Komodo Island, in West Nusa Tenggara; the Gili Islands, also in West Nusa Tenggara; Mount Bromo, East Java; Ijen Crater, East Java; Sumba Island, East Nusa Tenggara; and Derawan Island, East Kalimantan.

Hynes and Law (2020) recognized 16 top-rated tourist attractions in Indonesia. These are the beaches of Bali; Borobudur Temple, Central Java; the orangutans of Borneo; the Gili Islands, West Nusa Tenggara; Komodo National Park, West Nusa Tenggara; Sacred Monkey Forest, Ubud, Bali; Mount Bromo, East Java; Tana Toraja, South Sulawesi; Kalimantan Island; Lake Toba, North Sumatra; Mount Krakatau, West Java; Raja Ampat, West Papua; Mount Rinjani, West Nusa Tenggara; Pura Tanah Lot, Bali; Banda Islands, Maluku; and the Jatiluwih rice fields, Bali.

In 2021, to help the economic recovery in the tourism sector, the Indonesian government decided to focus on the development of five super-priority destinations: Borobudur, Central Java; Likupang, North Sulawesi; Mandalika, West Nusa Tenggara; Lake Toba, North Sumatra; and Labuan Bajo, West Nusa Tenggara. Improvements will focus on amenities, attractions, and accessibility. Also, "storynomics tourism" approaches and public–private partnership to build entertainment centers, such as theme parks, are expected to attract more travelers. Storynomics tourism is a tourism approach formula that puts forward narratives, creative content, and cultural life (Kominfo, 2021). The five super-priority destinations will have facilities with world-class infrastructure, such as airports, ports, and land routes. There will also be high-quality telecommunication networks and creative economy products as well as human resources. Lessons learned from the efforts of developing the five super-priority destinations will be the basis for improving the next priority destinations, which are yet to be decided.

Abundant Ethnic Foods and Drinks

The Sobat Budaya (Friends of Culture) Foundation, which consistently collects data on Indonesian traditional culture through the One Million Cultural Data Movement, stated that, to date, there are nearly 40,000 types of traditional Indonesian food and drinks from the western to the eastern part of Indonesia, and they are generally seasoned and spiced. This figure is still growing, but unfortunately, quite a lot are on the verge of extinction (NusaKuliner, n.d.). In relation to its biogeodiversity, the variety of food ingredients in Indonesia is vast. More than 30% of Indonesian delicacies consist of over 10 herbs and

52 *Amanda Katili Niode*

spices, with shallots, garlic, chili, lime, ginger, pepper, and turmeric being the most common.

Combination of herbs and spices may be considered Indonesian food innovation, as it can produce new dishes. Sobat Kuliner Foundation noted that, among the thousands of food items in its database, there are at least 100 types of hot sauce throughout the archipelago. Each sauce has different configurations and elements of food ingredients, creating unique, pungent tastes (BIFNews, 2016).

Sobat Budaya elaborated on a data-driven concept of culture and food. Culture exploration can provide new culinary frontiers. Most traditional foods require at least ten herbs and spices, and 90% are used exclusively in Indonesia, highlighting the effect of native plants in shaping local cuisine and the many functions surrounding the location. Traditional preserved foods such as meat floss, salted egg, and roasted sago may be viable food sources during extraordinary events like the current COVID-19 pandemic due to their locality and shelf life (Taufik, 2020).

Connecting Sobat Budaya's database to the five super-priority destinations, there are 5,013 selections of food and drink in Central Java, 1,445 in North Sulawesi, 1,241 in North Sumatra, and 418 in West Nusa Tenggara. Some or most of them may be strange foods to many visitors.

The culinary sub-sector makes a 30% contribution to the total revenue from the tourism and creative economy sectors. As it has a strong economic potential, the Indonesian government will work to strengthen food tourism in the country. As an example, the following are signature dishes from the five super-priority destinations that some visitors may consider strange (Kemenparekraf/ Baparekraf RI, n.d.):

Taliwang from Mandalika is a chicken dish, fried or grilled using jackfruit wood or coffee wood, creating a tempting aroma. The fresh ingredients consist of free-range chicken, chili, shallots, tomatoes, and shrimp paste.

Naniura from Lake Tobe is known as Batak sashimi. Rich in spices, *naniura* is a fish dish prepared without cooking. Usually, cleaned carps are soaked in tamarind and kaffir lime juice, immersed with a mix of herbs and spices for a unique taste. The major herbs and spices for *naniura* are *andaliman* (similar to Sichuan pepper) and *kecombrang* (torch ginger). Hence, the aftertaste of this lemony, chewy, soft, and delicious dish is a numb sensation in the mouth.

Tinutuan in Likupang is a bowl of rice porridge mixed with a variety of vegetables such as kale, spinach, basil, shelled corn, sweet potatoes, and pumpkin. Depending on the consumer's preference, other ingredients may be added, such as shredded skipjack, dried salted fish, and chili sauce. *Tinutuan* has a combination of pungent and savory flavors, with a hint of sweetness from the yellow pumpkin.

Kupat Tahu from the Borobudur area consists of tofu, rice cake, noodles, fried foods, bean sprouts, cabbage, and tofu, mixed with peanut sauce.

Labuan Bajo, the gateway to Komodo Island, has *se'i*, a meat dish with either beef, pork, or fish as its ingredient, processed with hot smoke. Its side dish, papaya leaves or blossoms, is quite pungent due to chili sauce. Those in the food business recognize the need for improvement in the process, including access to a one-stop business licensing process to make it easier for entrepreneurs.

Entry-level businesses, according to them, should be provided with guidelines, business training, licensing information, and legal assistance in the business establishment process. The Ministry of Tourism and Creative Economy provides facilitation such as business training, access to capital, and assistance in establishing food businesses. The Ministry will also assist in promoting the diversity of Indonesian food domestically and internationally (Kuliner, n.d.).

Dozens of Spices

De Gusman and Siemonsma (1999) mentioned the debate in the literature on the similarities and distinctions between herbs and spices. The food industry considers herbs to be soft-stemmed plants, mostly flavoring temperate plants; the whole herbaceous tops are collected and used either fresh or dried in the seasoning of food.

The word spices covers all other dried aromatic vegetable products used in food seasoning, usually of tropical or subtropical origin. It refers to only parts of the plant such as barks, rhizomes, flower buds, fruits, seeds, and other parts of fruits.

Citing De Guzman and Siemonsma (1999), Negeri Rempah Foundation noted that, in the course of time and on a world scale, there are about 500 types of plants that have been used and are known as spices. In Southeast Asia, the number is close to 275 plant species. Of the 126 commonly used spices, about half are already cultivated, and the rest still have to be harvested from the wild (Negeri Rempah, n.d.).

Intense focus-group discussions among stakeholders in major Indonesian islands, according to Vita Datau Messakh of the Indonesia Gastronomy Network, came up with "The Triangle Concept of Indonesian Gastronomy," which is expected to enhance travelers' experience through authenticity, locality, and novelty.

The unique selling proposition of Indonesian food tourism revolves around the interrelated aspects of history, culture, and food. Traditional rituals and ceremonies and the use of spices shape the characters of Indonesian foods. Culture depends on the food and history of Indonesia, directed by storytelling and cooking processes in rituals and ceremonies. Its history is heavily influenced by ancient cultures and the spice trade (Messakh, 2017).

In 2017, after a Facebook poll organized by CNN Travel, *rendang*, a meat dish from Sumatra, was voted as the world's most delicious food, with 35,000 votes. It is a tender beef stew, cooked in rich spices of lemongrass and ginger, with chili in creamy coconut milk and an authentic firewood aroma (Cheung, 2017). Celebrity chef Jamie Oliver, the world's richest chef, featured beef *rendang* in his book *Save with Jamie: Shop Smart, Cook Clever, Waste Less,* while Gordon Ramsay cooked *rendang* in West Sumatra. *Rendang* basically refers to a special process that makes beef tender, moistly dry, and flavorful. The complex cooking process gives it a unique taste, and maybe strange for some.

With eight hours required from the beginning until the end, beef as the main ingredient passes through three stages of cooking. *Gulai* is when the coconut milk is still in liquid form, followed by *kalio* after four hours of cooking, when the coconut milk thickens and becomes oily. When *kalio* is cooked on a low flame until moistly dried, it is called *rendang* and has a dark brown color (Indonesia Travel, n.d.-b).

Through personal communication (2022), Reno Andam Suri, the author of *Rendang: Minang Legacy to the World* explains the challenge of introducing *rendang* to international travelers coming to Indonesia. Tourists may appreciate the process of cooking *rendang* but not necessarily like the dish. Reno, who organizes food tours, suggests a prologue about *rendang* first and introduces the types of *rendang* that visitors may be curious about. There are all kinds of main ingredients for *rendang,* including beef, chicken, jackfruit, and vegetarian and vegan options made from leaves and vegetables. In the case of Reno's tourists, vegans would became more open to trying the strange dish and to cooking it back home.

Reno went further, as *rendang* is spicy, so those who would like less spicy food can be accommodated without reducing the core herbs and spices as the base. Hence, people who understand regional food in depth must guide food travelers, as they may have detailed and sometimes unusual questions. Reno said that to make *rendang,* there are at least five kinds of herbs and three types of spices required. This goes back to the *rendang* version from inland areas, called *darek*, which is minimalistic with less spices, as opposed to coastal *rendang,* which is rich in spices, with dozens of spices needed to cook the dish. Efriyanti, who has been cooking *rendang* for more than 40 years with recipes passed down from generation to generation, affirms that *rendang* is a traditional food presented in traditional ceremonies, and each region has different ingredients and cooking methods.

Darek is made from simpler spices and cooking techniques. Its ingredients are only chili, ginger, galangal, lemongrass, shallots, garlic, kaffir lime leaves, bay leaves, and turmeric leaves. Some even cook *rendang* using only red onions, garlic, chili, and spiced leaves. The cooking method is simple, involving mixing all the ingredients in coconut milk and stirring slowly until dry. In contrast, *rendang* from the coastal area is rich in flavor, and the ingredients can be sautéed. Efriyanti prefers cooking *darek rendang* by producing moist *rendang* (beef, chicken, fish, potatoes) and crispy *rendang* (corn, egg, beef lung, and cassava).

Tabu moitomo from Gorontalo may be the traditional dish with the most herbs and spices. It is a rich black soup using beef or poultry with all kinds of herbs and spices imaginable. This cuisine is commonly served at weddings, family gatherings, and special events. Preparing *tabu moitomo*, a comfort food for many, is a family affair, as it takes a long time and many people to grind the herbs and spices and to wait for the meat to become tender. The original *tabu moitomo* is blackish, due to the grated, toasted, and ground coconut as the basis. The cooking method is first to boil beef in a stew pan until cooked and set aside. Shredded coconut is toasted over a frying pan until lightly browned and ground until the oil is released. The next step is to grind and blend shallot, garlic, red chili pepper, cayenne pepper, coriander, pepper, galangal, lemongrass, turmeric, ginger, cumin, and salt. The ground spices are then mixed with scallions, basil leaves, pandan leaves, and lime leaves. Finally, the sautéed coconut and spices are poured into the stew pan and simmered until the spices seep into the meat.

One thing with traditional food is that it is usually served in abundance, in a pot full of what some people think of as strange food. The color is either black, brown, dark green, or dark yellow. It doesn't look appetizing unless combined with colorful garnishes and beautiful plating. Local people, however, may say that beautifully plated food is not authentic, and it is kind of scary to eat beautifully served food. This is a question that needs an answer: whether serving local food for visitors should be "as is" or presented in a sophisticated way.

Pungent Foods and Condiments

The taste of savory, hot and spicy, or even sour and spicy foods is very popular in several regions of Indonesia. In some areas, most foods are pungent and very hot, either from the use of ginger, black or white pepper, cayenne pepper, or red chili pepper. *Sambal*, spicy and hot sauce, is a condiment present in most Indonesian dishes. Considered as appetite enhancer, it is made from chili, salt, and other ingredients that are ground and mashed. Scoville Heat Units (SHU), indicating chili pepper's pungency and heat, measure the concentration of capsaicin, the substance that creates a sensation of heat on the tongue (Huitquist, 2020).

The average SHU score for cayenne pepper in Southeast Asia, including in Indonesia, is 50,000–100,000, and Indonesian red chili pepper has an SHU of 2,500–8,000, compared to Italian pepperoncini (100–500 SHU), and Mexican habanero (100,000–350,000 SHU) (Tempo, 2010). *Cabai hiyung*, a chili pepper that grows only in South Kalimantan Indonesia, however, is said to be 17 times hotter than the average Indonesian cayenne pepper and has an SHU of 1,512,000 (The Jakarta Post, 2017).

Some very hot dishes, enjoyed by many Indonesian youngsters, are called Satan food due to their high level of pungent spiciness. An example is *seblak mi setan,* made from noodles, sausage, eggs, vegetables, tomatoes, aromatic ginger, shallots, garlic, red chilies, and very hot cayenne pepper (Audina, 2020). Another popular one is *rawon setan*, a very pungent black soup made from, among other things, beef, galangal, lemongrass, lime and bay leaves, civet fruit, cayenne pepper, red chilies, hazelnut, turmeric, and ginger (Group, G. C. M., n.d.)

A research team from Gadjah Mada University identified at least 257 kinds of *sambal* in all parts of Indonesia, categorized into 138 cooked and 119 raw condiments. Among these 257 assorted chili sauces, there are 122 variations of spices, and the most widely used are shallots, garlic, palm sugar, refined sugar, and cooking oil (Gusti, 2018). According to Mudjiati Garjito, the research team leader, the variety of *sambal* should not just be considered from the point of view of taste: it should be seen as a reflection of heirloom elements in the formation of Indonesian culinary flavors. Each region has its own special *sambal,* and this must be researched further. Would travelers try pungent and hot food if they understood the philosophy behind it?

Arifasno Napu found, in a survey for his PhD dissertation, that hot food in Gorontalo means honesty. Respondents explained that, when they want to scold children who are disobedient, who lie, or who say bad words, parents will immediately rub their lips with cayenne pepper. This illustrates that the mouth is a tool to express good, civilized, and honest words (personal communication, 2018).

He explained further about the philosophy of hot food and honesty. When preparing hot food in Gorontalo, people traditionally only use cayenne pepper or red chili pepper, not mixed with any kind of sugar, so it is spicy from the beginning till the end of consumption; whereas, if it is mixed with sugar, the consumer will taste the sweetness first, followed by the spiciness (meaning "not honest"). In modern times, however, there have been many changes in the behavior of traditional food consumption because the old way is not taught anymore, and the philosophical meanings are not conveyed, so the element of honesty in practice is changing.

Plant-Based Delicacies

As Indonesia has 228 types of vegetables, variations of mixed plant dishes become daily food in many parts of the country. *Gado-gado* is a dish of steamed mixed vegetables and hard-boiled eggs served with a peanut sauce. The food usually consists of potatoes, spinach, beansprouts, cabbage, cucumber, tempeh, and tofu. The peanut sauce as the dressing is a mix of ground garlic, chili pepper, peanuts, brown sugar, and tamarind. Due to its creamy and brownish peanut sauce, *gado-gado* looks different than Western mixed salads but is quite universal, as global media such as *The Guardian, The New York Times, BBC Goodfood* and *Food52* have published *gado-gado* recipes.

Urap, another mixed-vegetable dish, consists of long beans, morning glory, spinach, basil, bean sprouts, carrot, young cassava leaf, papaya leaf, and cabbage. All the steamed vegetables are sliced and mixed with seasoned and spiced grated coconut for dressing. The grated coconut is usually peppered with ground garlic, shallot, chili, palm sugar, tamarind juice, salt, coconut sugar, lime leaves, and other things. It is very tasty and crunchy and can be consumed as a meal or side dish with rice, crackers, and other foods (Witaworld, 2019).

In Bali, a similar dish is called white *lawar,* prepared with boiled long beans, jackfruit, and shredded meat that could be chicken, pork, or duck. Grated coconut is added with mixed herbs and spices (Bali Travel Guide, n.d.-a).

White *lawar* is a typical Balinese food that is usually served as a daily meal and also in ceremonies to mark important life-cycle elements. Red *lawar*, considered extreme by some visitors, is similar but uses the blood of chickens, pigs, or ducks. One can still taste the blood even if the *lawar* is already mixed with herbs and spices (Bali Travel Guide, n.d.–b).

Other strange vegetable dishes are the smelly but delicious ones, adding *jengkol* or dogfruit (*Archidendron pauciflorum*), a member of the Fabaceae family, and *petai* or stinky bean (*Parkia speciosa*), also a member of the Fabaceae family. Muryanto (2021) categorized *petai* and *jengkol* as local and marginal vegetables; some of them can be more expensive than meat.

Consumers' behavior of avoiding smelly (not rotten) food may be changed if there is information on the health benefits of eating dogfruit and stinky bean. *Jengkol* is believed to purify blood, ease dysentery, and prevent diabetes (Kurniawan Ulung, 2018), whereas *petai* can reduce cholesterol, depression, hypertension, and the risk of heart attack (Siti, 2019).

Poisonous Tubers

Would travelers try poisonous food ingredients? Sumunar and Estiasih (2015) explained about wild yam (*Dioscorea hispida Dennst*), which contains cyanic acid; with simple processing, this tuber, which has bioactive compounds, carbohydrates, vitamins, and minerals, may play an important role in health and medical treatments. In Gorontalo, the wild yam is known as *bitule* or forest yam. *Keyabo*, a snack from the area wrapped in banana leaves, is made from *bitule*, palm sugar, grated coconut, garlic, and salt. Another poisonous tuber in Indonesia is *porang* (*Amorphophallus muelleri*). However, it is not as popular as it is in Japan, which utilizes this tuber as the basic ingredient for *shirataki* noodles or *konyaku*.

Besides containing carbohydrates, *porang* is rich in calcium; hence, it is good as baby food and as a substitute for breast milk. The key is to make *porang* safe to eat, and the way to do this could also be a tourist information item. The steps include soaking the grated tubers in water, replacing the water every 12 hours for three days to remove the poison. After being immersed in water many times, it is removed, dried, and made into *porang* flour (Abdullah, 2020).

Coconut Culture

In Indonesia, the coconut tree has as many uses and plays an important role in customs and folklore. Based on their local exploration, Ipong Niaga and Rosyid Azhar, a researcher and a journalist respectively, informed the author that the first human being, according to the legends of Gorontalo, Sulawesi, is not Adam but Bebe, who was created from a coconut seedling. There are 735 villages in Gorontalo, and more than ten of them are named after coconut, or *bongo*, as they say in Gorontalo. Some of these villages are Bongo, Bongo Nol,

Bongo Tua, Bongohulawa, Bongopini, Bongoime, Bongomeme, Tabongo, and Lombongo. Coconuts are always present in rituals involving the cycle of life. A baby has a ceremony with haircuts carried out by family members, who put the hair in a coconut and hang it outdoors. Coconut leaves are also part of decorations in coming-of-age rituals, marriage, and death.

Most traditional foods in Gorontalo are coconut-based, either cooked with coconut milk or home-made coconut oil. Coconuts are useful for condiments, appetizers, snacks, main courses, desserts, and drinks. Coconut milk is pressed from grated coconut produced by using *dudangata*, a traditional coconut grater. One sits on a wooden stool connected to a rod with a coconut grater. The grated coconut has a different texture compared to that produced by modern coconut grater. There is a saying in Gorontalo, *hiyambola dudangata debo mohangato:* "even a coconut grater requests a reward." This refers to corruption in society, showing how omnipresent coconuts are in society.

Ancient Ritual Cooking Methods

One of West Papua's tribal rites of peace and showing gratitude, considered a feast by international travelers, is *masak batu* (stone burning). It is a cooking method where locals use a pit of stone and light it with fire to cook some food. The ingredients include pork, yam, or other meat for those who do not eat pork products (Content, 2022.

Charles Toto, head of the Papua Jungle Chef Community, who has cooked for celebrities like Mick Jagger and Melinda Gates, mentioned there are many articles about stone burning in Papua, but he mapped the stone burning practice to seven customary areas consisting of four different methods (personal communication, 2022).

The first method is burning rock by digging a hole in the soil, generally practiced in highland areas of Baliem, Paniai, and the Arfak Mountains, with a range of altitude of 700–3,000 meters above sea level. The second is stone burning on the ground in the southern region of Papua Island, including Merauke, Bovendigoel, Mappi, and Timika. The third is stone burning with a pyramid shape in Biak and Raja Ampat, in the northern region of Papua Island. The fourth method is to burn papeda (sago porridge) in stones, usually in the Jayapura area and the Mamberamo River.

Some areas still use equipment such as pottery, bamboo, bark, and leaves, but there is an order in stone burning. According to Charles, the tubers are always at the bottom, the middle is vegetables or yams, and on top is always the meat, either pork or deer, so its juice can trickle down to the vegetables and the tubers (personal communication, 2022).

Another ancient ritual is *pa'piong* cooking from Toraja in Sulawesi. Some parts of the area are famous for death rites and burial sites. Noble people's burial ceremonies incorporate chants, the sacrifice of hundreds of water buffalo, skulls, and bones. The coffins of ordinary people are placed in caves and crevices in burial sites accompanied by *tau-tau* (wooden or bamboo effigies). In another area, a cliff burial site has galleries of ancestor statues, and coffins are not kept in caves or crevices. Deceased infants were buried in *tarra* trees (*Artocarpus sp.*, a tree species in the same family as jackfruit). One tree can hold 20 babies placed upright, each identified by a door-like structure. Eventually, the babies became one with the sap-flowing tree.

Pa'piong is the area's culinary specialty. It is made of meat (either pork, water buffalo, chicken, or fish) mixed with grated coconut and vegetables (sometimes cassava leaves or banana stems) and seasoned with garlic, shallots, lemon grass, red-eye chili, and some spices. The ancient cooking style with charcoal and bamboos presents an appetizing smell and distinct tastes and textures. *Pa'piong* can be served with steamed white rice or black rice.

Traditional Herbal Drinks

Ten years ago, there was an article in *Time* titled "Jamu: Why Isn't Indonesia's Ancient System of Herbal Healing Better Known?" (Neubauer, 2012). Historical analysis of temple reliefs shows that *jamu*, a traditional herbal medicine, has existed in Indonesia for more than a thousand years. Beers (2012) explained that Indonesian herbal medicine is part of the internal and external health and beauty system, which includes powders, pills, herbs, bark, ointments, lotions, cosmetics, and massages combined with ancient folklore.

The younger generation is now less interested in traditional herbal medicine processing because, apart from the bitter taste and distinct smell, it takes time and knowledge to produce the perfect concoction. Irma Haryadi, an art worker in Jakarta, has long tried to popularize herbal medicine among teenagers through herbal ice cream. One of the popular herbal drinks is *jamu beras kencur,* meant to treat fatigue and improve blood circulation. To make herbal ice cream, Irma uses wet rice, *kencur* (aromatic ginger), palm sugar, lemongrass, ginger, Javanese chili, fennel, cardamom, cinnamon, lime leaves, winged beans, cloves, tapioca flour, and mung bean flour, with a shaker to make the ice cream.

Students like *jamu* ice cream, which feels strange because the ice cream is cold in the mouth but warm in the throat because of the spices. After tasting it, some are then interested in learning more about the various herbal ingredients that can be made into ice cream. Suwe Ora Jamu, a simple shop in Jakarta serving those who want to enjoy delicious and healthy herbs, coffee, or traditional home-made snacks, made another effort. Popie Sutomo, from the shop, explained that most visitors are young people who come to drink herbal medicine. This shop tries to make young people happy with attractive packaging and presentation of herbal medicine, more acceptable flavors, and a comfortable place to drink it. What is provided is a bottle of house blend herbal medicine with a taste of turmeric and tamarind, *kencur* rice, rosella, ginger hot drink, and *alang-alang.*

Conclusion: Popularizing Strange Foods

Based on the observations and activities organized by the Omar Niode Foundation regarding traditional Gorontalo food, there are several ways that can be used to make traditional foods, including strange ones, liked and well known. The experience may be a reference to develop ways to popularize strange foods in order to increase the number of food travelers, in combination with other attractions.

First, the variety of traditional strange foods through the region can be explored and types of raw food materials by observers, researchers, and students as well as central and regional governments. Culinary tourism approaches, culinary diplomacy, and culinary history are also very helpful in identifying and exploring traditional strange food stories.

Second, central and local government intervention can be increased through policies and promotions involving public figures serving strange food at government meetings and state banquets. In addition, local governments need to be involved in encouraging local content of traditional foods in the education sector through regulation.

Third, the role of the business world can be expanded, both in terms of doing business and providing capital for strange food businesses/partnerships and sponsoring events, bazaars, festivals or education about traditional food in elementary schools, high schools, universities, and communities. The media industry, including print, electronic, and social media, is also a powerful partner in the promotion of strange food, especially when it comes to events.

Fourth, there can be active participation in global activities such as International Day, International Month, International Year, and International Decade that can be associated with traditional food. Thus, the benefits of mass media coverage and international social media can be obtained. Examples of activities are World Tourism Day, World Food Day, Terra Madre Day, International Year of Pulses, and United Nations Decade of Biodiversity.

Fifth, individuals and communities in various regions can intensify their efforts to raise awareness and to organize innovative public events related to traditional food. In Indonesia, some of these are the Indonesian Gastronomy Network, the I Love Indonesian Food Movement, and the Indonesian Food Blogger Association.

Sixth, there can be an emphasis on publishing books containing stories and traditional food recipes, both in English and other foreign languages, to raise the image and popularity of regional strange foods.

Seventh, international organizations can be joined, without forgetting to promote regional traditional food such as through the International Academy of Gastronomy, International Association of Culinary Professionals, Slow Food International, and The World Association of Chefs' Societies.

Eighth, there can be participation in national and international surveys related to traditional strange foods in order to determine public perceptions and develop appropriate programs. Surveys can also be designed to determine the success of programs related to traditional foods.

Ninth, there can be active promotion of food tourism or general tourism with local specialties highlighted. There can also be invitation of mass media and promotions on social media.

The essence of food festivals to popularize food is illustrated by the Ubud Food Festival (UFF) in Bali, launched in 2015 as a three-day cross-cultural culinary adventure with Indonesian food as its focus. In 2019, the festival organized more than 110 events featuring over 95 speakers and around ten performers. Organizers said that, unlike most food festivals, UFF is not just about eating. It is also about what food can teach travelers and the stories shared through food. Therefore, 90% of the festival audience of that year said they would attend again.

Over the years, the festival has had cooking demonstrations, food forums, special events, masterclasses, panel sessions, long-table lunches, dinners, food tours, free night-time entertainment consisting of film and music, and a food, beverage, and makers' market featuring food vendors where attendees consumed more than 20,000 plates of food. In its partnership proposal, the festival organizer revealed the number of visitors to the events. More than 15,000 food lovers came from the United States, Australia, Singapore, the UK, the Philippines, Thailand, India, and Indonesia. UFF is now considered a must-attend food event in the region (Ubud Food Festival, 2022).

Food for Thought

- What do you consider to be strange foods, and how can we identify them?
- Are herbs and spices necessary as food ingredients to attract food travelers to certain destinations?
- Should food stories and rituals be part of activities to change consumers' perception towards strange foods?

References

Abdullah, G. (2020, December 8). Porang Kaya Manfaat, Masih 'asing' di. Indonesia, Laris di Jepang. www.mongabay.co.id/2020/12/06/porang-kaya-manfaat-masih-asing-di-indonesia-laris-di-jepang/

Audina, W. (2020, July 9). Makanan "setan," Berani Coba? www.infobudaya.net/2020/07/makanan-setan-berani-coba/

Bali Travel Guide (n.d.-a). Visitbali - white Lawar: The typical Balinese foods rich in nutrition. https://visitbali.id/property/white-lawar-the-typical-balinese-foods-rich-in-nutrition

Bali Travel Guide (n.d.-b) Visitbali - taste the Balinese extreme culinary: Lawar Merah https://visitbali.id/property/taste-the-balinese-extreme-culinary-lawar-merah

Beers, S. J. (2012). *Jamu: the ancient Indonesian art of herbal healing*. Tuttle Publishing.

BFINews. (2016, November 9). Perlu Berapa Tahun Jamuan Makan Untuk Bisa menikmati Semua Masakan Khas Se-indonesia? *BFINews*. https://bfinews.com/news/2016-09-25_nusakuliner

62 Amanda Katili Niode

Cheung, T. (2017, July 12). Your pick: World's 50 best foods. *CNN*. https://edition.cnn.com/travel/article/world-best-foods-readers-choice/index.html

CNN Indonesia (2021, August 25). 7 tempat wisata di Indonesia yang Paling Sering Dikunjungi. *gaya hidup*. www.cnnindonesia.com/gaya-hidup/20210730104224-275-674188/7-tempat-wisata-di-indonesia-yang-paling-sering-dikunjungi/1

Content, W. P. (2022, February 22). Stone-burning ceremony, the west papua tradition, and feast. *West Papua Story*. https://westpapuastory.com/stone-burning-ceremony-the-friendly-west-papua-tradition-and-feast

De Guzman, C. C., & Siemonsma, J. S. (1999). *Plant resources of South-East Asia* (Vol. 13). Backhuys Publ.

Fauna & Flora International. (2019, February 28). www.fauna-flora.org/countries/indonesia/

Future Food Institute. (2022, May 26). https://futurefoodinstitute.org/

Group, G. C. M. (n.d.). Rawon Setan. *Primarasa*. www.primarasa.co.id/lauk-utama/rawon-setan-

Gusti, O. (2018, May 8). Peneliti UGM kumpulkan ragam sambal dari seluruh Indonesia. https://ugm.ac.id/id/berita/16174-peneliti-ugm-kumpulkan-ragam-sambal-dari-seluruh-indonesia

Hendijani, R. B. (2016). Effect of food experience on tourist satisfaction: the case of Indonesia. *International Journal of Culture, Tourism and Hospitality Research*.

Hultquist, M (2020, November 11). The Scoville Scale. *Chili Pepper Madness*. www.chilipeppermadness.com/frequently-asked-questions/the-scoville-scale/

Hynes, C. & Law, M. (2020). 16 top-rated tourist attractions in Indonesia: Planetware. www.planetware.com/tourist-attractions/indonesia-ina.htm

Indonesia Travel (n.d.-a). The Official Website of Indonesia Tourism. www.indonesia.travel/yachts/en/about-indonesia

Indonesia Travel. (n.d.-b). Fun Facts about Rendang As the World's Best Food. www.indonesia.travel/id/en/trip-ideas/rendang-minangkabau-one-of-the-world-s-best-food-s

Jakarta Post. (2017). South Kalimantan village home to Indonesia's Hottest Chili. *Jakarta Post*. www.thejakartapost.com/life/2017/01/14/south-kalimantan-village-home-to-indonesias-hottest-chili.html

Kemenparekraf/Baparekraf RI. (n.d.). Kuliner Khas Dari 5 destinasi super prioritas. www.kemenparekraf.go.id/ragam-ekonomi-kreatif/Kuliner-Khas-dari-5-Destinasi-Super-Prioritas

Khudori, K. (2010). Kondisi Pertanian Pangan Indonesia. *Jurnal Pangan*, *19*(3), 211–232

Klosse, P. R. (2019). The taste of a healthy and sustainable diet: What is the recipe for the future?. *Research in Hospitality Management*, *9*(1), 35–42.

Kominfo (2021). www.kominfo.go.id/content/detail/28599/menparekraf-pemulihan-ekonomi-pariwisata-secara-umum-jadi-fokus-di-2021/0/berita

Kuliner. (n.d.). https://kemenparekraf.go.id/layanan/Subsektor-Ekonomi-Kreatif/Kuliner

Kurniawan Ulung, A. (2018). More to "jengkol" than bad smell. *Jakarta Post*. www.thejakartapost.com/life/2018/04/10/more-to-jengkol-than-bad-smell.html

Maina, J. W. (2018). Analysis of the factors that determine food acceptability. *The Pharma Innovation*, 7(5, Part D), 253.

Messakh, V. D. (2017). The Triangle Concept of Indonesian Gastronomy. In World Tourism Organization. Affiliate Members Global Report, Volume 16 – *Second Global*

Challenging Consumer Culinary Expectations 63

Report on Gastronomy Tourism, UNWTO, Madrid. https://doi.org/10.18111/978928 4418701

Muryanto P. (2021, February 16). Indonesian local and marginal vegetables, 13 most common vegetables. https://legionbotanica.com/13-indonesian-local-and-margi nal-vegetables-some-of-them-can-be-expensive-than-meat/.html

Negeri Rempah. (n.d.) https://negerirempah.org/en/

Neubauer, I. L. (2012, February 29). Why isn't Indonesia's ancient system of herbal healing better known? *Time*. http://content.time.com/time/world/article/ 0,8599,2107489,00.html

NusaKuliner (n.d.) http://nusakuliner.sobatbudaya.or.id/

Siti, K. (2019, November 6). These are several benefits of consuming petai a.k.a stinky bean. *TIMES Indonesia*. www.timesindonesia.co.id/read/news/238054/these-are-several-benefits-of-consuming-petai-aka-stinky-bean

Sumunar, S. R., & Estiasih, T. (2015). Umbi Gadung (*Dioscorea hispida Dennst*) Sebagai Bahan Pangan Mengandung Senyawa Bioaktif: Kajian Pustaka. *Jurnal Pangan dan Agroindustri*, *3*(1), 108–112.

Taufik, Shadine (2020). Eating ethically during a global crisis. *The Jakarta Post*. www.the jakartapost.com/life/2020/07/20/eating-ethically-during-a-global-crisis.html

Tempo (2010). Cabai Ini 10 Kali Lipat Lebih pedas dari rawit. https://dunia.tempo.co/ read/238298/cabai-ini-10-kali-lipat-lebih-pedas-dari-rawit

Ubud Food Festival (2022). Partnership proposal. https://issuu.com/ubudwritersread ersfestival/docs/uff22_partnership_proposal_efc69208790aa0?e=28273674%2F9 2108189

von Braun, J., Afsana, K., Fresco, L., Hassan, M., & Torero, M. (2021). Food Systems–definition, concept and application for the UN food systems summit. *Sci. Innov*, *27*.

Wijaya, S., King, B., Morrison, A., & Nguyen, T. H. (2017). Destination encounters with local food: The experience of international visitors in Indonesia. *Tourism Culture & Communication*, *17*(2), 79–91.

Witaworld. (2019, July 9). *15 types Indonesia Vegetarian Food. Witaworld*. https://witawo rld.wordpress.com/2016/09/29/15-types-indonesia-vegetarian-food/

World Food Travel Association (n.d.). *The world's leading authority on Food & Beverage Tourism*. https://worldfoodtravel.org/

Part II
From Home to Media

5 Food as High Touch

F. Xavier Medina

Introduction

Food, in a wide sense of the word, embodies landscapes, natural resources, human relationships, biodiversity and associated occupations as well as the fields of health and welfare, creativity, leisure, and, at the same time and in a prominent place, social and cultural functions and values.

We know that the fact of "sharing food," eating with others or "close to" others, or even eating together, is in the basis of the cultural identity and continuity of peoples and communities around the world. In this regard, we can emphasize values of human contact, hospitality, neighborliness or strangeness, cultural borders, and intercultural dialogue, and/or respect for diversity (Medina, 2021).

On the other hand, we have that the concept of cultural heritage is today a shifting one, and our food culture is an outstanding part of this cultural heritage. Nevertheless, it needs to be pointed out that food as an intangible culture has been very late in joining the ranks of those things that are "heritagizable."

Furthermore, it should not be forgotten that cultural heritage is now also regarded as a tourism experience and a tourism resource with great potential, and the heritagization of "food culture" is currently taking place within the framework of tourism and of its eventual benefits for local economies and local development.

Having all those aspects in mind, the aim of this chapter is to approach the use and development of these concepts regarding food, commensality, heritage, and tourism, reflecting on some discourses and interests. Food tourism experiences should be an effective approach of the lifestyles of locals. This approach also relies on human relationship and is as a source of attraction for visitors. In this regard, the concept of "commensality" can provide a way of distinctive, qualitative contact with tourists that can allow the guests in some way to *feel part of* the local culture. It is from this perspective that commensality can add value to the experience beyond the economic mediation of tourism.

DOI: 10.4324/9781003282532-8

Sharing Food: Commensality, Identities, "Otherness," and Cultural Knowledge

According to the Merriam Webster Dictionary, the word commensality means: "The practice of eating together" or "a social group that eats together."[1] This practice seems to be universal, present probably in all cultures and in different spaces and periods of history. In an extended sense, French sociologist Michel Maffesoli (2013) points out that we rarely eat alone. On the other hand, and as the also French sociologist Claude Fischler (2011) says, commensality conveys the notion of sharing food, possibly with an assumption of dependence (or reliance) of one or several of the commensal parties upon another/others thus bringing commensals closer. Also the French anthropologist Maurice Bloch expresses himself in a similar way:

> In all societies, sharing food is a way of establishing closeness … Commensality, the act of eating together, is thus one of the most powerful operators of the social process. The reason is that the sharing of food is, and is always seen to be, in some way or other, the sharing of that which will cause, or at least maintain, a common substance among those who commune together.
>
> (Bloch, 2005: 45)

In this regard, and having all those considerations in mind, eating together has always been one of the foundations of any community (Maffesoli, 2013).

Following Sobal (2000), we can find three different dimensions in sociability around food: a) commensality, which means eating together with other people according to societal rules; b) interaction, which deals with social relationships during meals; and c) facilitation, which refers to the importance of social environment on food behavior. In this regard, commensality means sharing food with others, eating together (or close) and creating interaction in a context of facilitation through food.

But it is also true that the fact of eating together is usually strongly defined by rigid societal rules. As W. Robertson Smith[2] wrote more than a century ago: "The very act of eating and drinking with a man was a symbol and a confirmation of fellowship and mutual social obligations." People don't share food (and time) with just anyone. Sharing food is strongly patterned in different cultures based on important aspects such as gender (Tubiana, 2016), age (Andersen, 2015), class (Freedman, 2015; González Turmo, 2016), social stratification (Sébastia, 2016), otherness (Collinson, 2016). As Jönsson et al. (2021) pointed out: "Beyond the creation of commensality, the respect of these rules generates a sense of belonging to the same community"; and they also add that: "It is difficult to escape its (commensality) sociocultural desirability and idealization."

Food as High Touch   69

Nevertheless, and as those same last authors also argued:

> In social sciences and humanities, commensality is commonly used as a scientific concept for eating together. However, despite the wide usage of this term, especially in anthropology and sociology, its meaning remains a subject of debate. Does it mean sharing the food? The table? The place? The moment.
>
> (Jönsson et al., 2021)

Regarding tourism and from this perspective, this concept of commensality (conviviality *around* or *in relation to* food) is also an important element to consider. And even if the engine of this fact is that of an economic exchange and business. In this regard, there are different ways of sharing "around" food. In some cases, and as González Turmo (2016) pointed out, people can share food, but they don't share necessarily the fact of being together around a table. On the other hand, we can share food, drink, or spaces, even moments, but without necessarily being together. An example of this last fact should be when someone in a touristic destination recommends a typical or crowded local place to visit, where the visitor can go alone or with other visitors, without an explicit relationship with other costumers, but within a place and an atmosphere they can enjoy at the same time and in the same space.

In this regard, hospitality and friendliness are elements that different tourist destinations highlight in their promotions, offering to share cuisines and dishes, but also lifestyles, consumption manners. As Collinson (2016: 176) points out in reference to his fieldwork in rural Ireland:

> Some have argued that the commodification of culture in this way is a product of the post-modern society, one in which an erosion of traditional mechanisms of social organization has led to a loss of concrete identities and a search for grounded and 'authentic' modes of living which have become increasingly absent in the world's developed nations. Thus, the appeal of cultural marketing stems from the idea that the central economic contract between tourist and indigene can somehow be overcome, that the tourist will become a temporary part of the community in some fashion and will receive their host's hospitality as if they were an 'authentic' insider. A shift from balanced to generalized reciprocity, if you will. Indeed, in the post-modern society, the distinction between insider and outsider, indigene and tourist, authentic and inauthentic becomes increasingly blurred. From this perspective, the marketing image of rural Ireland is certainly a myth, but one which the tourist and indigene actively encourages and participates in.
>
> (Collinson (2016: 176)

As Blomstervik et al. (2021: 2921) points out: "Physical staging and human interaction influence behavioral intentions in experiences with varying levels of novelty." On the other hand, this human interaction leads us to a certain

70   F. Xavier Medina

co-creation of tourism from a local and close base. As Campos et al. (2016: 1311) says, a co-created tourism experience is "the sum of the psychological events a tourist goes through when contributing actively through physical and/or mental participation in activities and interacting with other subjects in the experience environment." In this same way, we have that

> human interaction provide support and can enable them (visitors) to take part in the co-creation process of the experience. Interactions with staff members, other tourists, and local people can make tourists feel more supported ... This can then have a positive influence on the tourist's willingness to come back but also recommend the experience to others.
>
> (Blomstervik et al., 2021: 2936)

On the other hand, Zgolli and Zaiem (2017: 44) shows that customer-to-customer interaction also influences the tourists' behavioral responses (desire of stay, satisfaction and loyalty).

As Jönsson et al. (2021) points out, we must go deeper into the contemporary evolutions and functions of commensality. In this regard, commensality around gastronomy can be an outstanding tool to add value to the visitor's experience. Commensality is much more than a shared meal, a shared moment, a shared experience, or even just a shared space, because it relates to "how" we eat and spend our time. The "how" involves socializing when eating and frequently provides communication, circulation of information, and inclusion (De la Torre-Moral et al., 2021; Medina, 2021; Scander et al., 2021).

After having very briefly set out all these arguments, and as a starting point, we can establish that commensality is universal; it's (normally) voluntary, but it is also strongly socially and culturally controlled; it is a means of mutual understanding, knowledge, and intercultural contact, but it is not exempt from conflicts; and it brings people closer, but always within identifiable social (and/or economic) rules and limits.

Gastronomy as a Food Heritage, as a Tourism Resource, and as a Socioeconomic Tool for Local Development

On Food, Cuisines, Identities, and Heritages

According to Everett (2019), the evolution of the gastronomic studies in the touristic field has shifted from an economic perspective towards a geographic analysis focused on space, place, and the tendency of the cultural and critical studies of identity and consumption. The products of the country (*terroir*) and local cuisines share both their uniqueness and complexity since they simultaneously refer to living practices and techniques, on the one hand, and to specific identities, affective links, and taste preferences, on the other. All this plays a role within a context of increasingly generalized heritagization.

Food as High Touch   71

Local (or not so local) societies have been able to identify themselves and even, today, define themselves in terms of heritage through the foods and dishes they select, cook, and eat. As noted more than forty years ago by French anthropologist Igor de Garine: "it is no coincidence that gastronomy is at the foreground of the panoply of regional demands" (Garine, 1979: 82).

However, if we focus our gaze upon a society's food culture, we can see that it is only recently that it has become worth "heritagizing." As the scope of heritage (regarded as a construction) has been expanding, aspects of intangible culture that were previously difficult to identify have joined the ranks of "heritagizable" things, and everyday aspects and knowledges such as those associated with food, which previously formed an intrinsic part of everyday life but not of Culture (with a capital "C") have been deemed worthy of becoming a heritage and, therefore, of being officially recognized as prompting a sense of belonging and identity (Medina, 2017).

In this regard, heritage (including intangible goods such as cuisines, food and culinary knowledge, lifestyles ...) plays a significant identificatory role, often fed by a feeling of belonging to a group with its own identity. As Prats notes, one of the core features of heritage is "its symbolic nature, its ability to represent, through a system of symbols, a particular identity" (Prats, 1997: 294). Nevertheless, the process of heritagization is therefore a feature of modern societies, which have a need to install sociocultural and identity benchmarks regarding their own conceptions of time and space (Contreras, 2022).

Following this premise and regarding food production, the notion of heritage raises undoubtedly complex issues, as this is a living, shifting heritage that is constantly evolving, with all the problems this implies for its management and maintenance. Sometimes, far from being inherent to a specific territory, these products or dishes may be the result of borrowings, interchanges and adaptations that interpret the culinary preferences of contemporary society, whether or not they are associated with any identity dimension (Contreras, 2022). Additionally, the interests of contemporary societies have an impact upon heritage products, upon production and consumption contexts, and upon their forms of expression, which may have changed considerably and even become divorced from local traditions (or the wishes of local authorities) or have transformed the ways in which they are communicated or disseminated towards less orthodox or hitherto unexplored methods.

All this places us on an unstable, still-forming and constantly evolving footing, in which the dictates of cultural evolution and social change itself call for flexibility and an ability to adapt, which, to date at least, have tended to lag behind the requirements created by everyday practices.

Food and Wine Tourism: Particularities and ... Benefits?

Gastronomy is a decisive factor in planning the journeys and carrying them out. Food is also one of tourists' main expenditure items (in the form local consumption, souvenirs, etc.). Additionally, gastronomic tourism possesses its own market, boosted by the development of the tourism sector and its need for diversification, without losing sight of the fact that tourism provides an exceptional platform for promoting local food products and brands (Fusté-Forné et al., 2020; Leal Londoño, 2015). The role of gastronomy in the definition and differentiation of tourism destinations is increasingly important at an international level. On one hand, the development of tourism in rural areas through agri-tourism, wine tourism, or community-based tourism is mainly based on the conversion of heritage attributes and territorial specificities into commodities available for consumption in the tourism sector (De Jesús & Medina, 2021: 416). On the other hand, one of the advantages of food and wine tourism is that it allows visitors to stay longer in the area, expand human contacts in the area, spend a little more money, and ultimately contribute positively to the regional economy (Kesar & Ferjanic, 2010; Pavlic et al., 2010). Recent research shows that there is an incentive in the purchase and consumption of food and beverages in rural and agricultural areas of great cultural and tourist value (Everett, 2019; Fusté-Forné, 2019; Hjalager, 2020).

However, the concept of "gastronomy" should always be as broad as possible, covering the entire agri-food chain, from production and productive landscapes to forms of preparation, consumption, dishes, restaurants, and even the use of resources. Sometimes, the definition of gastronomy covers, or attempts to cover, all or a significant part of this spectrum (Hjalager, 2002). However, it is often the case that "gastronomy" has been focused on the final links of the food chain, giving priority to the selection, preparation, consumption, and appreciation of foods and dishes. As Santich (2004) notes, for example, gastronomy refers to the rules or norms regarding food and drink, and can be expanded to include advice and guidance on what, where, when, and how to eat and drink, and in what combinations. Similarly, in Scarpato's words, gastronomy in a tourism destination refers to "the reflective cooking, preparation, presentation and eating of food in general" (Scarpato, 2002: 139). This is the reason why, from our perspective, we refer principally to food in tourism, aiming to cover the entire spectrum and, when we speak about gastronomy, we shall also try to give it this conceptual breadth, which it has been denied so often.

According to Gascón (2018), avoiding reductionist essentialisms and great modernizing policies that do not always fulfil their mandates, food-based tourism as a post-Fordist tourism proposal attaches value to the specificity of the food experience. And this specificity is based upon local agricultural varieties produced by peasants and the artisanal making of food. Food-based tourism is, in his words, about peculiar products rooted in the territory, and whose production is limited. Therefore, it avoids cosmopolitan gastronomies and homogenizing production that comes with the modern technically enhanced agriculture (Gascón, 2018: 28).

It is obvious that no kind of tourist activity, certainly no kind of activity dedicated to food and gastronomy, can ignore specific requirements such as effective food security and food safety. Nor can it avoid paying special attention to key aspects such as the destinations' load capacity, the agreement, collaboration, and active participation of those involved; a collective rather than solely individual socioeconomic benefit; or an unnecessary adaptation of specific recipes to an alleged tourist taste. Nevertheless, food-based tourisms appear, for the moment, to show a healthier balance in all the above aspects than other types of tourism. So, if care is taken and unnecessary tensions around them avoided, this type of tourism may end up giving rise to relatively positive symbioses. As noted by Medina et al. (2018: 219), food and wine tourism is an unexplored possibility that boasts a range of features regarded as highly favorable by specialists, to wit: less tourist pressure and greater sustainability; greater territorial integration and a greater impact on benefits in the territory; better social allocation of the benefits in local territories; a close relationship with certain products (foods, wines and other beverages, etc.) and *local* dishes, placing food and wine tourism squarely within the framework of cultural tourism; the networked relationship between tourism and agro-food companies; or a better-quality tourism with a higher spend per tourist and per day, among other aspects.

Following those premises, we have that food and wine tourism is particularly one of the economic activities most resilient to the socioeconomic crisis, which is showing signs of recovery and growth that are superior to other economic sectors (Casado et al., 2012; Eugenio & Campos, 2014; Monti, 2011; Stylidis & Terzidou, 2013; Suciu, 2012). Reducing seasonality in the sense of increasing the influx of public in the lowest seasons without decreasing it in the highest season is one of the objectives of a large part of the sector (Fusté-Forné, 2019; Hernández et al., 2012). To do this, it is necessary to establish effective and real alliances between agri-food producers and the tourism industry to promote gastronomic tourism as part of the growing segment of cultural tourism (Balalia & Petrescu, 2011; Tresserras & Medina, 2007; Urban & Verhaegen, 2011).

In this regard, and as Kesar and Ferjanic (2010) pointed out more than a decade ago in relation to food and wine tourism, much attention must be devoted to tourist motivation and the constant improvement of the product. Wine tourism areas use branding linked to the territory to highlight their unique and competitive character (Serrano, 2011). In this way, it is important to promote knowledge of the territory through tourist visits and, therefore, the development of tourism at a local level, promoting a better knowledge of the local territory and culture, and a more intensive contact with locals "around" food. Thus, aspects such as farmers' markets (Fusté-Forné et al., 2020), but also local shops or restaurants, that bring the visitor closer to the product, to local dishes, and even to local people; bet on the gastronomic product as a souvenir; the organization of special events (conferences, fairs …) or promotion, dissemination and even education programs are elements that bring interest and added value to the offer.

Kesar and Ferjanic (2010) add that a decrease in the quality of services is not permissible since the consequences are always negative in the medium and long term. It is advisable to encourage and take advantage of all forms of creativity and new ideas that do not require large investments. In this regard, a particular personal contact with visitors can add a special qualitative value that allows the

74   F. Xavier Medina

tourist to feel part of the local culture, and that ultimately results in greater customer satisfaction. It is from this perspective that the "commensality" we talked about at the beginning of this chapter, understood as the fact of sharing not only food, but also contexts or moments, acquires a greater meaning.

Once more we return to the critical appraisals of Collinson (2016) in relation to commensality between locals and tourists during his fieldwork in Ireland:

> It may be that the way in which Ireland is marketed distorts the gaze through which the tourist -and the anthropologist- views the country. Unduly influenced by the promoted image, the welcoming local, the friendly wave, the free breakfast, the glass of poteen assume a heightened prominence, because this corroborates and reinforces the experience that the outsider has been told to expect … But the fact that the Irish themselves see some truth in the cultural stereotype, and to some extent conform to it in rural areas of the country, means that it may not simply be a reflection of a marketeer's dream. The key to understanding how the complex relationship between image and reality intersect and influence each other is to focus on the lived experience of outsider and indigene, a project which ethnography is best placed to achieve.
>
> (Collinson, 2016)

Food as Local Heritage … and Tourism Experience

Talking about heritage, Espeitx points out that "products and dishes from a local cuisine become, when is successfully heritagized, a real tourism resource, comparable with other elements of cultural heritage" (Espeitx, 2004: 210). So it is that the heritagization that has been built from food culture is increasingly occurring within the framework of tourism and the local development discourse surrounding it. In addition to this, it should be noted that heritage is one of the main assets and attractions of tourism, especially that which is based around culture, as food/gastronomic tourism unquestionably is (Tresserras & Medina, 2007).

Food heritage also fully integrates into the economic and heritage-related field in another way: representative of a territory, its products can be given a boost by categories such as designations of origin, geographical indications, and other "quality" labelling that stimulates and preserves local production (Espeitx, 2004) and provides also a tourist appeal that is closely linked to the local *terroir*. Nevertheless, and as Tresserras, Medina and Matamala (2007) also note, political and tourism policies have helped bolster the role of food products as heritage and a symbol of identity, although, in some cases, the authenticity of food heritage and its place in the collective imaginary is the subject of some discussion (Tresserras, Medina & Matamala, 2007: 237).

So, today, gastronomic tourism is often defined as an activity created by agents (producers, processors, restaurateurs, etc.) whose chief goal is to provide tourists with an experience that may be enjoyed through food. The tourism

Food as High Touch   75

sector is increasingly recognizing the importance of emotional and relational aspects of tourist experiences, which is causing a profound transformation of this industry which, more and more, is becoming a market of emotions. Today's tourists demand sensations that are unique and exclusive and identify themselves as multiform and multisensory consumers (Di Clemente et al., 2014).

All these factors link concepts that, in our view, are of significant value: territory, gastronomy (agriculture-product-dish or production-sale-consumption), culture and heritage, and local development. Equally important are the relations with public, private, and civic power centres, and both political and economic players that are fostered by gastronomic heritage. The effects of heritagization on products, cuisines, or even on forms of consumption are, therefore, many and varied. The selection and preservation of heritage is also a productive activity, creating economic value, above and beyond any demands related to its belonging to what is symbolic and constitutive of memory, to territoriality and to identity. All these discourses can be used by all power levels, of whatever type. In this regard, and considering the above, we can affirm that heritage (the awareness of heritage and everything this implies with regard to the sense of cultural union between a product and a territory) holds a highly significant place within this context.

Local Food Culture, Local Heritage, Local Development

This differentiating ability of heritagized food culture can be—and very often is—an effective tool for developing tourism in any territory. Indeed, food culture appears in all the leaflets, guides, brochures, and television advertisements promoting a given location's tourist appeal. There are many examples of the food-focused heritage initiatives and, these days, no proposal for any tourism initiative can fail to include, on a central or complementary basis, local produce and dishes (Espeitx, 2004: 200). As Gascón (2018) states, from the perspective of local rural communities, the heritagization and conservation of food as a tourism attraction can help to enhance the value of the farming production supplying its raw materials. This is a model characterized by quality foods, sustainable agricultural production, and the creation of benefits for the ecosystem, unlike agroindustry, which is mostly unsustainable and homogenizes landscapes and foods. From this standpoint, the intentional creation of gastronomic heritage appears, for Gascón, to be apposite and fitting (Gascón, 2018: 28–29). The words of this author, who is usually highly critical of some forms of tourism and their impact, would appear to point towards a situation that, despite its obvious limitations (and risks), may end up becoming a factor for cultural heritage-based territorial development that involves local communities in both its construction and implementation and in the enjoyment of its benefits.

On the other hand, authors such as Kesar and Ferjanic (2010) and Suciu (2012) state that, in the case of food and wine tourism, integration with sustainable, responsible, and high-value development strategies is necessary, as well as further developing differentiation and innovation, emphasizing the

76   F. Xavier Medina

improvement of the image of the destination and looking for the added value that this type of tourism can offer.

Clearly, any tourism strategy associated with heritage and culture runs an obvious risk of banalization, commercialization, or even of commodification or loss of authenticity (Macleod, 2006: 177). Food heritage may easily lead to "translation," in the sense of the processes by means of which food becomes a tourist attraction, but also of how local cuisines are selected, modified, and translated so that they may be consumed by visitors (with the hypothetical loss of authenticity that this may entail). The debate is a long and complex one and it does not seem that it will be elucidated soon.

Conclusion

Over the course of this chapter, we have reviewed the intersections between food culture, heritage, human contact and sharing around food, and tourism, from both a critical and a practical standpoint.

We argued that through food, tourism experiences can represent an appropriation of the way of being and the lifestyles of locals which relies on human contact as a source of visitor attraction. In this regard, commensality (in a wide sense of the word) can provide a personal, distinctive, qualitative contact with visitors that can add value to the experience and allows the guests to *feel part of* the local culture. It is from this perspective that "commensality," understood as the fact of sharing not only food, but also contexts or moments, acquires its significance and becomes a means that allows sharing beyond the economic mediation of tourism.

On the other hand, food products and practices are benchmarks in self-representation and the building of identities, meaning that the vocabulary of heritage has become strongly associated with them in recent decades. Nevertheless, this is a relatively recent heritage for officialdom, which has been forced to include aspects of intangible culture once difficult to identify but now included amongst the ranks of what is "heritagizable."

The fact is that food heritage is regarded as a tourism resource with a great potential and food has become a core part of the management of culture and tourism, with the promotion of local products and culinary recipes that form part of the strategies for boosting local and regional economies.

To date, without ignoring possible limitations, just as cultural tourism, gastronomic tourism has been held as a form of leisure that seeks to fit with the local productive structure without subordinating it (for the moment, at least) to the tourist industry. Similarly, it is a form of tourism that tends to involve the local community more integrally with what tourism offers and its benefits and, at the same time, better integrates the experience of visitors and contact with locals.

Normally, it does not entail mass tourism and therefore does not exert excessive pressure on the territory. Proper monitoring of this point is, however, important, especially in urban destinations, some of which are already overcrowded. Differing experiences in the urban context, such as the huge number of tourist visits to some markets (like the Boqueria in Barcelona), call these claims into question and show the need for significant qualifications and specific studies.

There is no doubt that much is yet to be done. Food heritage is a unique form of heritage. Fungible and consumable, it must constantly be recreated within the cultural frameworks that are still being shaped and undergoing continuous evolution, calling for both flexibility and adaptability.

These qualities, to date at least, have lagged behind the needs created by everyday practices and that, when they meet tourism, need much more attention and explanation that they are currently receiving. The recognition of food-related heritage needs to be constantly redefined and honed, ensuring more specific analysis of how heritagization affects—both positively and negatively—different assets, what its practical relations with the powers that be are, how it is to be managed and conserved, how access and use are guaranteed, and how and in what way these assets become tourism resources. At the same time, on-the-ground analysis must be as critical as possible, detecting any points of friction and fostering practical debates and proper, speedy solutions to problems.

Nevertheless, and always under a critical eye and an attentive vision to the management, we cannot deny that food is a pivotal ingredient within the relationship between hosts and guests, between tourists and local territories, between different identities. Food is a sign of a close relationship between people and shows the values that local societies give to their own sense of place. The unavoidable (in a broad sense, sharing products, spaces, moments, cuisines …) act of sharing (commensality) that food implies, allows visitors to "be part" of the way of being and the lifestyles of locals. And this fact should result in a more frequent, informative, and close human contact and, consequently, in a better experience.

Food for Thought

- Can gastronomy tourism and wine tourism be a tool for local development?
- Should gastronomy linked to tourism be a significative factor to increase local product knowledge and consumption?
- Is gastronomic tourism a more sustainable type of tourism that respects the environment and local culture? Will it continue to be in the future?

Notes

1 Available online: www.merriam-webster.com/dictionary/.
2 Robertson Smith, W. (1894). Lectures on the Religion of the Semites: *First Series, the Fundamental Institutions; Religion of the Semites*. London: Adam and Charles Black (cited in Garine et al., 2016 and Chee-Beng, 2015).

References

Andersen, B. (2015). Commensality between the young, in S. Kerner, C. Chou, & M. Warmind (Eds.), *Commensality from everyday food to feast*, pp. 43–50. London: Bloomsbury.

Balalia, A. E., Petrescu, R. M. (2011). The involvement of the public and private sector: Elements with influence on travel y tourism demand during the crisis period. *Tourism and Hospitality Management*, 17(2): 217–230.

Bloch, M. (2005). *Essays on Cultural Transmission*. Oxford, Berg.

Blomstervik, I. H., Prebensen, N. K., Campos, A. C. & Pinto, P. (2021). Novelty in tourism experiences: the influence of physical staging and human interaction on behavioural intentions. *Current Issues in Tourism*, 24(20): 2921–2938. DOI: 10.1080/13683500.2020.1854197

Campos, A. C., Mendes, J., do Valle, P. O., & Scott, N. (2016). Co-creation experiences: Attention and memorability. *Journal of Travel and Tourism Marketing*, 33(9), 1309–1336.

Casado, E., Ruíz, L.M & Rodríguez, L. (2012). The European Tourism in a post-crisis scenario. *Journal on GSTF Business Review*, 1(4): 164–168.

Chee-Beng, T. (2015). Commensality and the organization of social relations. In S. Kerner, C. Chou, & M. Warmind (Eds.), *Commensality from everyday food to feast*, pp. 13–30. London: Bloomsbury.

Collinson, P. (2016). Hospitality in Western Ireland: Myth or reality, or something in between? In E. Garine, M. L. Rodrigo, C. Raymond & F. X. Medina (Eds.), *Sharing food*, pp. 175–189. Guadalajara (Mexico): University of Guadalajara.

Contreras, J. (2022). *¿Seguiremos siendo lo que comemos?* Barcelona, Icaria.

De Jesús, D. & Medina, F. X. (2021). Food and wine tourism in rural areas: a critical theoretical reflection from the anthropology of food perspectives, *International Journal of Tourism Anthropology*, 8(4): 416–435.

De la Torre-Moral, A., Fàbregues, S., Bach-Faig, A., Fornieles-Deu, A., Medina, F.X., Aguilar-Martínez, A. & Sánchez-Carracedo, D. (2021). Family Meals, Conviviality, and the Mediterranean Diet among Families with Adolescents. *International Journal of Environmental Research in Public Health*, 18, 2499. DOI: https://doi.org/10.3390/ijerph18052499

Di Clemente, E., Hernández Mogollón, J. M. & López Guzmán, T. (2014). La gastronomía como patrimonio cultural y motor del desarrollo turístico. Un análisis DAFO para Extremadura. *Monográfico*, 9, 817–833.

Espeitx, E. (2004). Patrimonio alimentario y turismo: una relación singular. *PASOS, Revista de turismo y patrimonio cultural*, 2(2), 193–213.

Eugenio, J. L., Campos, J.A. (2014). Economic crisis and tourism expenditure cutback decision. *Annals of Tourism Research*, 44, 53–73.

Everett, S. (2019). Theoretical turns through tourism taste-scapes: the evolution of food tourism research. *Research in Hospitality Management*, 9(1), 3–12.

Fischler, C. (2011). Commensality, Society and Culture, in *Social Science Information*, 50, 528–548.

Freedman, P. (2015). Medieval and modern banquets: commensality and social stratification, in S. Kerner, C. Chou & M. Warmind (Eds.), *Commensality from everyday food to feast*, pp. 99–108. London: Bloomsbury.

Fusté-Forné, F. (2019). Seasonality in food tourism: wild foods in peripheral areas. *Tourism Geographies*, 2019, 1–21. DOI: 10.1080/14616688.2018.1558453

Fusté-Forné, F., Medina, F. X. & Cerdan, L. M. (2020). La Proximidad de los Productos Alimentarios: Turismo Gastronómico y Mercados de Abastos en la Costa Daurada (Cataluña, España). *Revista De Geografía Norte Grande, 76*: 213–231.

Garine, E., Rodrigo, M. L., Raymond, C., Medina, F. X., Garine, I. de & Garine, V. de (2016). Introduction: Is sharing food an option or a duty? In E. Garine, M. L. Rodrigo, C. Raymond & F. X. Medina (Eds.), *Sharing food*, pp. 11–20. Guadalajara (Mexico): University of Guadalajara.

Garine, I. de. (1979). Culture et nutrition. *Communications, 31*: 70–92.

Gascón, J. (2018). Turismo, agricultura y alimentación. De la Teoría del Enlace a la patrimonialización de la gastronomía. In F. X. Medina & P. Leal Londoño (Eds.) *Gastronomía y turismo en Iberoamérica*. Gijón: Trea.

González Turmo, I. (2016). Compartir, en el límite del significado. In E. Garine, M. L. Rodrigo, C. Raymond & F. X. Medina (Eds.), *Sharing food*, pp. 99–114. Guadalajara (Mexico): University of Guadalajara.

Hernández, M., Muñoz, A. & Rodríguez, A. (2012). Impact of the International Financial Crisis on the Spanish Tourism Sector. *Journal on GSTF Business Review, 1*(4): 149–152.

Hjalager, A.-M. (2002). A typology of gastronomy tourism. In A.-M. Hjalager & G. Richards (Eds.), *Tourism and Gastronomy* (pp. 21–36). London: Routledge.

Hjalager, A.-M. (2020). The coevolution of tourism and agriculture. *Journal of Gastronomy and Tourism, 4*(4): 175–191.

Jönsson, H., Michaud, M. & Neuman, N. (2021). What Is Commensality? A Critical Discussion of an Expanding Research Field. *International Journal of Environmental Research and Public Health, 18*, 6235.

Kesar, O. & Ferjanic, D. (2010). Key aspects of managing successful wine tourism development in times of global economic crisis: A case of Croatia. *Acta turistica, 22* (1): 99–131.

Leal Londoño, M. P. (2015). *Turismo gastronómico, impulsor del comercio de proximidad.* Barcelona: Editorial UOC.

Macleod, N. (2006). Cultural tourism: aspects on authenticity and commodification. In M.K. Smith & M. Robinson (Eds.), *Cultural tourism in a changing World. Politics, participation and (re)presentation*. Clavedon: Channel View Publications.

Maffesoli, M. (2013). Éthique de l'esthétique. In M. Maffessoli (Ed.), *Manger ensemble.* Paris: CNRS Éditions.

Medina, F. X. (2017). Reflexiones sobre el patrimonio y la alimentación desde las perspectivas cultural y turística. *Anales de Antropología, 51*(2): 106–113.

Medina, F. X. (2021). Looking for Commensality: On Culture, Health, Heritage, and the Mediterranean Diet. *International Journal of Environmental Research and Public Health, 18*, 2605.

Medina, F. X., Gómez Patiño, M., Puyuelo, J. M. & Tomás, C. (2018). Turismo enogastronómico en España: cultura, patrimonio, economía y capacidad de reacción ante la crisis socioeconómica. In F. X. Medina & P. Leal Londoño (Eds.), *Gastronomía y turismo en Iberoamérica*, pp. 201–223. Gijón: Trea.

Monti, E. (2011). La crisis económica internacional de 2008 y el turismo: Efectos y medidas de respuesta en Rio Grande do Norte, Brasil. *Investigaciones Turísticas, 1*, 93–106.

Pavlic, I., Perucic, D. & Portolan, A. (2010). Towards reducing the negative effects of the economic crisis by using market segmentation based on tourist expenditure: The case of Dubrovnik-Neretva County. In L. Galetić, M. Spremić & M. Ivanov (Eds.),

80 F. Xavier Medina

5th International conference: An Enterprise Odyssey: From Crisis to Prosperity. Challenges for Government and Business, pp. 1666–1682. Opatija: Faculty of Economics and Business.

Prats, L. (1997). *Antropología y patrimonio*. Barcelona: Ariel.

Santich, B. (2004). The study of gastronomy and its relevance to hospitality education and training. *International Journal of Hospitality Management, 23*: 15–24.

Scander, H., Yngve, A. & Lennernäs Wiklund, M. (2021). Assessing Commensality in Research. *International Journal of Environmental Research and Public Health, 18*, 2632.

Scarpato, R. (2002). Sustainable gastronomy as a tourist product. In A.-M. Hjalager & G. Richards (Eds.), *Tourism and Gastronomy* (pp. 132–152). London: Routledge.

Sébastia, B. (2016). 'I Hate Sharing Food'. Partage de la nourriture en Inde: de la commensalité à la convivialité. In E. Garine, M. L. Rodrigo, C. Raymond & F. X. Medina (Eds.), *Sharing food*, pp. 237–251. Guadalajara (Mexico): University of Guadalajara.

Serrano, D. (2011). El turismo del vino: la lectura espacial de un binomio estratégico. In F. X. Medina, D. Serrano & J. Tresserras (Eds.), *Turismo del vino. Análisis de casos internacionales*. Barcelona: Editorial UOC.

Sobal, J. (2000). Sociability and meals: Facilitation, commensality, and interaction. In H. L. Meiselman (Ed.), *Dimensions of the meal: the science, culture, business, and art of eating*, pp. 119–133. Gaithersburg (MD), Aspen Publishers, Inc.

Stylidis, D. & Terzidou, M. (2013). Tourism and the economic crisis in Kavala, Greece. *Annals of Tourism Research, 44*: 210–226.

Suciu, A. (2012). Tourism development in the member States of the European Union during economic crisis. *Managerial Challenges of the Contemporary Society, 4*: 177–179.

Tresserras, J. & Medina, F. X. (Eds.) (2007). Introducción, in *Patrimonio gastronómico y turismo cultural en el Mediterráneo*. Barcelona: Universitat de Barcelona-Ibertur.

Tresserras, J., Medina, F. X. & Matamala, J. C. (2007). El patrimonio gastronómico como recurso en las políticas culturales y turísticas en España: el caso de Catalunya. In J. Tresserras & F. X. Medina (Eds.), *Patrimonio gastronómico y turismo cultural en el Mediterráneo*, pp. 217–242. Barcelona: Universitat de Barcelona-Ibertur.

Tubiana, M. J. (2016). Être femme et partager la nourriture en milieu musulman: Témoignages. In E. Garine, M. L. Rodrigo, C. Raymond & F. X. Medina (Eds.), *Sharing food*, pp. 253–265. Guadalajara (Mexico): University of Guadalajara.

Urban, V. & Verhaegen, I. (2011). The Influence of Economic and Financial Crisis on Tourism Services in Romania. *Economy Transdisciplinarity Cognition, 14*(1): 187–196.

Zgolli, S. & Zaiem, I. (2017). Customer-to-customer interaction in tourism experience: Moderating role of nationality. *Arab Economic and Business Journal, 12*(1): 44–56.

6 Food as High Tech

Roberta Garibaldi and Andrea Pozzi

Introduction

Today technology has become increasingly pervasive, gradually changing people's way of living and that of relating. However, not all the technology has been adopted within the industry, only that able to generate added value for both businesses and consumers. Tourism, as for other service-intense sectors, has gone hand in hand with technology and has embraced its latest developments (Buhalis & Law, 2008) – from non-interactive websites and reservation systems to social networking tools, Augmented and Virtual Reality, the metaverse. Today, technology is adopted throughout all travel stages and serves a variety of functions: for instance, it supports the tourist in choosing and booking the tourism experience; it establishes a closer relationship and interaction between the provider, the tourist, and other tourists; it enriches the onsite experience, etc. (Neuhofer et al., 2014; Zhang et al., 2018).

The growing relevance of food tourism (Garibaldi, 2021; Stone et al., 2020) has led destinations and attractions to its increasing adoption, gradually changing the way this experience is produced, communicated, purchased, created, and consumed (Flavián et al., 2019; Garibaldi, in-press; Garibaldi & Sfodera, 2019). The present chapter analyzes the (evolving and increasing) use of technology in each travel stage of the food tourism experience, highlighting its main functions also with empirical evidence. Its increasing adoption is here regarded as linked to the evolution of food tourism in its nature (experientiality) and structure (co-creation). In conclusion, an integrated use of technology is presented, offering a useful tool for the food tourism industry to embed different applications within the experience.

The Evolution of the Food Tourism Experience

Since its emergence, food tourism has been a visible area within tourism literature (Ellis et al, 2018). Diverse definitions have appeared, alternatively placing a major emphasis to the physical experience that travellers can do (e.g., Hall & Mitchell, 2001; Hall & Mitchell, 2004) and to the cultural value embedded in this practice (e.g., Horng & Tsai, 2012; Long, 1998). Food tourism deals

DOI: 10.4324/9781003282532-9

with the enjoyment of a set of various activities on holiday, which ranges from the most consumptive/passive (e.g., dining at local restaurants) to the more engaging (e.g., attending themed festivals and events) and learning (e.g., visits to wineries, breweries). It also means a direct experience of the cultural, social, and economic practices related to the production and the consumption of food and, to a general extent, of the sense of the place and the society.

The literature review allows us to identify an evolution in the experiential nature of food tourism as the result of a growing interest on the part of tourists. From merely being a physical necessity, food on holiday has become a multifaceted experience with different meanings and dimensions. Its consumption involves multi-sensory and emotive aspects that generate a sense of personal enjoyment (Andersson & Mossberg, 2004; Therkelsen, 2015). The hedonic nature that food tourism holds is closely connected with socialization aspects. The act of consumption often happens with other members of the travelling party and/or the members of the host community, providing opportunities to create or strengthen interpersonal relationships (Fernandes, 2021; Walter et al., 2010). Food tourism has also a learning dimension. It can foster personal development through activities that introduce to the characteristics of food, the historical and contemporary practices, and, to a wider extent, the food culture of the destination (Ignatov & Smith, 2006; Mak et al., 2012). It has therefore the potential to be a transformative experience. Gaining knowledge can encourage a change in daily habits moving towards e.g., more conscious food choices and/or healthy lifestyle (Balderas-Cejudo et al., 2019; Bertella, 2020; Lean, 2009).

Such changes follow a transformation in the structure of the food tourism. Early studies generally noticed that the offering development was a supply-led process, where producers had a primary role and travellers were only receivers (Richards, 2015). The quality of the products and services delivered was found to deeply influence satisfaction and revisit intention of tourists, while interaction and engagement appeared to be of less importance (Cohen & Avieli, 2004; Tse & Crotts, 2005). More recent contributions observed a shift towards co-creation, as highlighted also in the general tourism literature (Mossberg, 2007; Ryan, 1997). This process implies an increasing interaction between tourists and providers in the offering development, with the former now having greater control over the experience they are pursuing (Boswijk et al., 2007). Technology has intensified this change, empowering tourists to generate and share contents on an unprecedent scale, therefore influencing reputation and branding of destinations and attractions (Mkono & Tribe, 2017; Richards, 2021; Seeler et al., 2019). Emotions, personal fulfilment, and sociability have risen as relevant attributes to be embedded within the food tourism experience as to increase its memorability. New activities incorporating some or all these elements (such as e.g., cooking classes, grape/olive oil harvest for tourists) have then emerged to satisfy travellers' willingness for pleasure, socialization, and learning (Campos et al., 2018; Rachão et al., 2020; Walter, 2017).

The theoretical framework of food tourism appears under development due to its constant evolution. Technology is now transforming and revolutionizing this practice, becoming increasingly used in all travel stages. It has acquired new functions that go beyond the supportive role of assisting the tourist in finding information and booking the experience (Okumus, 2021). Despite that, studies of its current application are few and fragmented (Flavián et al., 2019; Garibaldi, in-press; Garibaldi & Sfodera, 2019), leading to just a partial comprehension of the role of technology in the current and future evolution of food tourism.

Technology Applications to the Food Tourism Experience

Technology is among the most studied topics in tourism. The literature review shows its contribution to the transformation of the experience. The proliferation of technology has initially facilitated the role of tourism providers in assisting and supporting the tourist to access information and booking through e.g., websites, reservation systems, emails, etc. (Cho et al., 2002; Green, 2002). Subsequently, improvements in technology have empowered the tourist in the pre-travel, during-travel and post-travel stages (Neuhofer et al., 2014; Sfodera, 2011). The growing emergence of social networks, interactive websites, virtual marketplaces, and real-time communication tools have enabled a co-creation process where the tourist and the provider develop together the experience, leading to a more personalized and meaningful offering (Inversini et al., 2010; Sigala, 2009; Tussyadiah & Fesenmaier, 2007; Zhang et al., 2018). The appearance of Virtual Reality, Augmented Reality, interactive touch screens, multitouch tables, 180° and 360° projections, and other technological tools has changed the way the experience is lived by the tourist, providing him/her access to new and/or more engaging contents (Flavián et al., 2019; Guttentag, 2010). There emerges that technology has acquired more sophisticated and relevant functions through times, becoming increasingly pervasive to the tourism experience in all stages and contributing to its transformation (Neuhofer et al., 2014).

As in other travel segments, the adoption of technology is transforming and revolutionizing food tourism. The present paragraph analyzes its use while highlighting the main functions in the pre-travel, during-travel and post-travel stages. Empirical evidence through examples from both food tourism destinations and attractions are provided, allowing us to understand its current application within the experience.

The Pre-Travel Stage

Technology, at this level, plays both a supportive and enhancing role to the food tourism experience (Neuhofer et al., 2014). When supporting, it assists the tourist to find (personalized) information, and it facilitates the booking process. Destinations and attractions' websites serve these scopes, providing textual and video contents to inspire and to buy their proposals (Duarte Alonso et al., 2013; Richards, 2021). The official website of wine tourism in France *Visit French Wine* (http://visitfrenchwine.com), for instance, encourages tourists to discover wines, wineries, and wine regions within the country, inspiring them with attractive photos and engaging contents while providing the opportunity to choose experiences according to their needs (but without directly selling). Moving to attractions, *Castello di Amorosa* winery in the United States (https://castellodiamorosa.com) embeds a digital tour in its website, allowing tourists to take a virtual walk through its courtyard, chapel, and barrel room, etc. and to draw inspiration for their future visits (which can be booked directly on the website).

When enhanced, technology allows a higher level of interaction: it encourages discussions and/or feedbacks between the provider, the tourist, and other tourists, and it establishes a closer relationship among them (Haller et al., 2020; Richards, 2021). Many technological applications are available, differing in the level of tourist engagement. Social media and review sites allow virtual interactions, enabling the co-creation process. For instance, the destination management organization of Napa County in the United States *Visit Napa Valley* (www.visitnapavalley.com) uses Facebook, Instagram, Pinterest, Twitter, YouTube, and TripAdvisor to publish trip ideas and quizzes for discovering places, restaurants, producers, etc., while encouraging tourists to generate text and visual content and share their opinions with experience providers and other tourists. Virtual concepts like live digital tastings and tours create a face-to-face interaction with tourists, therefore intensifying the co-creation process. Such technology-based experiences have become popular in 2020 due to mobility restrictions caused by the pandemic emergency. From merely offering live events with tasting, they have become increasingly sophisticated by pairing e.g., food and wine boxes and kits, relaxing activities and/or courses, etc. (Garibaldi & Pozzi, 2020; Garibaldi, in-press. Today, virtual concepts are less common and are used not to replace the onsite experience, but to establish a closer relationship with tourists and to encourage future visits. For instance, the New Zealand winery *Cloudy Bay* (www.cloudybay.com) includes in its current offering digital tasting along with a set of different tours, visits, and tastings to be enjoyed in the real places. The 'Cloudy Bay Virtual Wine Tasting @Home' introduces to its vintages through a guided tasting via Zoom platform. A brand ambassador explains the wine-making process, the wine characteristics and tells anecdotes and stories around the winery. In doing so, the ambassadors and the customers establish a face-to-face interaction, share their own opinions and comments around wines, etc.; definitively, they act together and co-create the digital experience.

During the Travel

At this stage, technology enhances or empowers the food tourism experience (Neuhofer et al., 2014). Enhancing means that the tourist actively participates and interacts with virtual content that enriches the experience he/she is enjoying, making it more attractive and memorable. Many technological tools are used, e.g., interactive touch screens and multitouch tables, 180° and 360° projections, Virtual and Augmented Reality, etc. For instance, *Inamo Restaurant* in London (www.inamo-restaurant.com) uses a combination of table touchpads that allows customers, e.g., to see the food and drinks menu projected onto the table surface, change table clothes accordingly to their mood and preferences, manage their order and watch in real time their food being prepared in the kitchen through a webcam. *Ultraviolet* restaurant in Shanghai (https://uvbypp.cc) and *Alchemist* in Copenhagen (https://alchemist.dk) combine different technological tools to create unique, high-impact settings that make the dining experience distinct and memorable. *Ultraviolet* serves its avant-garde menu in a dining room fully covered by video screens, with lights, scents, atmosphere, projections that change according to each dish. *Alchemist* combines high-end cuisine and audio-visual installations to transport guests through each course by means of taste, imagery, performance, and sound. Moving to production sites, the Spanish winery *Bodegas Ramòn Bilbao* (https://bodegasramonbilbao.com) has started offering a VR-based experience (the so-called 'Experiencia Oculus') that allows visitors to be virtually introduced to the entire wine-making process and its vintages during the guided tours to its cellars. The Italian wine estate *Castello Banfi* (www.castellobanfiwineresort.it) offers an onsite tour enriched by AR contents. Visitors can enjoy traditional scenes of the wine-making process coming to life by framing the markers placed in specific areas through their smartphone.

Empowering means that technology needs to exist for the food tourism experience to happen (Neuhofer et al., 2014). It is pervasive throughout all stages of the experience, becoming an essential part of what is enjoyed onsite. A new generation of wine museums use multimedia technology extensively to create an experiential approach to wine culture (Bellini & Resnick 2018). *La Cité du Vin* (www.laciteduvin.com), for instance, is a renowned French museum that has conceived the permanent tour as a modular journey with twenty themed spaces explaining the culture of wine through history, geography, geology, oenology, and the arts. Each is characterized by the extensive use of digital and interactive technology – e.g., multitouch tables, 180° projections, interactive PODs, etc. – that create immersive and high-impact settings and allow visitors to be introduced to the culture of wine in a more dynamic and engaging way (Garibaldi & Sfodera, 2019). Similarly, *Il Tempio di Montalcino* (www.orodimontalcino.it/tempio-del-brunello) is an Italian museum that extensively adopts technology to engage visitors with one of the most renowned red wines of this country. Among other things, it offers a VR-based experience ('InVolo') to virtually visit and discover the wine area, its vineyards and winescapes, while listening to their stories. Within the foodservice sector, service robots are increasingly used in many roles, e.g., bartenders, waiters, chefs, etc. Their main (and expected) function is to assist both providers and customers with (a varying level) of autonomy; however, they also serve (implicitly or explicitly) as 'attractions' for the amusement of the clients. For instance, the *Avatar Robot Café* (https://dawn2021.orylab.com/en/) is a Japanese bar where avatar robots – which are remotely guided by people with disabilities – take the orders and serve at the tables. Technology becomes a means not just to assist workers, but to create new opportunities for those who want to work but cannot do due to medical or physical conditions. In the case of the *Robot Theme Restaurant* in India (www.robotrestaurantomr.in), the idea of replacing humans with robot waiters has the different purpose of creating the 'reason why' to come and dine at the restaurant. Their adoption mainly contributes to making the experience unique and distinctive, while also providing a certain level of support to the restaurant activities.

The Post-Travel Stage

After the onsite experience, technology plays an enhancing role allowing a higher level of interaction between the tourist, the provider, and other tourists (Neuhofer et al., 2014). Social media are used by destinations and attractions to stimulate and to facilitate a positive and open conversation around the food tourism experience, which can also lead other tourists to buy. The destination management organization of the Australian wine region of *Hunter Valley* (www. winecountry.com.au), for instance, has decided to show its places and wines through the eye of the real customers. It engages tourists with publishing their videos and/or pictures of their holiday (and tagging the Hunter Valley destination) on its social media accounts and embeds these contents on the home page of their website. This enables the creation of common memories and fosters a positive word of mouth.

Food tourism destinations and attractions are also often present on different online marketplaces (e.g., TripAdvisor, Viator, etc.) not just to promote and sell their offering, but also to allow tourists to review the experience purchased and influence other customers (Richards, 2021).

Technology for a Never-Ending Food Tourism?

Although limitative, the above-mentioned examples demonstrate that technology plays a relevant role within the food tourism experience. But, often, its current use is limited at single stages. Adopting technology in a more integrated way can blur the existing time and space boundaries, transforming food tourism in a never-ending process during which the tourist is constantly engaged and actively involved with the real and the virtual experience. It appears useful to obtain a complete view of the process (Figure 6.1) that summarizes different technological applications by the travel stages, the (main) tourist needs, the function(s) of the technology. This view is not exhaustive, as new technological developments will appear, but can help both destinations and attractions to maximize their potential thorough all the travel stages.

The Pre-Travel: Deciding to Buy the Experience

The tourist motivation to purchase the food travel experience becomes manifest when his/her internal needs and external stimuli work together. Technology

Food as High Tech 87

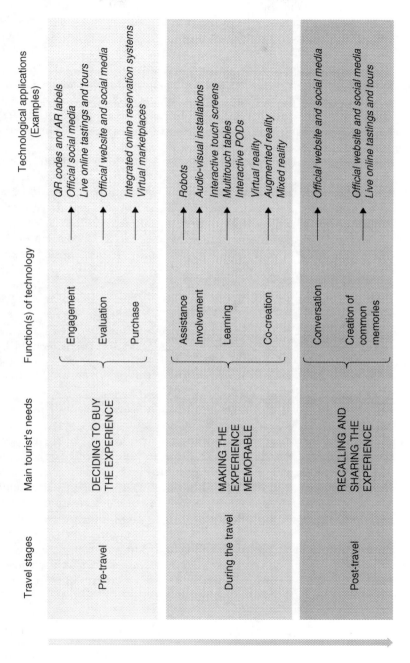

Figure 6.1 Summary of the technological applications by the travel stages, the (main) tourist needs, the function(s) of the technology

helps to emotionally engage as it can create a first and meaningful contact between the provider and the consumer. Different technological applications can be used in an increasing intensity. QR codes and augmented reality labels on food products – which today are mainly used for non-tourist scopes (Garibaldi, in-press) – can capture the attention of the tourist and lead him/her virtually in the places while engaging with e.g., captivating stories, mini-games, etc. The same contents can be published on social media platforms, which also allows the provider to directly interact with the tourist. Live online tastings and tours can reinforce this interaction by establishing a face-to-face contact (although virtually), which can bring him/her to discover the product, the places and the people, creating a stronger motive for the future onsite visit.

The decision to purchase is preceded by a careful evaluation of the characteristics of the experience (e.g., price, quality, perceived benefits, and risk, etc.). At this stage, different technology assists the tourist to find information and to facilitate the booking process. Official websites and social media accounts can provide what he/she needs to make a more conscious choice, e.g., by publishing trip ideas starting from their preferences, etc. Integrated online reservation systems and/or virtual marketplaces (linked to the website) can help the tourist to easily finalize the purchase.

During the Travel: Having a Memorable Experience

The tourist wants that the experience purchased fulfils his/her needs of being emotionally engaged, learning, and co-creating. Onsite, different technology increasingly reinforces the related dimensions of the food tourism experience, contributing to its memorability. Audio-visual installations can create an immersive setting that captures the attention of the tourist, emotionally involving him/her. Interactive touch screens, multitouch tables, interactive PODs, etc. can provide (a more personalized) access to different visual and textual contents, while mixing elements of entertainment and learning. Virtual, Augmented and Mixed Reality, etc. can overcome physical barriers and virtually introduce to the products, the places, and the people in a more dynamic way.

But the tourist needs also to be assisted during the entire experience. Robots can interact with him/her and address single- and multi-information requests, as well as to provide more complex services (e.g., serving at the tables, cooking, assisting the food and/or wine tasting, etc.). Their adoption can also make the experience worth purchasing contributing to its distinctiveness. However, different to above-mentioned technology, robots can partly affect the participatory nature of the food tourism experience, as well as its capability to engage the tourist and to provide him/her with new knowledge.

The Post-Travel: Recalling and Sharing Memories

Finally, the tourist wants to share the experience. And, explicitly or implicitly, to express his/her satisfaction or dissatisfaction of what was enjoyed on holiday.

Technology facilitates open conversations and the creation of common memories. Different applications can be used in an increasing intensity. Official websites, social media, etc. allow the tourist to publish the videos and/or pictures of the holiday (and/or being tagged in) and to review the food tourism experience, partly influencing other tourists' decisions. Live online tastings and tours can be used to recall the memories and share what was enjoyed with parents and friends. They therefore contribute to reinforce the positive e-WOM previously generated through social media, blogs, etc., and make the tourist an 'ambassador' of the destination or the attraction.

Conclusions

That technology has become increasingly adopted in tourism, revolutionizing the way of producing, promoting, communicating, creating, and selling is widely acknowledged in literature. From simply assisting and supporting the tourist to access information and to finalize the purchase, it has taken on more sophisticated functions, becoming an enhancer and enabler of the tourism experience. Because of its potential for disruption, little attention has been devoted to the use of technology in food tourism although there appears to be evidence of a number of examples.

Case studies analyzed in this chapter show that technology serves the scope of supporting, enhancing, and empowering the food tourism experience throughout all travel stages. Applications currently used widely vary, encompassing both Internet-based communication (e.g., websites, social media, live virtual concepts) and physical technology (e.g., audio-visual installations, interactive tables and touchscreen, AR and VR, robots). To exploit its benefits technology should work integratedly, and not just be applied at a single travel stage and/or to achieve a specific goal, as often happens. Different applications can be used in an increasing intensity as: to encourage the tourist to choose and buy the experience; to deeply involve and engage him/her during the onsite visit, making it memorable; to allow the co-creation of shared memories afterwards. Satisfying the diverse tourist's needs along the entire food tourism experience also with the use of technology can transform it in a never-ending process, where he/she is constantly engaged with virtual and real contents.

It must be argued that new technological developments will appear on the market, further revolutionizing the food tourism experience. Particularly, the metaverse – which can be defined "as a parallel, virtual universe that uses ambient intelligence to enhance physical spaces, products and services, emerges as a collective, virtual shared space of value cocreation" (Buhalis & Karaty, 2022: 16) – appears to largely change the way in which the tourism sector operates in future. Despite the fact its applications are still few, new virtual experiences are appearing on the market enabling the tourist to overcome physical barriers while putting him/her in the main role of creator (Gursoy et al., 2022). Food tourism destinations and attractions should not only recognize this change in future (and are partly doing it), but also to develop strategies to actively participate in this "new world" and leverage this opportunity to build a competitive advantage. Bearing in mind that, similar to other technological applications, the metaverse will not completely replace the real food tourism experience. It will change the way the tourist perceives and consumes it.

Food for Thought

- How to find the right 'balance' virtual and physical moments within the food tourism experience?
- What technological developments will be crucial for the food tourism industry in the next years?
- How will the use of technology be perceived by different tourists? What factors can mostly influence its acceptance among younger and older generations?

References

Andersson, T., & Mossberg, L. (2004). The Dining Experience: Do Restaurants Satisfy Customer Needs? *Food Service Technology, 4*(4), 171–77.

Balderas-Cejudo, A., Patterson, I. & Leeson, G. W. (2019). Senior foodies: a developing niche market in gastronomic tourism, *International Journal of Gastronomy and Food Science, 16*, art. no. 100152.

Bellini, N., & Resnick, E. (2018). The luxury turn in wine tourism. Still good for local development? In N. Bellini, C. Clergeau & O. Etcheverria (Eds.), *Gastronomy and Local Development The Quality of Products, Places and Experiences, 1st Edition.* London: Routledge.

Bertella, G. (2020). Re-thinking sustainability and food in tourism, *Annals of Tourism Research, 84*, art. no. 103005.

Boswijk, A., Thijssen, T. & Peelen, E. (2007). *The Experience Economy: A New Perspective.* Amsterdam: Pearson Education.

Buhalis, D., & Karaty, N. (2022). Mixed Reality (MR) for Generation Z in Cultural Heritage Tourism Towards Metaverse. In J. L Stienmetz, B. Ferrer-Rosell, D. Massimo (Eds.), *Information and Communication Technologies in Tourism 2022 - ENTER 2022* (pp. 16–27). Cham: Springer.

Buhalis, D., & Law, R. (2008). Progress in information technology and tourism management: 20 years on and 10 years after the Internet—The state of eTourism research, *Tourism management, 29*(4), 609–623.

Campos, A. C., Mendes, J., Valle, P. O. D. & Scott, N. (2018). Co-creation of tourist experiences: a literature review, *Current Issues in Tourism, 21*(4), 369–400.

Cho Y-H, Wang Y, & Fesenmaier, D. R. (2002). The Web-based virtual touri in tourism marketing, *Journal of Travel & Tourism Marketing, 12*(4), 1–17.

Cohen, E. & Avieli, N. (2004). Food in tourism: attraction and impediment, *Annals of Tourism Research, 31*(4), 755–778.

Duarte Alonso, A., Bressan, A., O'Shea, M., & Krajsic, V. (2013). Website and social media usage: Implications for the further development of wine tourism, hospitality, and the wine sector. *Tourism Planning and Development, 10*(3), 229–248.

Ellis, A., Park, E., Sangkyun, K., & Yeoman, I. (2018). What is food tourism?, *Tourism Management, 68*, 250–263.

Fernandes, C. (2021). Quale gastronomia dopo la pandemia? In R. Garibaldi (Ed.), *Rapporto sul Turismo enogastronomico italiano 2021. Trend e tendenze* (pp. 36–39).

Flavián, C., Ibáñez-Sánchez, S., & Orús, C. (2019). The impact of virtual, augmented and mixed reality technologies on the customer experience, *Journal of Business Research*, 547–560.

Garibaldi, R. (in-press). The role of technology in wine tourism. In S. K. Dixit (Ed.), *The Routledge Handbook of Wine Tourism*. London: Routledge.

Garibaldi, R. (2021). *Rapporto sul Turismo enogastronomico italiano 2021. La domanda italiana.*

Garibaldi, R., & Pozzi, A. (2020). Gastronomy tourism and COVID-19: technologies for overcoming current and future restrictions. In F. Burini (Ed.), *Tourism facing a pandemic: from crisis to recovery* (pp. 35–40). Bergamo: Università degli studi di Bergamo.

Garibaldi, R., & Sfodera, F. (2019). Technologies for enhancing wine tourism experience. In S. K. Dixit (ed.), *The Routledge Handbook of Tourism Experience Management and Marketing* (pp. 409–417). London: Routledge.

Green, N. (2002) On the Move: technology, mobility, and the mediation of social time and space, *The Information Society, 18*(4), 281–292.

Gursoy, D., Malodia, S., & Dhir, A. (2022). The metaverse in the hospitality and tourism industry: an overview of current trends and future research directions, *Journal of Hospitality Marketing & Management, 31*(5), 527–534.

Guttentag, D. A. (2010). Virtual reality: Applications and implications for tourism, *Tourism Management, 31*, 637–651.

Hall, C. M., & Mitchell, R. (2001). Wine and food tourism. In N. Douglas, N. Douglas, & R. Derrett (Eds.), *Special Interest Tourism: Context and Cases* (pp. 307–329). Brisbane: John Wiley & Sons Australia.

Hall, C. M., & Mitchell, R. D. (2004). Gastronomic tourism: Comparing food and wine tourism experiences. In B. Griffin (Ed.), *Niche Tourism. Contemporary Issues, Trends and Cases* (pp. 89–100). London: Routledge.

Haller, C., Thach, L., & Olsen, J. (2020). Understanding eWinetourism practices of European and North America wineries, *Journal of Gastronomy and Tourism, 4*(3), 141–156.

Horng, J., & Tsai, C. (2012). Culinary tourism strategic development an Asia-Pacific perspective, *International Journal of Tourism Research, 14*(1), 40–55.

Ignatov, E., & Smith, S. (2006). Segmenting Canadian culinary tourists, *Current Issues in Tourism, 9*(3), 235–255.

Inversini, A., Cantoni, L., & Buhalis, D. (2010). Destinations information competitors and Web reputation, *Information Technology and Tourism, 11*, 221–234.

Lean, G. (2009). Transforming travel: Inspiring sustainability, in R. Bushell, & P. Sheldon (Eds.), *Wellness and tourism: Mind, body, spirit, place* (pp. 191–205). New York: Cognizant.

Long, L. M. (1998). Culinary tourism: A folkloristic perspective on eating and otherness, *Southern Folklore, 55*(3), 181–204.

Mak, A. H. N., Lumbers, M., & Eves, A. (2012). Globalisation and food consumption in tourism, *Annals of Tourism Research, 39*(1), 171–196.

Mkono, M. & Tribe, J. (2017). Beyond reviewing: uncovering the multiple roles of tourism social media users, *Journal of Travel Research, 56*(3), 287–298.

Mossberg, L. (2007). A marketing approach to the tourist experience, *Scandinavian Journal of Hospitality and Tourism, 7*(1), 59–74.

Neuhofer, B., Buhalis, D., & Ladkin, A. (2014). A typology of technology-enhanced tourism experiences, *International Journal of Tourism Research*, *16*(4), 340–350.

Okumus, B. (2021). Food tourism research: a perspective article, *Tourism Review*, *76*(1), 38–42.

Rachão, S., Breda, Z., Fernandes, C. & Joukes, V. (2020). Cocreation of tourism experiences: are food-related activities being explored?, *British Food Journal*, *122*(3), 910–928.

Richards, G. (2015). Evolving gastronomic experiences: from food to foodies to foodscapes, *Journal of Gastronomy and Tourism*, *1*(1), 5–17.

Richards, G. (2021). Evolving research perspectives on food and gastronomic experiences in tourism, *International Journal of Contemporary Hospitality Management*, *33*(3), 1037–1058.

Ryan, C. (1997). *The Tourist Experience. A New Introduction*. London: Cassell.

Seeler, S., Lück, M., & Schänzel, H. A. (2019). Exploring the drivers behind experience accumulation – the role of secondary experiences consumed through the eyes of social media influencers, *Journal of Hospitality and Tourism Management*, *41*, 80–89.

Sfodera, F. (2011). *Turismi, destinazioni e internet: la rilevazione della consumer experience nei portali turistici (Tourisms, destinations and internet: the consumer experience recognition on tourism web portal)*. Milano: Franco Angeli.

Sigala, M. (2009). E-service quality and Web 2.0: expanding quality models to include customer participation and inter-customer support, *Service Industries Journal*, *29*(10), 1341–1358.

Stone, M. J., Migacz, S., & Garibaldi, R. (2020). *2020 Food Travel Monitor*. Oregon, US: World Food Travel Association.

Therkelsen, A. (2015). Catering for yourself: Food experiences of self-catering tourists, *Tourist Studies*, *15*(3), 316–333

Tse, P. & Crotts, J. C. (2005). Antecedents of novelty seeking: international visitors' propensity to experiment across Hong Kong's culinary traditions, *Tourism Management*, *26*(6), 965–968.

Tussyadiah, I. P., & Fesenmaier, D. R. (2007). Interpreting Tourist Experiences from First-Person Stories: A Foundation for Mobile Guides, in *15th European Conference on Information Systems*, St. Gallen, Switzerland.

Walter, P. (2017). Culinary tourism as living history: staging, tourist performance and perceptions of authenticity in a Thai cooking school, *Journal of Heritage Tourism*, *12*(4), 365–379.

Walter, U., Edvardsson, B. & Öström, Å. (2010). Drivers of customers' service experiences: a study in the restaurant industry, *Managing Service Quality, An International Journal*, *20*(3), 236–258.

Zhang, H., Gordon, S., Buhalis, D., & Ding, X. (2018). Experience value cocreation on destination online platforms, *Journal of Travel Research*, *57*(8), 1093–1107.

Sitography

Alchemist restaurant: https://alchemist.dk

Avatar Robot Café: https://dawn2021.orylab.com/en/

Bodegas Ramòn Bilbao: https://bodegasramonbilbao.com

Castello Banfi: www.castellobanfiwineresort.it

Castello di Amorosa: https://castellodiamorosa.com

Cloudy Bay winery: www.cloudybay.com
Hunter Valley Wine Country: www.winecountry.com.au
Il Tempio di Montalcino: www.orodimontalcino.it/tempio-del-brunello
Inamo restaurant: www.inamo-restaurant.com
La Cité du Vin: www.laciteduvin.com
Robot Theme restaurant: www.robotrestaurantomr.in
Ultraviolet restaurant: https://uvbypp.ccm
Visit French Wine: http://visitfrenchwine.com
Visit Napa Valley: www.visitnapavalley.com

7 The Influence of Media on Food Travel

Jonatan Leer

Introduction

In the digital era, media consumption is increasingly woven into and shaping other forms of consumption and disrupting traditional consumption structures. Tourism is no exception, and neither is, obviously, food tourism. A few generations ago, guidebooks and maps were the predominant (and relatively limited) media products used by tourists and food tourists. Today, these are progressively replaced by apps, digital search engine, online platforms etc. With this digitalization of food tourism, media are integrated in a rising number of food and tourism practices, including locating interesting food experiences and reviewing them, finding information relating to local food cultures, understanding traditional foodways and novel trends, sharing food photos and impressions from the food travel etc.

In this chapter, I will situate the present relation and reciprocal influence of food, travel and media in a historic perspective. The goal is to highlight the uniqueness of the current situation as well as the continuities. Furthermore, I will pinpoint central debates, dilemmas, and tendencies in the correlation between food, media and travel. Particularly, I will argue that the current omni-presence of media in food and traveling has three major consequences. First, the present digital mediascape is arguably more democratic and co-creative, but this development also involves more complex and rapidly shifting structures in relation to authoritative voices and economic systems. This development has altered the role of both the food travelers and the food entrepreneurs offering food tourism experiences. Second, I argue that there is a paradox in the digital age of food and traveling, namely that the new media open the world to new food destinations and food cultures while at the same time facilitating the pro-duction of analogous food spaces, designs and aesthetics around the world. Third, as researchers and practitioners in the field of food and tourism, we need to understand that media is not just reporting on what is going on in food and travel. Media are increasingly shaping food experiences and culinary destinations.

It is obviously impossible to cover all that has been written on the topic of food, media and travel in a single chapter, so rather than superficially doing

DOI: 10.4324/9781003282532-10

The Influence of Media on Food Travel   95

a literature review, the present account is somewhat selective as I focus more in depth on a series of studies, I find help us best to understand the principal tendencies and dynamics in field. The methodological approach of the chapter is thus theoretical. I do not present new empirical data or analyses. Rather, I try to outline and theoretically discuss some overarching themes in recent studies of food, media and travel. Hence, I discuss a mix of international studies and studies that I have been involved with. The studies I focus on are selected because I believe they can serve as illustrations of more general tendencies. Due to this selective approach, it might be relevant to situate myself and my work. I have entered the field of food tourism via food studies and cultural studies of food consumption and food cultures. My work has mostly been based on qualitative methods (ethnography, interviews, media analyses) and is driven by a desire to understand food practices in context and in depth. Hence, most of the studies discussed here are based on qualitative methodology and, in terms of the geographic scope, most of my work has addressed a European and Nordic context. In this chapter, most of my examples will reflect this geographical context. Notably, examples from my hometown Copenhagen will play a predominant role. This choice is not just a practical one, Copenhagen is a particularly enlightening example in relation to food, media and travel as the city in the last 20 years has undergone a radical transformation from a culinary no-man's-land 20 years ago to become one of the most hyped food destinations in the world (Leer, 2016a). This development is in part due to clever use of media.

Despite these methodological and geographical constraints, I believe the theoretical perspectives and discussions offered here are much broader and can inspire people from around the globe studying and working in the field of food, travel and media, notably as many of these media-driven trends I discuss are transnational and even global phenomenon.

Media in Food Traveling: From Guidebooks to Influencers

There is a fascinating dialectics between food traveling and media as we find a lot of traveling in food media and a lot of media use in food traveling. Travel literature is an old genre which covers a range of subgenres. For instance, travel diaries like Montaigne's iconic Renaissance travel account of his trip to Italy in the 16th century (Montaigne, 1962). Many other modern and colonial writers followed up and popularized their exotic explorations to their national public, who were often confined to explore a limited geographical sphere in their life-span. Other subgenres are more instructional like the 19th-century Canadian settlement narratives with guides for other potential settlers (Alexander, 2016). More recently, guidebooks have been a growing genre throughout the 20th century. The guidebook can be traced back to a pilgrim's guide in the Renaissance, and later for students ambitioning to do their formative "grand tour". (Gassan, 2005). With the continued rise of cultural and later mass tourism, the genre has flourished until the 21st century where digital technologies have presented a more updated and rapid form of searching for information. However, the material guidebook seems to remain relevant for a number of tourists (Mieli & Zilinger, 2020).

Food is obviously a recurrent theme in this travel literature. Montaigne has countless descriptions of what and where he ate during his travel to Italy in 1580–1581. In his journal of the tour, we find detailed accounts of truffles in Rovereto and Trento to his elaborated analyses of differences in water quality from holy sources he drank for health reasons (Montaigne, 1962). Modern guides also tend to have food recommendations. In the 20th century, specialized culinary guides became more common. Founded in the early part of the 20th century (Lane, 2014: 13), the Michelin guide is often considered one of the foundational ones with the famous star system. One star implies a "very good restaurant in its category", two "excellent cooking worth a detour" and three "exceptional cuisine, worth a special journey". The guide was motivated by the Michelin tire factories' ambition to stimulate car traveling to sustain and expand their business (Henderson, 2017). Due to its role as first mover, the general acceptance of its sense of quality as well as the mystique concerning its inspectors and the secrecy regarding their modus operandi, it has retained a leading position in the market for almost a century. Currently, it has expanded far beyond France and covers 28 countries and rates more than 40.000 establishments, and has become increasingly online with 25 million visits in 2018 (Montargot, Kallmuenzer & Kraus, 2022).

Various attempts have been made to challenge the Michelin guide's unique status and it has repeatedly been subject to criticism, most severely due to the secrecy and perceived unfairness (Hoa & May, 2021). In the 1970s in France, two journalists Gault and Millau found the guide out of touch with new trends in gastronomy and established their own guide named after themselves (Montargot, Kallmuenzer & Kraus, 2022). In their ratings, they distinguished between traditional and modern gastronomy. More recently, the world's 50 best restaurants list (W50) with its more global focus has challenged the French dominance in the global field of fine dining and the taste hierarchies of the Michelin guide (Beaugé, 2013). The W50 list has for instance helped the Nordic restaurants gain international recognition, notably NOMA which has topped the list five times. This attention sparked a significant rise in food tourists to the region.

In recent years both the Michelin Guide and the W50 have launched their guides with mediatized events where celebrity chefs and the food intelligentsia glamorize the products and generate international media attention to the guides, the individual businesses, and the industry. The media attention for such events are both from traditional and social media. The competitive nature of the events as well as the presence of celebrity chefs work well on both kinds of media.

Such mediatized culinary award events are an interesting example of how a traditional food media genre such as the guidebook try to adapt to the contemporary digital age and modern ways of communicating. In their eagerness to attract attention to the guides, they combine experiential, digital and print communication. This is a way of maintaining some form of recognition in a digital age where travelers' individual and idiosyncratic searches on social and digital media increasingly seem to replace the material guidebook.

Food Travels in the Media: The Search for Authenticity

Food travels have been a major part of food media. Notably in the post-war period where numerous food authors from the global North explained "exotic" cuisines to a growing readership. The exoticism of these cuisines varied and included old colonial terroirs, but most often Mediterranean cuisines were favored. In Elizabeth David's iconic cookbooks from the 1950s, we discover numerous accounts of the uniqueness of the Mediterranean food cultures which are often mixed with colorful narratives of the spaces and the locals. Many have copied this form and invited the reader to travel via anecdotal travel accounts mixed with recipes. With the rise of food television in the 1970s–80s (Leer, 2017), the travelogue cooking show genre became particularly popular. Keith Floyd was one of the first to pioneer this genre with his humorous and lively style of presenting and cooking around the world from the British islands to exotic destinations like Australia, Africa and the Far East (Inglis & Almila, 2019; Rousseau, 2012).

The travelogue food shows allowed the viewer to experience more or less exotic food cultures and visually meet the people, landscapes and the traditions of specific food regions from home. The genre has nonetheless been accused of romanticizing the local cultures and shaping these according to a Western gaze. Food philosopher Lisa Heldke argues that mediatized food adventurers like Keith Floyd are problematic because of the social hierarchies his shows reproduce: "For Floyd, the food of the Other remains exotic, exoticism often standing as evidence not of the fascination of other cultures, but of their inferiority" (Heldke, 2015, 129). In this perspective, food traveling is not a gateway to equal cultural exchange, but rather a means to reproduce stereotypical hierarchies between Western chefs and locals from less Westernized cultures.

Leer and Kjær (2015) are also critical of televised food shows of newer generations, including Gordan Ramsay and Jamie Oliver. Inspired by social theorist Sara Ahmed, they argue that the white, male TV chefs in their encounters with "exotic" food cultures perform acts of "stranger fetishism". This means that the hosts reduce locals to embodiments of their preconceived fantasies of authenticity. Furthermore, these male culinary adventurers establish themselves as "subjects who can evaluate this authenticity as well as distinguish between what is 'too authentic' and what is 'not authentic enough.'"(Leer & Kjær, 2015, 324). Although these culinary encounters in food travel media might be democratizing culinary knowledge about these cultures and cuisines, these narratives risk – like food tourism experiences – being reductive of the plurality of local culture and echoing the visitors' fixed expectations.

Authenticity is – and has been for some time – the dominant buzzword in the media's food travel discourses and a controversial one due to its many meanings. In their book *Foodies*, sociologists Johnston and Baumann (2010) make one of

98 *Jonatan Leer*

the more convincing descriptions of the concept. The authors try – on the basis of a major analyses of foodie media discourses – to describe how good taste is defined in an era where French gastronomy no longer is synonymous with good taste. Their point is that the modern foodie is often described as an omnivore, e.g. someone who embraces a variety of cuisines and food repertoires. However, this does not mean that "anything goes" according to the sociologists. They argue that exoticism and authenticity are the new modes of distinction that work to ascribe value to food products and food experiences. So, if you as a Western tourist buy a fish sauce from a small, local producers during a trip to Thailand and bring it home, it will have a higher "culinary capital" (Naccarato & LeBesco, 2013) than the mass-produced fish sauce from a global brand in the local, Western supermarket. Both fish sauces might be defined as exotic, but the latter lacks authenticity. Johnston and Baumann list five qualities of the authentic food product or experience: Geographic specificity, simplicity, personal connection, history and tradition, and ethnic connection. These reoccur frequently across central food travel media and add to the prestige of a product and an experience. If the fish sauce you bought when traveling in Thailand is from specific region, made with simple tools by the person you bought it from, and the product reflects a traditional craft that the producer's family have passed on from generation to generation for centuries and maybe even ties in to the history of an ethnic community, then you are truly buying authenticity and you can proudly flag it in front of your foodie friends.

Mediatized Celebrity Chefs as Reason to Go

In recent years, many high-end chefs are no longer just cooks working in the kitchen, but also brands sustained by personalized storytelling (Ulver & Classen, 2018). This also means that chefs have entered the sphere of celebrities (Johnston & Goodmann, 2015), and they take up more space in the media and are featured in new types of media. For instance, when Danish chef René Redzepi was on the cover of *TIME* magazine in 2012 as one of the first chefs on this magazine cover, which are usually reserved for political and cultural icons (Leer, 2016a). The Netflix series *Chef's Table* (2015–) is a clear example of the idolization of the contemporary (often male) chefs and their restaurants. Whereas traditional food media seemed to disseminate information and guidance in relation to cooking, these novel chef-centered portraits rather "work to democratize knowledge about the chef's brand image" (Hollows & Jones, 2010: 523). Through this personality-driven hype, these establishments become destinations for foodies' pilgrimage (Lee, 2014). Such pilgrimages are in no way easy to accomplish. These high-end restaurants are not only expensive, but the costumers often have to invest quite a bit of time in booking tables and organizing the trip.

We find a description of such a pilgrimage in Australian media and food studies scholar Nancy Lee's dissertation (Lee, 2014). She describes how she as a not very affluent PhD student decided to try to visit NOMA during a trip to the US and Europe. In her description, there is an interesting interplay between the media and the visit. The very idea to visit NOMA was inspired by W50 recognition which led her to follow Redzepi on Twitter (it was in 2011, now Instagram works as his and NOMAs primary communication channel). Following Redzepi's account, she was intrigued by the transgressive stories about dishes with ants and living, but anaesthetized prawns.

Reservation dates for NOMA were released three months in advance at midnight for each month. At the time of release, Lee and a friend called the restaurant over Skype 47 times in 45 minutes before getting through and being able to accomplish the reservation. Five minutes later the entire month was fully booked. This dramatic reservation process added a unique value the visit. Nonetheless, Lee concludes after the visit that "My visit to NOMA turned out to be underwhelming. I had been carried away by the hype. Even so, I felt like I had made a significant pilgrimage as a member of the culinary community" (Lee, 2014: 14).

In this example, we see how closely novel media technologies are shaping the experience both practically and mentally. Lee's description interestingly points out some of the dilemmas of this development and notably the risk of building up so much hype that even the allegedly best restaurant in the world turns out underwhelming.

I have found similar ambivalences in my studies of NOMA's burger pop-up (see Figure 7.1) following the COVID-19 lockdown. For a couple of months in the summer of 2020 when restaurants were allowed to reopen, NOMA was transformed into a burger joint/wine bar reducing their menu and pricing dramatically. In this form, reservations were not possible, but people had to show up and wait in line. The story of one of the world's best restaurants turning into a burger joint went viral and people flocked to try it. Locals and travelers would stand in line for up to 2–3 hours. This called for a new wave of media attention describing the endless lines. The customers we interviewed for a case study were all intrigued by this hype phenomenon and those who got a chance to see Redzepi or his wife were particularly thrilled. Some, however, were also like Lee a little underwhelmed because they found the relatively traditional cheeseburger too plain for the innovative and edgy brand of NOMA (Leer & Hoff-Jørgensen, 2022).

This shows how much of mediatized hype and the presence of mediatized celebrity chefs shape food experiences and make them worth traveling and standing in line for, but also that there is a risk of a mismatch between branding and the actual product. The NOMA burger case is nonetheless a great example of how chefs can use the media to generate attention and expand their brand. The NOMA burger was a good story and generated attention. It also showed that René Redzepi continues to transgress the norms of fine dining: serving an American cheeseburger at a locavore, Nordic restaurant is almost as transgressive as the earlier transgressions of serving a living, but anaesthetized prawn. The stunt cemented the audacity and unpredictability of Redzepi's brand. The media bought the narrative and generated international hype. The queue as

Figure 7.1 The NOMA burger

a symbol of the success of the story extended the hype for another round of media attention. Also, the experience design with the queue system gave costumers a lot of time to take photos and share them on social media … and many did.

Digital Media and Democratization of Food Authorities: The Examples of Foodies and Restaurant Reviewing

Among food tourists, the figure of the foodie is increasingly an important one (Getz et al.,, 2014). The foodie was first defined in the Foodie Handbook as a person who was "very, very, very interested in food" (Barr & Levy 1984: 6). More recently, the term has been taken up by the academic literature. De Solier (2013) links the concept to that of serious leisure to understand the difference between a foodie and ordinary consumers who like eating well. The concept of serious leisure (Stebbins, 2007) implies that a leisure activity is performed with a higher degree of dedication than the average consumer and a focus of accumulating skills and knowledge. Serious leisure is also central to the practitioner's identity. Most leisure activities from sports to sewing could become a serious leisure activity if it is practiced in a "serious" manner. So, it is not as much a matter of the type of practice, but a matter of how this practice is performed.

For instance, drinking a glass of wine in a wine bar can be casual leisure or serious leisure depending on the context and the way it is performed. For many, drinking a glass of wine would just be a pleasant moment, maybe even just an excuse for socializing, but for the wine connoisseur, this would be a quite different experience where the wine is analyzed in depth and compared to a whole catalogue of previous tastings and wine travels. The result of the analysis would in many cases be shared on SoMe, blogs and on accounts in wine apps. There is a thin and fluid line between leisure and work. There are many examples of wine enthusiasts who become semi-professionals, either as an expert or consultant or as a wine importer.

Digital media play a major role in the development of foodie identity in relation to food and traveling. Foodies are increasingly taking over what used to be done by professionals. Restaurant reviewing is an illustrative example. Just a few decades ago, a few journalists in print media would be dominant authorities in food in specific cities, regions or countries (Naulin, 2017). They would also go on culinary tours to important food destinations and present their recommendations to the local audiences upon return. They could be what French sociologist Pierre Bourdieu has described as cultural intermediaries taking on a role of divulging "legitimate culture" (Kobez, 2018). However, with the rise of digital media, the traditional structure of cultural intermediaries in the culinary field has been disrupted, and print media and television no longer monopolize the role as cultural intermediaries (Kobez, 2018). They must share this position with a rising number of food bloggers and foodies with direct access to the public via social and digital media.

Various restaurateurs in Copenhagen have informally confirmed to me that whereas a review in one of the major Danish newspapers could make or break a restaurant in the 2000s, this is no longer the case. Fewer and fewer read the newspapers, and most costumers – tourists and locals – search information in online media when looking for options to eat out. A picture that has been confirmed even by the critics.[1] This also means that the restaurateurs in Copenhagen (and elsewhere) now must consider the rising numbers of international food bloggers who pass by their establishments. The number is important in Copenhagen as the city has gained international culinary fame.

Among the people I talked to, the views on bloggers and foodies differed. Some pay extra attention to these lonely diners in hope of positive mentions on their media outlets. Others find that it has gone too far because these bloggers often dine alone but take up a table that could have served a couple or more guests. Some restaurateurs are also annoyed by the elaborated camera equipment some bloggers bring to the table, and by certain food bloggers' expectations of free treats in exchange for media attention. There have been some cases of chefs

102 *Jonatan Leer*

even raising this topic publicly. The notoriously provocative Danish chef Umut Sakarya (Leer & Krogager, 2022), called out a known influencer for "begging for free food" which he found particularly provoking as the restaurant industry had suffered great loses during the pandemic.[2]

In other restaurants, the development has affected restaurant design. When I visited restaurant KOKS at the Faroe Islands, I discovered that they had created a communal table where all the lonely eaters were seated. This initiative ensured that the relatively small restaurant would maximize its capacity and not let tables for two or more be occupied by one person. Also, they said that after a few dishes (and glasses of wine), there was always a very vivid ambience at the communal table. I was told that the Michelin guide inspector was seated at that table and the two stars in the Guide testify that he/she enjoyed it.

So digital media restructure the whole mediascape around food and travel and even restaurants' interior design. But is this new mediascape a good or bad development? It is arguably a democratization that allows new voices to talk about and judge food. This democratization assures that the public culinary debate is no longer reserved for a few selected authorities (Getz et al., 2014: 189). Also, travelers going to a new destination can be inspired by numerous blogs and Instagram accounts by local voices and culinary globetrotters. On the other hand, these "old" authorities might claim that the so-called democratization in nothing short of a dumping down of their métier which is now conduct by a bunch of laypersons with limited skills, experience and insight to the local context (Kobez, 2018). There is certainly some truth in both perspectives. The contemporary food traveler needs to be a critical reader, but she/he also has a unique possibility to access a variety of perspectives.

Is Social Media Homogenizing Food Destinations? The Example of Hipster Food Culture in World Cities

One might imagine that the increased number of food travel media and the multiplication of voices in food media (locally and globally) should make the world of food more diverse and help the food traveler to explore more unique food spaces around the world. However, some researchers also argue that an increased homogenization of food culture is one of the consequences of this development. This is, for instance, a central idea in food scholars Mateusz Halawa and Fabio Parasecoli's theory of Global Brooklyn (Halawa & Parasecoli, 2019). Their argument is that a certain Brooklynesque model of food aesthetics and ideology has spread across world cities. Around the world, old industrial areas are transformed into gentrified zones for food, craft and creative milieus. The ideal type of Global Brooklyn, which the authors sketch in a 2019 essay (Halawa & Parasecoli, 2019), is characterized by a post-industrial design where industrial buildings are redesigned for food and recreation. The industrial feeling is, however, maintained in the rough, yet carefully curated interiors. Bricks and metal tubes remain visible, rather than masked. These eateries also share a palate

The Influence of Media on Food Travel   103

characterized by challenging flavors like the fermented, sour and bitter. Iconic foods include craft beer, artisanal pizzas, third wave coffee, kombucha ... Global Brooklyn nostalgically evokes the past and rediscovers old-fashioned crafts (making bread dough by hand) and old technology (fetishizing vinyl records). The atmosphere is casual, and staffers are not wearing uniform, but they hold a high degree of connoisseurship and skills which are often displayed as they perform and talk about their food products.

Chances are that you might have a local version of Global Brooklyn nearby. A place where an industrial area is transformed into a funky zone for craft beer, sour dough and expensive coffee sold by tattooed hipsters wearing beanies who are eager to share their knowledge about coffee roasting or the age of their sour dough. Halawa and Parasecoli argue that although these different versions of Global Brooklyn have certain unique local features, they remain quite similar in aesthetics, ambience and ethics. They cater to a global, cosmopolitan, middle-class clientele. An important point for the authors is that the spread of this global trend is distinct from previous forms of globalization of food régimes which were anchored in national cuisine (French food, sushi) or in global brands (Starbucks or McDonald's). According to Halawa and Parasecoli, Global Brooklyn is spreading so fast due to new media and networked communication:

> Spaces and meals are designed in response to the global circulation of images, values and ideas deployed into local things, and then are in turn further photographed, discussed and disseminated on Instagram and pinned on Pinterest. They become part of a coherent aesthetic that may nevertheless look out of place in their physical context.
>
> (Parasecoli & Halawa, 2021: 14)

As a follow up to their original essay, the authors edited an anthology where researchers from around the world would empirically explore the local version of Global Brooklyn in their big cities. The result was striking: Global Brooklyn milieus were found with local modifications in Cape Town, Paris, Rio De Janeiro, London, Tel Aviv, Mumbai and many other cities. The authors shared their photos from their ethnographic work and they are now accessible on Fabio Parasecoli's website.[3] When reviewing this imagery, it is surprisingly difficult to guess in which city or part of the world the photos are from, if you don't look at the text. All pass as variants of a collective aesthetical régime rather than adhering to any national or regional aesthetical code. This is of course very interesting in relation to food tourism. Contrary to the old travelogue food shows mentioned above where local uniqueness was highlighted and even essentialized, this fad of Global Brooklyn seems to detach the spaces from the local nature, culture and traditional foods to adopt a "decentralized sameness" anchored in an urban post-industrial feeling and foodscape. Here again media's role is not just to represent food travel to new audiences, the

Figure 7.2 Global Brooklyn in Copenhagen

media-based circulation of imagery shapes food tourists' experiences locally and globally.

I contributed to the Global Brooklyn anthology with a chapter on my town, Copenhagen, where various previously important industrial areas have been transformed into hip food and leisure spaces (see Figure 7.2). One of the most prominent examples is Refshaleøen and the street-food market Reffen. In the words of the Lonely Planet 2019 guide: "the city's booming street-food scene is smashing it on Refshaleøen, where a former shipyard is now rebooted food and craft market Reffen."[4] Here we find containers turned into street-food outlets and Mikkeller craft beers by the sea side. It is thought-provoking in the Lonely Planet's 2019 description and accompanying promotion video that this Brooklynesque food scene plays a more prominent role than the New Nordic which otherwise had shaped the city's local food identity for the last decade. The guide highlights something that is also found in numerous world cities, rather than something unique to the local community. So what are we really looking for as food travelers? The unique or the recognizable? Or some form of recognizable uniqueness? This is of course a matter of differences among food tourists, but it is remarkable that many food tourists seem attracted to experiences that have a certain recognizability to them.

Conclusion

Media have been a central part of food traveling as I have tried to demonstrate in this chapter. Nonetheless, it seems fair to say that the relationship has intensified with the arrival of digital media. Media no longer just report on food travels, but seem increasingly to be a player in shaping the food experience design as we saw in several of the examples here. At the same time, digital food media disrupt and democratize traditional hierarchies in the culinary field and invite the food traveler to participate in the booming field.

It should also be noted that despite the constant innovation in a rapidly changing mediascape around food and travel, the digital world also give us, researchers and practitioners, some possibilities for gaining new insights and perspectives on food and tourism consumers' attitudes and practices. These insights include quantitative data as well as new qualitative data in the form of discussions in online fora, posts on social media platforms and online reviews. As with all data, this data should be read critically, but it might offer new perspectives on food, travel and media for both practitioners and researchers alike and we should think of it as a way to develop the field (Leer & Krogager, 2021).

Food for Thought

- How can media contribute to more equal meetings between food tourists and members of local food communities which are not framed by global inequalities or stereotypes?
- Is the democratization of restaurant reviewing in the digital era of food traveling a good or a bad development? And who might benefit from it? And who might suffer the consequences?
- Do you recognize the description of the Global Brooklyn aesthetical régime in your local context? And do you think that media generally make the world of food and travel more diverse or more homogenic?

Notes

1 https://podimo.com/en/shows/c60d6e23-19e2-4cb9-870b-cb00361b37fb/epis ode/9c7e8b82-6b6c-40cd-8fc1-07af1506ebc8.
2 www.bt.dk/kendte/caroline-fleming-haengt-ud-paa-kendiskoks-instagram-som-tig ger-det-var-ikke.
3 Visit the gallery at https://fabioparasecoli.com/global-brooklyn-gallery/
4 www.lonelyplanet.com/best-in-travel/cities.

References

Alexander, V. (2016). Transcultural food and recipes for immigration: Susanna Moodie and Catharine Parr Traill. In J. Leer & K. K. Povlsen (Eds.), *Food and Media: Practices, distinctions and heterotopias* (pp. 38–61). Routledge.

Barr, A., & Levy, P. (1984). *The Official Foodie Handbook*. Timbre Books.

Beaugé, B. (2013). *Plats du jour*. Paris: Métaillé.

De Solier, I. (2013). *Food and the self: Consumption, production and material culture*. Bloomsbury Publishing.

Gassan, R. (2005). The First American Tourist Guidebooks. *Book History, 8*(1), 51–74.

Getz, D., Robinson, R., Andersson, T., & Vujicic, S. (2014). *Foodies and food tourism*. Goodfellow Publishers Ltd.

Halawa, M., & Parasecoli, F. (2019). Eating and Drinking in Global Brooklyn. *Food, Culture & Society, 22*(4), 387–406.

Heldke, L. (2015). *Exotic appetites: Ruminations of a food adventurer*. Routledge.

Henderson, J. C. (2017). Street food, Hawkers and the Michelin Guide in Singapore. *British Food Journal. 119*(4), 790–802.

Hoa, N. V., & May, I. (2021). A reflection on the story, current positioning, offerings and the darker side of the luxury gastronomy book, the Michelin Guide. *Research in Hospitality Management, 11*(1), 59–65.

Hollows, J., & Jones, S. (2010). Please don't try this at home: Heston Blumenthal, cookery TV and the culinary field. *Food, Culture & Society, 13*(4), 521–537.

Inglis, D., & Almila, A. M. (2019). Creating and routinizing style and immediacy: Keith Floyd and the South-West English roots of new cookery mediatizations. In *Globalized eating cultures* (pp. 221–244). Cham: Palgrave Macmillan.

Johnston, J., & Baumann, S. (2010). *Foodies: Democracy and distinction in the gourmet foodscape*. Routledge.

Johnston, J., & Goodman, M. K. (2015). Spectacular foodscapes: Food celebrities and the politics of lifestyle mediation in an age of inequality. *Food, Culture & Society, 18*(2), 205–222.

Kobez, M. (2018). 'Restaurant reviews aren't what they used to be': digital disruption and the transformation of the role of the food critic. *Communication Research and Practice, 4*(3), 261–276.

Lane, C. (2014). *The Cultivation of Taste*. Oxford: Oxford University Press.

Lee, N. (2014). *Celebrity chefs: class mobility, media, masculinity*. University of Sydney.

Leer, J. (2016). The rise and fall of the New Nordic Cuisine. *Journal of Aesthetics & Culture, 8*(1), 1–20.

Leer, J. (2016). What's cooking, man? Masculinity in European cooking shows after The Naked Chef. *Feminist Review, 114*(1), 72–90.

Leer, J. (2017). Gender and food television: A transnational perspective on the gendered identities of televised celebrity chefs. In K. Lebesco & P. Naccarato (Eds.), *The Bloomsbury Handbook of Food and Popular Culture*, 13–26.

Leer, J. & Hoff-Jørgensen (2022). Consumers' Attitudes to Gourmet Burgers. *British Food Journal*, 1–16

Leer, J., & Kjær, K. M. (2015). Strange Culinary Encounters: Stranger Fetishism in Jamie's Italian Escape and Gordon's Great Escape. *Food, Culture & Society, 18*(2), 309–327.

Leer, J., & Krogager, S. G. S. (2021). *Research Methods in Digital Food Studies*. Routledge.

Leer, J. & Krogager, S. G. S. (2022). Transgressive Food Practices on Instagram: The Case of Guldkroen in Copenhagen. In E. J. H. Contois & Z. Kish (Eds.), *You Are What You Post: Food and Instagram*. Bloomsbury Academic.

Mieli, M., & Zillinger, M. (2020). Tourist information channels as consumer choice: The value of tourist guidebooks in the digital age. *Scandinavian Journal of Hospitality and Tourism, 20*(1), 28–48.

Montaigne (1962): *Oeuvres Complètes. Bibliothèque de la Pleiade*. Paris: Gallimard.

Montargot, N., Kallmuenzer, A., & Kraus, S. (2022). Haute cuisine three-star restaurants' representation on websites and dining guides: a lexicometric analysis. *International Journal of Contemporary Hospitality Management*.

Naccarato, P., & LeBesco, K. (2013). *Culinary capital.* Bloomsbury Publishing.

Naulin, S. (2017). *Des mots à la bouche. Le journalisme gastronomique en France.* François Rabelais.

Parasecoli, F., & Halawa, M. (Eds.). (2021). *Global Brooklyn: designing food experiences in world cities.* Bloomsbury Publishing.

Rousseau, S. (2012). *Food Media.* London: Bloomsbury.

Stebbins, R. A. (2007). *Serious leisure.* Routledge.

Ulver, S., & Klasson, M. (2018). Social Magic for Dinner? The Taste Script and Shaping of Foodieness in Netflix's Chef's Table. In Z. Arsel & J. Bean (Eds.), *Taste, Consumption, and Markets* (pp. 26–44). Routledge.

8 The Role of Digital Marketing in the Future of Food Tourism

Andrea Wintergerst

Introduction

Travelers use social media and digital resources in all the stages of travel (Expedia Group, 2016). From obtaining inspiration from wanderlust-worthy Instagram posts and reading comments on travel forums to help plan itineraries, to sharing updates during the trip and posting reviews on TripAdvisor after returning home. This same prevalence has allowed food tourism to grow exponentially over the past years.

Remember the days when *#foodporn* and *#travelgram* dominated your social media feed? As of 2022, there are over 286 million public posts for the former, and about 159 million for the latter on Instagram *alone*. These hashtags are still being used, and there is no indication of them disappearing. Currently, there are 131,000 posts using *#foodtourism* but expect this number to grow in the coming years.

Accompanying travelers through the entire travel cycle will help achieve consumer satisfaction, attract new fans, and increment loyalty in returning users. To achieve this, there needs to be a well-laid-out marketing strategy that aligns with your organization's goals. This chapter examines steps a business can take to ensure that its digital marketing efforts are coherent and effective.

Social Media Usage in Travel by the Numbers

The use of consumer technology for travel-related endeavors is widespread. According to a study by Yahoo (Bahadur, 2014), 74% of millennials use their smartphone to research travel. Another study shows that 84% of millennials and 73% of non-millennials are very likely to use social media as a source of inspiration when planning travel (AMP Agency, 2016). Nearly all (97%) travelers post on social networks when traveling (Shankman, 2014).

Gen Z, on the other hand, reports 58% use of a mobile device to research travel, according to European Travel Commission (2020). The same study shows that 53% of Gen-Zers share on social media during their trip. Social media influences almost 90% of their travel decisions, with Facebook influencing 64% of these decisions (Expedia Group, 2018). And 55% of all travelers will like

DOI: 10.4324/9781003282532-11

social media pages related to their trip (Del Gigante, 2018) after returning from it. By continuing to engage with users, an organization can reinforce positive opinions and drive repeat visits.

What Value Are You Providing to Consumers?

We have heard about our unique selling propositions and added value. This applies not only to a destination, business, or product but to marketing as well. Why? Digital content relating to food tourism is immense. To reach consumers through the noise, businesses need to add value to that content. A nice picture of a traditional dish is no longer enough to captivate and maintain user attention since this is what most other travelers and brands are posting too. At best, simple content like this will prompt a user to find out more and arrive at a destination or business, and at worst, will garner passing likes that will not convert to bookings, reservations, or visits.

Adding value does not have to be complicated. Anything useful to consumers is valuable. Short recipes, fun facts, tutorials, checklists, stories, etc. all add to what could be an easily ignorable post.

It is worth mentioning that whatever you choose to share with consumers does not necessarily need to be in the same vein as your main service or product. What matters is its usefulness to your chosen market segment. For example, a restaurant need not limit itself to telling stories about the local ingredients used in their preparations. They could share a list of interesting places to see in the neighborhood before stopping by for a meal. And vice-versa, a museum could share a list of their team's favorite places to get a drink and a bite after work.

Every destination is unique in its traditions, gastronomy, and people. Weaving these stories into your content will not only provide users with something valuable but also reach people with whom those stories truly resonate.

It is also important to know which platforms are best suited for the value provided. Do you represent a culinary destination seeking to provide evergreen content, such as information about local dishes and gastronomic traditions? Pinterest and a dedicated blog are excellent options. Is your business a pop-up food truck traveling through the country? Instagram and Facebook will visually inform where and when diners can find you. Are you managing a visitor center? A complete, up-to-date Google Business page with operating hours and services offered is necessary.

A Platform for Each Purpose

As previously mentioned, some platforms are best suited for specific types of content. Regardless of which platforms the organization chooses to incorporate into its digital marketing strategy, keeping them up to date, accurate, and complete should not be overlooked. Users expect to be able to find basic information about the business. In terms of service expectations (Parasuraman, Berry and Zeithaml, 1991) it is the bare minimum they would expect. If users run into outdated information and profiles, the perceived quality of the services lowers significantly, driving users to the competition that has properly maintained their platforms.

Facebook

If a business had to choose a single platform for marketing, it should be Facebook. Not because it is the best, but because it incorporates several of the elements that define other platforms. Pictures that could be shared on Instagram, reviews that belong on TripAdvisor, news updates, basic information usually found on a website, as well as the ability to send and receive direct messages from users. The overall functionality, combined with the widespread use (there are 2.93 billion monthly active users (Statista, 2022a) which is just over one-third of the world's population), makes it necessary within the growing portfolio of platforms.

Facebook has done a decent job of designing templates that a business can use to best suit a specific need, including those such as business, venues, services, shopping, and restaurants and cafes. Each template has a series of predetermined tabs, but the administrator can always activate or deactivate specific tabs according to their needs. Tabs include About, Photos, Shop, Reviews, Offers, Guides, and more. When fully and correctly populated, these tabs can easily substitute a full-fledged website, if it is monitored and updated constantly.

Appointments on Facebook also allow a business to manage bookings, such as time slots for culinary tours and sending confirmations to customers. Although not the most comprehensive scheduling solution, the ease of access and management make it a valuable tool, especially for startups without the resources for a full booking solution.

Instagram

The most direct and visually appealing way to reach out to consumers, Instagram is the tool that propelled food tourism into the spotlight. It has about 1.4 billion monthly active users (Statista, 2022b).

Beyond the post feed, Instagram has added many features over the years, like a separate profile tab for longer videos which can, in turn, be categorized into series; a tab for Reels (which are Instagram's answer to TikTok); a section for Guides (a group of posts with a theme and featured image that can also include locations and additional text); Filters (which can be applied in Stories); and Tagged posts.

But how might a culinary destination or restaurant make the most of these tools? Repurposing content they have already created is one way to start. A destination board may have a diverse collection of videos that can be posted and organized into series such as Meet The People, Welcome To our Neighborhood, etc. Any shorter videos with punctual information would be well suited for Reels. Posts old and new can become relevant again by thoughtfully grouping them into guides such as Top 10 Most Famous Dishes or Hidden Culinary

Gems. With enough time, creating a Filter for your destination or organization is a fun, effortless way to motivate consumers to share.

And lastly, there are always the questions of how many and which hashtags to use. Five or six are usually enough to categorize and segment your content. Any more can start to look cluttered and too broad. Hashtags have become extremely specific, but it is this same specificity that allows your brand to reach the right people. Instead of simply using the generic hashtags *#food*, *#tourism*, *#travel*, and – for example – *#poland*, it might be better to use *#polandfoodtours*.

TripAdvisor

TripAdvisor is arguably still the largest travel community and website out there. Mostly known for its ranking of attractions, restaurants, museums, and other points of interest based on users' ratings and reviews, TripAdvisor – from the perspective of a business – allows one to manage a business's general information, upload images, access guides, and articles, and even view a performance dashboard with key indicators about the listing. Most importantly, TripAdvisor allows a business to respond to reviews and questions posted by users.

Setting up TripAdvisor is a straightforward process, and having a proper listing not only gives the business credibility but also provides it with valuable insights and metrics.

Any relevant business or organization with a physical location can be listed. If, for example, a local or national tourism board has a location that travelers can visit, it can be added to TripAdvisor. The "Visitor Centers" category is available as a property type. This is especially useful in aiding travelers with their questions before visiting a destination. A notable example is the Hong Kong Tourism Board's Visitor Center in Kowloon. It is rated so highly that it is recommended on TripAdvisor as #7 of 1,379 things to do in Hong Kong (TripAdvisor, n.d.).

One last way to use TripAdvisor is with a profile (not listing) for an organization. Profiles can contribute to forums, post links, pictures, videos, and maps, and create trips that use TripAdvisor's listings, providing users the option of doing most of their planning within a single platform.

There are over four hundred verified profiles for Tourism Boards (VisitJapan, VisitOrlando, and VisitSpain, to name a few) around the world and in a variety of languages as well, and what better way to find information than directly from the source?

Twitter

Built for news and entertainment and the accompanying social discussion, Twitter's defining feature is speed. It updates quickly, efficiently, and constantly. So much so, that 53% of users expect to hear back from brands within the hour (Lee, 2013).

Tweets can be up to 280 characters long and include photos, videos, and animated GIFs. Links included in Tweets count towards Tweet length, so URL shorteners are recommended. Tweets then must be extremely direct and visually appealing. Because of this, Twitter is best suited for public relations, news, resharing content from other platforms, links to articles, urgent updates, and public dialogue with users. Actively monitoring mentions and responding quickly to consumers is important across all platforms, but especially here.

Every Tweet has a unique URL, including public responses. This makes it easy to track, revisit, and manage any inquiries made directly to a profile, although private messages exist on the platform as well.

Retweets make it easy to share any relevant posts from across the platform with users, so resharing content that can be useful or otherwise interesting to them is encouraged. Follow relevant hashtags, industry leaders, and fellow businesses and organizations to keep your finger on the pulse.

Pinterest

The nature of Pinterest allows content posted here to have a longer shelf life than most other platforms. Still, Pins need to be thoughtfully designed to achieve their full potential. Images used on Pins should be a visual summary of what users can expect to find inside, complete with a title. When these Pins are shared across the platform and the general internet, users can quickly and easily find what they need.

The Boards created here will depend on the exact nature of the organization, but Pinterest's visual essence and its intended use as an online idea board make it an ideal tool for the inspiration and planning phases. A culinary destination might create Boards for itineraries and road trips, while food tour companies can put together foodie guides and checklists.

Pinterest also offers a great resource, Pinterest Trends, which allows a destination to see how certain keywords have performed over the last year. The administrator can analyze multiple trends at a time, and popular Pins related to those keywords are shown at the bottom of the page. Not every keyword is available to be searched, but according to the interface, new terms are added frequently.

Pinterest Ads Manager has several personas that a business can target their efforts at (as do most platforms), but one that stands out for our industry is "The Foodie Traveler" (previously the Eating Explorer).

Adding a Pin! Button to a destination or business website is another way to make it easy for users to save content to their inspiration Boards, straight from the source.

TikTok

The most popular of the newest apps that live on users' phones, TikTok excels at what it does: shorter-form, easily-bingeable videos. Stories, news, tutorials, or skits, you can find them all on TikTok.

Food tourism content on TikTok usually includes glimpses of food tours, recommendations of places to eat, rankings, short reviews, recipes, and factoids.

On TikTok's main screen, you scroll through full-screen videos the way you would endlessly scroll through posts on Instagram. TikTok's algorithm and user controls, though, mean that if a user expresses interest in your organization and industry (food tourism, in our case), they will be served content that matches these criteria constantly, whether they follow specific accounts or not. With the introduction of Reels, however, Instagram is poised to achieve the same. This contrasts with Instagram's main feed where you would have to actively follow accounts to see their content, and even then, Instagram-generated recommendations only appear around every ten posts or so.

TikTok has already overtaken Instagram in terms of popularity with the Gen Z crowd (a whopping 41.7% of the app's one billion users are aged 18–24) (Statista, 2022c), but new and shiny does not necessarily mean it will suit your market. It is unlikely that younger TikTok users will have the spending ability most destinations aim for. So, unless your target market is specifically Gen Z, the recommendation would be to stick to Instagram. This is especially true since viral and well-performing TikTok videos still make their way to Instagram.

It is worth noting that TikTok is a Chinese company and there are serious concerns over privacy, leaks, and especially data mining. It has been reported that this information is shared with the Chinese government, effectively allowing them to spy on users.

Search Engines

For many users, a quick web search is the way to go when looking up basic information about a place or company. Regardless of search engine preference, most have a business module that displays available information for the place in question.

Google Search has Google Business, Yahoo! has partnered with Yext PowerListings, Bing Search has Bing Places for Business, and even DuckDuckGo will display information pulled from TripAdvisor – one more reason to make sure your TripAdvisor listing is complete, and up to date.

As with TripAdvisor, a business can claim the listing and make sure the information presented to users is accurate and complete. The process to do so across search engines is similar. In all cases, you provide details to verify your identity and can then make necessary changes.

SEO (Search Engine Optimization) is another key element of a destination's search engine strategy and will be discussed later.

Official Website

A website is a digital brochure for a business, organization, or destination. It should contain everything users may need: up-to-date, accurate, and complete information; prices; menus; visual content; a booking engine; frequently asked questions; email sign-up forms; and a chatbot set up to receive messages and provide quick answers even when admins are away. With a Facebook Messenger widget, businesses can consolidate their messaging.

Website design is just as important as content and can influence whether a user stays on a website and how long for, and ultimately whether that visit leads to a sale, visit, or booking. With a growing number of website builders, you can set up an effective website in no time.

61% of travelers use hotel websites to plan their trip, and 37% use a destination's website (AMP Agency, 2016). Considering these numbers, a mobile-friendly responsive website is essential. Especially during travel, when laptops and desktops are limited.

As destinations strive to become more accessible, so should their websites. Everyone should be able to easily interact with the site, regardless of disabilities. This includes:

- Captions and transcripts for all media elements
- Colors with proper contrast
- Clearly outlining hyperlinks
- Clear, legible fonts
- Alternative text for images
- Audio descriptions

Although it is easier to build an accessible website from the start, many tools allow an administrator to check how accessible the site currently is and make necessary changes. Having an accessible website benefits everyone.

Ultimately, the quality of the website will reflect the quality of the business in consumers' minds.

Email

Commercial email has been around for almost three decades. It will continue to be used for a long time.

Email is the most direct and most customizable way to reach your customers. To receive emails from an organization, a user must have directly interacted with them. They might have subscribed to a newsletter, or they booked an experience and are receiving transactional emails.

Catchy subject lines are the first thing users will see once that email lands in their inbox.

The exact content of the emails will depend on the nature of the organization, but should include:

- News and important updates, both from the organization and, if relevant, the industry as a whole
- Inspirational images and/or videos
- Advice on how to best experience the service or destination

The Role of Digital Marketing in the Future of Food Tourism   115

- Calls to action
- Any upcoming events or dates visitors should be aware of
- Deals and discounts
- Social media links

Email personalization goes beyond addressing customers by name. Administrators can segment users by their interests, geographic area, whether they are already a customer or not, and more. Dynamic content will also change based on these data to further personalize emails. Asking a few questions during sign-up will ensure that only relevant emails reach users, increasing conversions and reducing unsubscribe rates.

Newsletters can be quarterly, monthly, weekly, or even daily, while transactional emails are triggered by specific events and actions.

Special occasion emails, however, can be for any good enough reason: a food tour sale, a reservation opening at a restaurant, or even a freebie on a visitor's birthday.

Making Content Easy to Find with SEO

With so much content on the internet, it is more important than ever to make your content as easily accessible to consumers as possible.

SEO is the process of optimizing every aspect of your website to rank higher in search engines, reaching a wider audience. Keywords, having a responsive site, alt text and captions on images and videos, having a complete Google Business listing, landing pages, and other actions you take outside of your website all have an impact. SEO is not hard per se, but it does take time to properly build and requires research and thoughtful planning. Results of proper SEO will show up in the long term.

Evergreen content – content that remains consistently relevant – is good for SEO, too. If it stands the test of time, then it can potentially continue to drive traffic to your site for a long time, which in turn gives you a better ranking.

Most of the content that the food tourism industry produces is already evergreen by nature: traditional recipes, must-visit places, and stories about your community's people are all things that barely change over time, if at all.

This ranking can be improved by using long-tailed keywords. Instead of using a keyword such as "New Orleans tours" you could instead use "Vegan food tours in New Orleans". As the internet keeps growing and more content is churned out, expect to have to use even longer-tailed keywords in the future.

It is important to use keywords naturally and avoid "keyword stuffing" which is the practice of using them in as many places as possible, which sounds unnatural and inauthentic.

On social media platforms that accept hashtags you can include general ones such as *#food*, *#drinks*, and *#travel*, but also narrow down to more specific hashtags the way you would with keywords, for example, *#napavalleywinetrail*. Every platform has a limit to how many hashtags can be used before being flagged as spam, as well as lists of hashtags that are banned. Keep this is mind when writing copy.

Due to consumer protection legislation, such as the GDPR and CCPA, as well as measures designed to mask users' activity and interests (like Virtual Private Networks and search engines that don't track you), it has become harder to accurately target consumers with ads across the internet, and many sites inform users of this when prompting them to select cookie preferences. But travelers are always searching, so as long as you have optimized your content and platforms, your target audience will find you, and even better, because they *choose* to.

There's an App for That

With the emergence of new platforms like TikTok, as well as new features in older networks (such as Instagram Reels and YouTube Shorts), it might seem tedious to have to learn how to use another app. Although it might take some time to master and fully incorporate new systems into the organization's strategy, consider this: it is much easier to meet travelers where they already are than it is to persuade them to follow you somewhere else. Why? App fatigue. Basic needs and desires have already been met by the same apps you likely have on your phone yourself. The top ten most downloaded apps in 2021 were TikTok, Instagram, Facebook, WhatsApp, Telegram, Snapchat, Zoom, Messenger, Capcut, and Spotify (Koetsier, 2021).

Take a moment and think if the information and value that the business seeks to provide its users with can be placed into an existing app. If the answer is yes, one is better off making sure they have covered their bases on those platforms. The business might consider creating a new platform if they have a unique process or system that cannot be incorporated into an existing one. Do keep in mind that this process is time-consuming and costly.

Larger destinations like Paris, France, and businesses like OpenTable might be able to justify the cost and maintenance of a dedicated app, but there is still a good chance these apps will be used to satisfy an immediate need and deleted afterward. Rarely will they occupy a permanent place on the phone screen real estate of consumers.

Take for example the app "Too Good To Go". Many food delivery apps exist on the market, but Too Good To Go's uniqueness lies in connecting restaurants and other food establishments that have leftover food at the end of a shift with diners looking to save money on their deliveries. It is a solution that benefits everyone.

How Digital Marketing Strategy Informs a Business's Image

How are guests greeted when they step into a restaurant? What kind of verbiage is used in brochures? Are there set protocols and guidelines for any type of guest interaction? If an organization already has standards like this in place in other areas, extending them into digital marketing is easy.

The Role of Digital Marketing in the Future of Food Tourism   117

A fine-dining restaurant might use highly curated photos, a color theme, and formal language in their printed advertisements. Their social media might then look like a cohesive Instagram with a defined color story, and answers to inquiries are structured and polite. On the other hand, a food tour company owned and operated by locals might post Stories, have friendly and fun engagements with visitors, and sign posts and interactions with the name of the person responding. Tourism offices that publish quarterly destination magazines can design a newsletter that offers additional tips and secrets with the same style and tone.

Take for example Universal Studios' Twitter account. They have become known for their sarcastic, funny, and often shady interactions. Is this surprising when looking at the brand as a whole? Not really. It would be quite jarring, though, to have the same kind of response when writing to inquire about availability at the Four Seasons.

A marketing calendar also plays a role in building this image. Frequent, regular posting transmits confidence to consumers, who know to expect those updates. Occasional posting could instead convey feelings of uncertainty in some cases, or surprise and excitement in others. It is especially important when opting for the former, to plan and schedule what content will be released. If an organization is having trouble figuring out where to begin, consider any local or national holidays to create content about. Start with some history and a traditional recipe centered around winter festivities, for instance.

Of course, one cannot forget branding. Brand assets such as fonts, colors and color palettes, logos, and other specific visuals must be carried over for consistency. Regardless of company size, it is worth having a style guide that specifies the correct usage of brand assets, as well as examples of voice and tone.

It does not matter what image the organization wants to convey to its consumers as long as that image is intentional *and* coherent with every other aspect of the business.

Establishing a Dialogue with Consumers

Previously discussed was the type of content that should be shared across digital platforms. By itself, content is a one-sided conversation. The wording that accompanies content, however, can create an active discussion that users can participate in. Ending posts with a question is a straightforward way to do so.

Actively interacting with users is another way of creating a dialogue. Although it is unrealistic to engage with every single user, an organization should aim to have a 100% response rate for direct inquiries, complaints, and reviews. A customer who walks into a visitor center or restaurant would not be ignored; in the same way, one should not leave any user's online queries unanswered.

Always answer the user's specific inquiry when responding to questions. Template responses are impersonal, and if they could find the answer easily elsewhere, they would not ask questions in the first place. Greet users, answer their questions, and offer further assistance.

When dealing with complaints, especially on Twitter, an immediate solution should be offered to avoid the complaint turning into a negative review.

When replying to a negative review, acknowledge the guest's feelings, apologize for the situation, and if possible, offer to rectify it. Positive reviews are equally important to reply to, as this shows that you are committed to all guests.

Essentially, engaging with customers should be done promptly and in a friendly manner. A casual conversation from a human being who understands the guest and their situation will always yield better results than a default, corporate response.

Not every interaction with consumers needs to be a response to something. Proactively engaging in a conversation with users by liking and commenting on their content can provide insights otherwise unavailable.

Increasingly, companies are using social media as an additional way of helping visitors. While travelers can find information and recommendations online, organizations could provide immediate assistance in other matters if travelers required it. A guest might need to know if certain allergens are present on a menu. A family following certain dietary standards could be unable to find suitable establishments. A visitor making a brief stop in a destination may be looking for the single food item they absolutely cannot miss.

Receiving Feedback

In addition to reviews and ratings, most platforms have polls or quizzes. This is a simple and casual way to ask for feedback from users. These can reach a larger audience in a shorter amount of time than it would take to gather survey respondents, for example. However, they are usually limited to one question. Furthermore, they should not be used when hard, analyzable data is needed. Instead, simple topics such as what kind of content users would like to see featured next, or what their favorite foods are can provide information to act upon for day-to-day content planning, while at the same time engaging with users and making them feel heard.

Occasionally, it is important. (i.e., when launching a new service or planning a yearly digital marketing strategy) to obtain more thorough and structured data from users. Many tools are available for different needs and budgets, including SurveyMonkey, Google Forms, and Typeform. Other useful platforms include Formaloo, Zoho Survey, and GetFeedback. Regardless of which platform is used, messaging here should be consistent with the organization's other platforms. Consumers need to feel heard and share valuable information, so keep questions direct, clear, and friendly in tone. If possible, provide incentives for completing the survey.

The Risks of Giveaways and Influencer Marketing

Picture this: a destination creates a giveaway across its platforms. Overnight, the number of followers grows. But a short time after the giveaway has ended, those

The Role of Digital Marketing in the Future of Food Tourism   119

followers are nowhere to be found. Even worse, during the giveaway period, there were no new bookings, reservations, or visits to the destination's site. Another scenario: an organization has a high follower count, but an extremely low engagement rate, which in turn likely means a low conversion rate. These scenarios happen too often. Why? The content provided was not resonating with customers, or worse, they found no value in the content *at all*.

Because travel is quintessentially experiential, the industry is prone to partnering with influencers. Several things should be analyzed when considering collaborations with an influencer as part of a digital strategy. A shady and unfortunately widespread practice is to inflate follower counts with bots and fake accounts that continuously provide likes and meaningless comments to appear engaging. But these accounts do not consume services or purchase products.

Accounts are also inflated through giveaways which ask users to follow not only the account running the giveaway but also several other accounts. Using these impressively high followings, many "influencers" will present themselves to unsuspecting companies or brands who erroneously believe that this large following will result in more visitors, bookings, and reservations. But having followers is *not* the same as having influence. These users like free stuff and will rarely book anything. A business may reach new consumers, but there are far more cost-efficient and congruent ways of doing so.

If choosing to work with an influencer, keep the following in mind:

Look at their metrics. What does their engagement rate look like? Are these interactions meaningful?

Consider their niche. Are their interests, personality, and content aligned with the message the organization wants to transmit?

It bears repeating that big follower counts should not blind you. Consumers who are solely interested in the influencer themselves are unlikely to be the destination's target market and will have low interest in your partnership efforts.

What Digital Marketing Might Look Like in the Future

As mentioned before, there are only so many apps and platforms that can be created to be used with current consumer-accessible technology. However, as newer technologies like Augmented Reality and especially Virtual Reality – as well as a variety of devices that utilize them – become more common at a consumer level, digital marketing will find its way onto them. Virtual Reality is already used to let travelers preview a destination before committing, and in some cases, bookings have increased by 190% (Visualise, 2015).

Currently, social media ads are served to a specific user on a specific device at a time. But in a Virtual Reality world where one might be having a conversation with another user, a digital billboard may be able to tailor its content to both users at the same time within that virtual space.

Part of making Virtual Reality more immersive is involving all senses. Digital content currently appeals to sight and sound, and there are some levels of haptic feedback depending on the device. Now, take another form of marketing that involves a different sense: scent marketing. In the tourism industry, hotels and theme parks have notoriously and effectively used this form of marketing by strategically releasing smells in key areas and moments of their service. Smell is the sense most closely linked to memories and emotion (Walsh, 2020). Have you ever noticed how Miami smells like saltwater and freshly washed cotton sheets? Or how Brussels smells like beef tallow and burnt sugar?

It is this author's opinion that digital content will soon be able to tap into the sense of smell. Imagine sharing a post about the best local dishes in a destination, while allowing users to experience the scents. You would be creating a memory that spans from the time travelers were planning their trip to when they finally experienced a meal.

Even influencer marketing has suffered big changes, with many countries passing laws that hold them accountable and require full disclosure of paid advertising. With it being such a big part of digital marketing nowadays, this will no doubt have an impact on how users perceive influencers, especially in terms of credibility and authenticity.

Conclusion

Digital marketing and technologies will continue to advance, and currently established platforms, despite recent pushback, are not going anywhere soon. The sooner a business sets up a complete, coherent digital marketing strategy, the more prepared it will be for new platforms that become available.

However, before jumping in and committing to any new technologies it is important to fully understand their utility and analyze if it is a piece that fits in the puzzle of the long-term strategy. As tempting as it may be to be the first to participate in the newest thing, not everything might be suited to a destination or organization's unique needs and segment.

Food for Thought

- Do you believe the abundance of visual content has done more to hurt or to help travelers' expectations? Why?
- What platforms or technologies do you believe have been underutilized in digital marketing? How may these be used in the future?
- Think of a culinary destination, organization, and business that have been extremely successful in their digital marketing efforts. What do they have in common? What have they done differently?

References

AMP Agency (2016). *Targeting Moments of Need in the New Travel Landscape*. AMP Agency.
Bahadur, M. (2014). *The Role of Content in the Millennial Traveler Journey*. Yahoo! Travel.
Del Gigante, M. (2018). Vacationing the social media way [infographic]. Retrieved from www.mdgadvertising.com/marketing-insights/infographics/vacationing-the-soc ial-media-way-infographic/

European Travel Commission (2020). *Study on Generation Z Travellers: A Handbook Produced for the European Travel Commission (ETC) by TOPOSOPHY Ltd*. European Travel Commission (ETC).

Expedia Group (2016). The Traveler's Path to Purchase. Retrieved from https://info.advertising.expedia.com/2016-travelers-path-to-purchase

Expedia Group (2018). American Multi-Generational Travel Trends. Retrieved from https://info.advertising.expedia.com/hubfs/Content_Docs/Rebrand-2018/American_Multi-Generational_Travel_Trends.pdf

Koetsier, J. (2021). Top 10 Most Downloaded Apps And Games Of 2021: TikTok, Telegram Big Winners. Retrieved from www.forbes.com/sites/johnkoetsier/2021/12/27/top-10-most-downloaded-apps-and-games-of-2021-tiktok-telegram-big-winners/?sh=335f0dd43a1f

Lee, J. (2013). Brands Expected to Respond Within an Hour on Twitter [Study]. Retrieved from www.searchenginewatch.com/2013/11/01/brands-expected-to-respond-within-an-hour-on-twitter-study/

Parasuraman, A., Berry, L. L. & Zeithaml, V. A. (1991). Understanding customer expectations of service. *Sloan Management Review, 32*(3), 39–48.

Shankman, S. (2014). Three-Quarters of Millennial Travelers Update social media once a day. Retrieved from https://skift.com/2014/06/10/three-quarters-of-millennial-travelers-update-social-media-once-a-day/

Statista (2022a). Facebook: Number of monthly active users worldwide 2008–2022. Retrieved from www.statista.com/statistics/264810/number-of-monthly-active-facebook-users-worldwide/

Statista (2022b). Global social networks ranked by number of users 2022. Retrieved from www.statista.com/statistics/272014/global-social-networks-ranked-by-number-of-users/

Statista (2022c). TikTok: distribution of global audiences 2022, by age and gender. Retrieved from www.statista.com/statistics/1299771/tiktok-global-user-age-distribution/

TripAdvisor (n.d.). Hong Kong Tourism Board - All You Need to Know BEFORE You Go. Retrieved from www.tripadvisor.com/Attraction_Review-g294217-d548040-Reviews-Hong_Kong_Tourism_Board-Hong_Kong.html

Visualise (2015). Thomas Cook Try Before You Fly | Virtual Reality Holiday | VR Case Study. Retrieved from https://visualise.com/case-study/thomas-cook-virtual-holiday

Walsh, C. (2020). *What the nose knows – How scent, emotion, and memory are intertwined – and exploited*. Harvard Gazette.

Part III

Important Old and New Influences

9 Sustainability Issues at the Local Level

Isabel Coll-Barneto and Francesc Fusté-Forné

Introduction

While regenerative tourism has gained recent attention as a response to the effects of the pandemic derived from the spread of COVID-19, the notion of tourism regeneration was mentioned earlier (Owen, 2007) as a response to the unsustainable growth of tourism. In particular, a preoccupation towards regenerative tourism is grounded in a need to achieve a systemic change within the tourism sector (see, for example, McEnhill, Jorgensen, & Urlich, 2020). This chapter builds on the notion of regeneration not only as a step to strengthen sustainable practices but also as a step beyond sustainability (Pollock, 2019). Tourism systems rely on limited natural resources and on valuable cultural and social capital (Hussain, 2021). Both sustainable and regenerative tourism acknowledge that continuing tourism business as usual would lead to the degradation of natural, cultural and social resources, the basis on which tourism is developed and managed. This chapter argues that doing tourism sustainably is not enough and tourism systems need to do tourism regeneratively, which requires a holistic approach towards the creation of meaningful impacts by all the stakeholders: from the hosts, guests, community and place to its natural and socio-cultural capital.

In the regenerative tourism model, humans are part of nature. Humans need to harness the potential of tourism as a vital force in making communities regenerative (Ajoon & Rao, 2020) where local food and drinks play a key role (Ateljević, 2020; Sheller, 2021). In this sense, the hospitality sector can contribute to this still unexplored regenerative potential of the relationships between food and tourism at the local level. This is especially relevant in accommodation options which are interested in developing an organic product (Bellato et al., 2022). The aim of this chapter is to understand food-based sustainable practices from the supply perspective. This chapter focuses on the design of the gastronomic offer of ecological hotels in order to discuss to what extent local environmental-based accommodations contribute to the sustainability, and regeneration, of tourism systems. As described in the methodology, the study adopts a qualitative design which is based on in-depth interviews with the managers of eight ecological hotels located in Catalonia, northeastern

DOI: 10.4324/9781003282532-13

Spain. Results show the design of sustainable food experiences from the environmental practices adopted by the establishments. After this introductory part, we develop the theoretical background, the methods and the results. Later, the discussion and conclusion serve to analyze the implications of the research within the context of food tourism.

Theoretical Background

This section discusses the notions of regenerative, conscious and transformative (food) tourism. It is divided in three parts which specifically deal with the understanding of regenerative food tourism, the role of hosts in tourism systems, and the creation of transformative experiences from the perspective of food.

Community Collaboration towards Regenerative Food Tourism

Previous research shows that there is not a unique way to make a (tourist) community regenerative. Regenerative tourism cannot be achieved using the same pathway for different communities because communities have their local idiosyncrasies, which are based on both the cultural heritage and the natural environment. Every place and community are different. Therefore, actions, policies and strategies must be in line with the characteristics of each destination, as each one has its own social, cultural and environmental processes (McEnhill, Jorgensen & Urlich, 2020). According to the regenerative tourism model (see Hussain, 2021), in order to make a destination regenerative, it is necessary to heal and restore the degradation suffered by its environmental, cultural and social capital. When the system becomes healthy, it is possible to create the conditions in order for human and natural systems to regenerate (Axinte et al., 2019).

Regeneration in tourism cannot happen without a change in humans' mindset. Several experts agree on the fact that we as humans should stop thinking that we are separate from the natural world (Du Plessis & Brandon, 2015). Humans should realize that destinations are embedded in the natural environment (Hussain and Haley, 2022). Moreover, as Anna Pollock (2019) reveals, humans should be aware that we are not superior to other life forms and that each of us is able to contribute to the Earth's health. Instead of thinking that the planet is full of resources that can be exploited, we should change the way we perceive the world and discover the capacity of the living system to evolve and self-generate (Pollock, 2019) where food plays a pivotal role to engage visitors with responsible practices.

Added to this, collaboration is one of the key elements in the design and implementation of (regenerative) tourism. It is necessary that all the participants in the tourism system collaborate. Local authorities, regional governments, tourists, destination management organizations, tourist establishments and host communities should work together to create the conditions for the destination

Sustainability Issues at the Local Level 127

to adapt to continuous changes (McEnhill, Jorgensen & Urlich, 2020). In this sense, to apply a regenerative tourism model, tourism stakeholders must pay attention to residents' aspirations, experiences and needs. There should be a greater involvement of the destination's community in the tourism decision-making (Pollock, 2019). Nowadays we live in a global world characterized by continuous technological advancements. This technology enables destinations to be connected and visible through the internet and social media, as other chapters in this book explore. This contributes to the fact that the residents of a place have a lower control of their town, city or region when it becomes a popular destination and attracts a lot of tourism (Hussain, 2021).

Hosts Must Lead the Conscious Changes

The concepts of collaboration and community are linked with the urgent need for considering tourism as a system instead of an industry. Drawing from a mindset change, there should be a shift from an industrial approach to a system approach that engages with the community and works in a collaborative networking (Ajoon & Rao, 2020). As Pollock (2019) stresses, tourism products and services cannot be considered as a result of industrial production because tourism is not only a system subject to nature's operating rules and principles, but also to personal relationships.

> Every aspect of travel is about human beings encountering other human beings while moving from home to a foreign place in order to have an experience. As it's all about people meeting, serving, taking care of, and entertaining other people, the primary unit of activity is a relationship not a transaction.
>
> (Pollock, 2012: 8)

The role of hosts and guests is crucial to sustain a regenerative tourism model (Hussain, 2021) because conscious travel as regeneration within the tourism system takes place when tourists are conscious consumers (Pollock, 2013). In the last two decades this concept has gathered growing attention, especially from the perspective of environmental conscious travel (Škrinjarić, 2018). Conscious travel is a new way of 'doing' tourism that positively impacts the communities and places. Conscious travel transforms tourism into a positive contributor to wellbeing of all the stakeholders involved in the tourism system. This approach helps with the preservation of the environmental and cultural resources providing food-loving traveler experiences which are aware of the local landscapes, local people and local practices. The creation of food and drink experiences in their cultural and natural environment are crucial in sustainable food tourism management and marketing (Sharma, Thomas & Paul, 2021; Sims, 2009). In particular, food-based experiences are a source of "deeper human connections, wellbeing, and a greater sense of reciprocity with the natural environment" (Chassagne and Everingham, 2019: 1911).

128 *Isabel Coll-Barneto and Francesc Fusté-Forné*

Anna Pollock (2013) stresses the main role of hosts as change agents. Conscious travel considers that hosts should be the leaders of the tourism model transformation. They are the ones responsible for the type of tourism that will be developed in their community. Moreover, if hosts change their behavior, they have the power to change tourists' mindset and travel habits. The protection of the environmental and cultural values by hosts will lead to the promotion of a sustainable and regenerative tourism. In this sense, the main role of a conscious host is to "help the guest slow down in a destination, learn to fully savor their experience by stimulating and satiating all their senses and making them feel more fully alive" (Pollock, 2013: 14). Therefore, hosts need to attract, engage and create a conscious traveler by designing experiences that transform (Cheer, 2020; Pung, Gnoth & Del Chiappa, 2020). This chapter advocates that this can be done through food-based experiences (see Fusté-Forné & Hussain, 2021; Morón-Corujeira & Fusté-Forné, 2022).

The Creation of Transformative Food Experiences

Transformative tourism consists of "a process" where tourists experience an internal journey that "is part of the awakening of consciousness, and creates more self-awareness, more self-inquiry into the purpose of life, living by a higher set of values, and making greater contributions to others" (Sheldon, 2020: 2). Reisinger also affirms that tourist transformative experiences bring a higher "awareness of one's own existence and a stronger connection with self and others" (Reisinger, 2013: 27). Hosts, such as tourist accommodations, should create the right conditions for transformation to occur. Soulard, McGehee, and Stern (2019) highlight a need for the promotion of social contact between tourists and locals, encouraging cultural understanding and sensitivity, and engaging in environmental and socially responsible experiences.

Moreover, these same experts propose a glocalization strategy with the key elements for organizations that want to provide transformative tourist experiences (Soulard, McGehee, & Stern, 2019). In this sense, it is important that the community's natural and cultural values must be integrated in the design of the tourists' experiences. Also, the role of employees in the creation of transformative experiences is crucial because they are the bond between the tourists and the host culture. Hosts are responsible not only to show what are the features of their 'food' experience, but also to connect with a physical environment that facilitates human contact, community involvement, and interaction with nature in order to create places that encourage transformation.

In this sense, "food provides a context to learn – new skills, new flavours, and new cultural understandings – and to pass on those skills to younger generations" (Fountain, 2021: 9). A transformative travel experience based on food must also be understood as a way of reshaping the tourist understanding of experiences (Živoder, Ateljević, & Čorak, 2015) which are rooted in the local cultural and natural heritage and which allow visitors to gather for a taste of the place (World Food Travel Association, 2021). This must be planned as a process that "creates more self-awareness, more self-inquiry into the purpose of life, living by a higher set of values, and making greater contributions to others" (Sheldon, 2020: 2). Is this manifested in the food experiences offered by ecological accommodations? If so, how? This chapter adds texture to these conversations in the following sections.

Methodology

This chapter is based on a qualitative design which is focused on in-depth interviews with the managers of eight ecological hotels in Catalonia. The researchers developed two sub-samples. The first is formed by ecological hotels which were awarded an environmental certificate (EU Ecolabel) and the second is formed by hotels which, while not having a specific environmental certificate, show a pro-environmental business behavior. For the first sample, all the accommodations with the EU Ecolabel certificate in Catalonia were contacted, six of them agreed to participate and four of them have gastronomic services. Later, drawing from a non-probabilistic convenience sample, the researchers selected six environmental-based accommodations without environmental certificates. These were selected based on expert opinion and the communication of their business strategy through their websites. While all the accommodations agreed to participate, only four of them have gastronomic services.

The interviewed accommodations are family businesses where the founders are at the forefront of the establishments. They have added their sustainable way of life to the way of working. Although the accommodations are located in different regions of Catalonia, all of them are located in small villages with few inhabitants in the countryside. They are also small accommodations of no more than twelve rooms. The interviewed businesses recognise that neither the current tourism model nor its operations are sustainable and they strongly believe that both accommodations and tourists need to be responsible in order to build a better tourism model where food acts as a cornerstone to transformative travel experiences.

It must be noted that this study is part of a project which seeks to understand environmental actions in tourism systems and, specifically, to analyze the role of ecological tourist accommodations for a regenerative tourism development. As part of this project, the current research explores the configuration of food experiences from an environmental perspective. The interviews with the managers of the establishments were conducted between February and March, 2022, and the results are focused on how the businesses promotes (or not) a sustainable and regenerative food tourism at the local level, drawing from the gastronomic-based environmental practices.

Results

The results show the role of ecological tourist establishments in generating transformative food tourism experiences through environmental practices. The analysis of the interviews conducted with the eight accommodations that have gastronomic services reveals the main features of their food-based offerings are a local-based product which relies on the values of the local landscapes and lifestyles, the creation of synergies between producers, suppliers and the ecological establishments, and finally the development of organic practices where food waste management also reveals the engagement of the businesses with sustainability at the local level.

They Develop a Product for a Visitor Who Looks for a Taste of Place

All the accommodations seek for tourists that have food-based interests. From a gastronomic perspective, the Catalan accommodations interviewed assure they want guests who are keen on integrating their experience into the place they are visiting. According to the businesses, the ideal tourism model is the one that adapts to the idiosyncrasies of each place. They facilitate tourism experiences that show visitors, respectfully, the authentic way of life of each place, the local landscapes and lifestyles while respecting the environmental and socio-cultural heritages (see Figure 9.1). Therefore, the interviewed representatives think that, in a regenerative tourism model, the establishments should "promote tradition and local products" and "be integrated in the place where they are located in natural, cultural and gastronomic terms". In order to structure their food experiences, the main criteria that the accommodations use when choosing their food providers is the proximity of products. They look for local products which are cultivated and grown in the region where they are located. "Basically, we make sure that everything comes from the territory, that the products we buy are Km 0".

The accommodations try to plan their gastronomic offer based on traditional products because by buying local products they protect and promote traditional recipes, minimize their ecological footprint and improve the wellbeing of the local community and the environment. In this sense, the establishments prepare menus based on seasonal products and traditional dishes such as the 'carreretes' (a local type of wild mushroom) omelette, and the preparation of themed menus such as the forest breakfast. Vegetarian and vegan options are also available in many of the establishments. The use of organic products is essential to build a culinary offer that respects the environment where the food comes from – the river from which a wild trout is sourced, and the people who take care of it – a local grower that provides local tomatoes –.

They Support Local Stakeholders to Build Regenerative Food Travel Experiences

The food-selection criteria are also based on community working and collaboration between businesses. The participants affirm that they must network

Figure 9.1 A Catalan ecological accommodation philosophy

with the producers and suppliers that are also located in the region. One of the owners says that

> we use local products and small suppliers. We try to boost the networking between the providers of the region. We buy our cheese in Albió from a small cheese factory. Wines and beer also come from the region and we also buy the bread from a local bakery.

In this sense, another avenue towards the collaboration between local actors is through agricultural associations. For example, "in terms of suppliers, I am a member of the Cerdanya Agri-food Association and I always try to use the products from the Association that are local and from the region", reported one of the interviewees who owns an ecological accommodation in the Cerdanya.

Getting to know the suppliers first-hand is another way for the producers to add value to their offering. In this sense, it is not only important that the products have an organic certificate (for example, a quality label such as the Protected Designation of Origin and the Protected Geographical Indication),

132 *Isabel Coll-Barneto and Francesc Fusté-Forné*

but what really matters to the accommodations is to observe that the suppliers produce in an environmentally friendly way and, thus, the products they offer are of high quality. For example, a manager affirms that:

> we have everything under control: we have visited the farms where we buy the meat from, also the farm where we buy the milk … we don't believe much in what a piece of paper or a label tells us, we like to go and see for ourselves. We are very happy with our food suppliers.

In addition, another participant reports that "I can give products a name and a surname. I know who produced it and how. They don't bring me the food, I go and get it". This is crucial to deliver an authentic storytelling based on the local values of food, which are not only based on the places where the food grows, but also on the people and practices behind the products, and where the establishments are located (see Figure 9.2). In turn, the products are the basis towards the configuration of traditional, and transformative menus, which are not only respectful of the supply chains but also of food waste, as explored in the next section.

They Minimize Food Waste and Contribute to the Destination Wellbeing

For the ecological accommodations interviewed in this study, minimizing food waste is a priority. They use different strategies that take place in three different moments: when buying the products and designing the menus, when cooking, and when partially eaten plates return to the restaurants' kitchens. In this sense, techniques to reduce waste start with shopping. They use cloth bags and buy products without plastic packaging. Moreover, the accommodations use fixed menus which help to reduce the diversity and quantity of food that they need to purchase. While this may limit the variety of dishes in the menus, it also contributes to the minimization of food waste.

> We make traditional cuisine, the way our grandmothers used to make it. My grandmother used to make the most of everything, and we also do a type of cooking where we use all the kitchen's leftovers. From the ripest fruit we make jam and from the offal we make 'chireta' [a typical sausage produced in the Pyrenees]. We offer typical dishes. It is a type of cooking where food waste is minimized, which is very important for us.

This is not only important for the accommodations, but also for visitors who are increasingly interested in the sustainable management of the tourism experiences in general and the food experiences in particular.

In this sense, the cooking of Catalan traditional recipes allows accommodation owners to offer a zero-waste cuisine which uses all the products (for example in the case of fruit peel to make marmalade), exemplified in the pork-based products with the idiom 'everything but the oink'. In addition, some

Sustainability Issues at the Local Level 133

Figure 9.2 A Catalan ecological accommodation integrated to the environment

establishments ask customers in advance for their menu choices, thus reducing leftovers. One of the participants says that:

> Before the customers come, I send them the menus. At dinner time we offer a menu of two starters, two main courses, dessert and wine. We can accommodate 8 people here. And I don't have eight portions of each dish. I ask them what their choice is going to be. In this way I can prepare the right portions for what they want to order.

Finally, leftover food from customers' plates is used as compost or given to the animals, or to local farmers. "We don't generate organic waste. What is left over goes to the chickens, the sheep or the dog." In addition, customers have the

134 *Isabel Coll-Barneto and Francesc Fusté-Forné*

possibility to take away the rest of their meals in cardboard containers known as 'doggy bags'.

Discussion and Conclusion

This chapter analyzed the role of ecological accommodations in the creation of sustainable practices as part of their gastronomic experiences. Results of this research show that ecological accommodations, both environmentally certified and not, are engaged in food experiences that promote regenerative, conscious and transformative values that bring tourists closer to the culture and nature of the place they are visiting. Results also show the local-based vision of the establishments when structuring their food-based services. This is manifested both in terms of products and menus, which are integrated in the region where they are located in natural (they use seasonal food), gastronomic (they cook dishes that have always been cooked in that area), and cultural terms (traditional dishes allow guests to learn part of the culture of the place). These factors offer a food experience which protects and promotes sustainability at the local level.

The management and marketing of sustainable-based tourism experiences is a challenge in a regenerative context (Hussain, 2021). In other words, there must be a shift from superfluous management and marketing which promote mass tourism and unsustainable practices towards a management and marketing that has a deeper purpose and uses its regenerative potential to improve the wellbeing of tourism stakeholders. Both businesses and destinations must promote responsible production and consumption, encourage the preservation of the natural environment and influence tourists to leave the destination better than they found it (Pollock, 2019). These practices must involve collaboration and community work in order to create the necessary conditions for places to flourish (McEnhill, Jorgensen & Urlich, 2020).

Results show that the businesses develop a gastronomic experience which is rooted in the land, and offers a genuine taste of place based on the local culinary tradition. The use of products which are fresh, organic and seasonal, and products which are cultivated by local producers, contextualizes the food experience in a local context and contributes to the destination's wellbeing from a food tourism perspective (Fusté-Forné and Jamal, 2020; Hall and Gössling, 2016). This reveals the commitment of the accommodations with the creation of local-based menus which are also a path to teach guests about the culture and nature of the place. Therefore, ecological accommodations can act as change agents through sustainable food experiences. In this sense, food and drink experiences help destination's "economic, social and environmental sustainability and should not be peripheral to tourism research" (Everett and Aitchison, 2008: 150).

From a demand perspective, conscious travelers search for a deep meaning of places through their experiences. Tourists with conscious travel habits want to be transformed when traveling. They look for tourist experiences that bring them

Sustainability Issues at the Local Level   135

a new way of seeing the world (Pollock, 2013). This chapter revealed how this can be achieved through the gastronomic offer of ecological accommodations. Tourists can also play the role of change agents by using sustainable criteria when making their travel decisions. The accommodations with environmental concerns have the ability, through the planning and management of their dining services, to promote responsible tourism practices. This is not only manifested in the products available, but also in the source of the products. They come from the local stakeholders which means that they are based on short supply chains which have a positive impact on the planet.

The purchase of local products by the accommodations allows local people to continue to make a living from their agricultural, livestock and commercial activities. This community collaboration allows the environmental and socio-cultural heritages of the place to be preserved and promoted. For example, the traditional dishes cooked by the establishments bring tourists closer to the landscapes and the lifestyles of the local communities. Moreover, practices aimed at eliminating or minimizing food waste are extremely necessary if we want to achieve a regenerative tourism that promotes a circular economy. While this chapter is limited to the study of a small sample of establishments, it offers relevant insights into the regenerative, conscious and transformative potential of the organic practices in the food services.

Future research should analyze from both qualitative and quantitative methodologies how the hospitality sector can contribute to the still unexplored potential of the relationships between food and tourism at a regenerative, conscious and transformative level. This will help to provide a more robust understanding of the implications of this chapter, which will help both academics and practitioners to implement sustainable practices that contribute to the wellbeing of communities and places at the local level.

Food for Thought

- What is the potential of sustainable food experiences for a regenerative tourism development?
- How can environmentally concerned accommodations transform their guests into change agents for a regenerative tourism model through their dining services?
- Why 'green' food experiences can help businesses to satisfy, and exceed, the visitors' gastronomic expectations?

References

Ajoon, E. J., & Rao, Y. V. (2020). A study on consciousness of young travelers towards regenerative tourism: with reference to Puducherry. *Journal of Tourism Economics and Applied Research, 4*(1), 1–10.

Ateljević, I. (2020). Transforming the (tourism) world for good and (re) generating the potential 'new normal'. *Tourism Geographies, 22*(3), 467–475.

Axinte, L. F., Mehmood, A., Marsden, T., & Roep, D. (2019). Regenerative city-regions: a new conceptual framework. *Regional Studies, Regional Science, 6*(1), 117–129.

Bellato, L., Frantzeskaki, N., Fiebig, C. B., Pollock, A., Dens, E., & Reed, B. (2022). Transformative roles in tourism: adopting living systems' thinking for regenerative futures. *Journal of Tourism Futures*, 1–18.

Chassagne, N., & Everingham, P. (2019). Buen Vivir: Degrowing extractivism and growing wellbeing through tourism. *Journal of Sustainable Tourism, 27*(12), 1909–1925.

Cheer, J. M. (2020). Human flourishing, tourism transformation and COVID-19: A conceptual touchstone. *Tourism Geographies, 22*(3), 514–524.

Du Plessis, C., & Brandon, P. (2015). An ecological worldview as basis for a regenerative sustainability paradigm for the built environment. *Journal of Cleaner Production, 109*, 53–61.

Everett, S., & Aitchison, C. (2008). The role of food tourism in sustaining regional identity: A case study of Cornwall, South West England. *Journal of sustainable tourism, 16*(2), 150–167.

Fountain, J. (2021). The future of food tourism in a post-COVID-19 world: insights from New Zealand. *Journal of Tourism Futures*, 1–14.

Fusté-Forné, F., & Hussain, A. (2021). Looking through a tourist gaze: the joy of missing out (JOMO) and the case of mussels. *Journal of Tourism, Hospitality and Culinary Arts, 13*(2), 1–8.

Fusté-Forné, F., & Jamal, T. (2020). Slow food tourism: an ethical microtrend for the Anthropocene. *Journal of Tourism Futures, 6*(3), 227–232.

Hall, C. M., & Gössling, S. (2016). *Food tourism and regional development.* Routledge.

Hussain, A. (2021). A future of tourism industry: Conscious travel, destination recovery and regenerative tourism. *Journal of Sustainability and Resilience, 1*(1), 1–11.

Hussain, A., & Haley, M. (2022). Regenerative tourism model: challenges of adapting concepts from natural science to tourism industry. *Journal of Sustainability and Resilience, 2*(1), 4.

McEnhill, L., Jorgensen, E. S., & Urlich, S. (2020). *Paying it forward and back: Regenerative tourism as part of place.* Lincoln University.

Morón-Corujeira, N., & Fusté-Forné, F. (2022). Visiting a furancho: local lifestyles as drivers of (food) tourism transformation. *Journal of Tourism Futures*, 1–4.

Owen, C. (2007). Regenerative tourism: a case study of the resort town Yulara. *Open House International, 32*(4), 42–53.

Pollock, A. (2012, September). Conscious travel: signposts towards a new model for tourism. *2nd UNWTO Ethics and Tourism Congress Conscious Tourism for a New Era.* Ecuador: Quito.

Pollock, A. (2013). Six reasons why mass tourism is unsustainable. *The Guardian*, August 21.

Pollock, A. (2019). *Flourishing Beyond Sustainability.* Krakow, Poland: ETC Workshop.

Pung, J. M., Gnoth, J., & Del Chiappa, G. (2020). Tourist transformation: Towards a conceptual model. *Annals of Tourism Research, 81*, 102885.

Reisinger, Y. (2013). *Transformational tourism: tourist perspectives.* CAB International.

Sharma, G. D., Thomas, A., & Paul, J. (2021). Reviving tourism industry post-COVID-19: A resilience-based framework. *Tourism Management Perspectives, 37*, 100786.

Sheldon, P. J. (2020). Designing tourism experiences for inner transformation. *Annals of Tourism Research, 83*, 102935.

Sheller, M. (2021). Reconstructing tourism in the Caribbean: connecting pandemic recovery, climate resilience and sustainable tourism through mobility justice. *Journal of Sustainable Tourism, 29*(9), 1436–1449.

Sims, R. (2009). Food, place and authenticity: local food and the sustainable tourism experience. *Journal of Sustainable Tourism, 17*(3), 321–336.

Škrinjarić, T. (2018). Evaluation of environmentally conscious tourism industry: Case of Croatian counties. *Tourism: An International Interdisciplinary Journal, 66*(3), 254–268.

Soulard, J., McGehee, N. G., & Stern, M. (2019). Transformative tourism organizations and glocalization. *Annals of Tourism Research, 76*, 91–104.

World Food Travel Association (2021). *State of the Industry. Food and Beverage Tourism.* World Food Travel Association.

Živoder, S. B., Ateljević, I., & Čorak, S. (2015). Conscious travel and critical social theory meets destination marketing and management studies: Lessons learned from Croatia. *Journal of Destination Marketing and Management, 4*(1), 68–77.

10 Responsibility and Sustainability: Everything Has Changed

Divya Vaghela and Ulpa Chauhan

Introduction

Everything has changed. It is time to reimagine and rethink absolutely everything. What we do right now has an impact. Every decision you make, every item you buy, every meal you cook. There is a before and an after. As you sit there (or stand) reading this chapter, we want you to look around you. OK, it means taking your eyes off this page for the moment. But go ahead and then come back right here to this point. THIS POINT. Absolutely everything around you at some point was impossible. It took creativity, imagination and innovation for each and every item around you to exist and be. From the clothes you are wearing, to the device you are reading this book on, to the chair you are sitting on was at some point in time impossible. Even the food you might be eating as you read could be something that at one point didn't even exist.

We show you how the way we have imagined responsibility and sustainability to be is not quite what you think. As we acknowledge and move towards wanting to be more sustainable and taking responsibility for our part, we realise that there is an even more sustainable and planet friendly way to do this. We will show you why the circular economy model is the answer.

We have come a long way. Technology has advanced so quickly in such a short space of time. And to give you an aspect of time and how long we as humans have been around then think about this. The Tyrannosaurus Rex is closer to the invention of the iPad than the Stegosaurus. Dinosaurs were around for so long without as much advancement as what we as humans have achieved in what is a nanosecond compared to the existence of planet earth. So, what have we been doing in such a short space of time that has meant that we have moved along the evolution of the planet quicker than it has ever done before. Understand that the planet will survive. We are not killing earth but moving along (at a faster pace than we would like) the existence of humans. Earth will continue to evolve and thrive.

Everything that has happened until this point has been helpful to get us exactly where we need to be at this very moment. Let's look at nature. Everything in nature works symbiotically together to help and nourish everything else. There is nowhere in nature where anything is seen as bad. We have so

DOI: 10.4324/9781003282532-14

Responsibility and Sustainability   139

much to learn from everything around us that we haven't even really started to understand how it works and how we can benefit. We are the only consumers on this planet. The goal has been to produce as many products as possible with very little regard for the consequences which occur at each step: *taking* natural resources, *making* the product through processing and manufacturing, *using,* or *consuming* the product, and finally *disposing* of the product – waste and environmental impacts.

We know we need to take responsibility around sustainability. That's nothing new. But everything moves at a faster pace here on earth and technology has helped us accelerate everything. Take the simple art of growing food. Many years ago, we would forage for food and eat what was available. We then learnt how to grow food which was on our doorstep and in our communities and we grew what was native to the land and survived in the climate we were in. Then we learnt to travel, and this meant we discovered foods we had never seen or heard of before. Food was then travelling across continents to supply the needs of our ever-growing palates. To the point now where we no longer understand what seasonal means. And the outrage if there was ever a shortage of strawberries available in the middle of December in the UK. And then the pandemic of 2020. It has shown us just how fragile our food system is. Shelves became empty as food could no longer be shipped around the world. The shortage of labour meant whole crops were wasted and thrown away. Food waste and food shortage took on whole new meanings. For the first time ever for many people they had to rethink about how they shopped and what they cooked. But people got creative. They grew their own food on their patios and in their gardens. People learnt to be a part of their communities again and shared food with neighbours and family that would have gone to waste. New apps emerged that let you know if your local supermarket had anything going to waste which you could take away and consume. We are getting there. But what this did highlight was the growing gap between food waste and food shortage.

Sustainability has been around a lot longer than you probably think. It is now a buzz word and many more of us are aware of what it means. To sustain something means to do no more harm. However, it is time to think beyond sustainability and reimagine, rethink, and rejuvenate.

What's New in Sustainability?

There is a word that we want to introduce you to and it's a word that is not new or never heard of before but is really where everything has absolutely changed. And that is the word *circular*. You've heard of the word and maybe have an idea of what it means (see, for example, Masi et al., 2018; Witjes & Lozano, 2016). This has taken over from the word sustainability and got us thinking about how we can be more circular with the way we live; how can we be more planet conscious and connect with nature and everything living on it in a way we have never done before. Everything in nature is interrelated and connected. It has a rhythm and pattern and it's circular. We are part of nature so we can be part of being circular.

So, let's dissect this a little. What we know and do now is a linear model (Taşnadi et al., 2018): Make – Sell – Consume – Throw. Let's take tofu for example (Fournier, 2017; Hickman, 2010; Horler, 2021). Soybeans are one of the most produced crops globally, playing a large role in the livestock industry, are the main ingredient in soybean oil production, and more recently are skyrocketing in popularity as part of meat alternatives like tofu. Starting from the beginning, soybeans take up large swaths of land to grow and take up more resources than crop-based proteins like lentils and chickpeas. Following the emissions created during the raw production process by extracting resources like fresh water, which could be used at a lower rate for similar crops, the soybeans next need to travel (often) thousands of miles to a facility where they will become tofu. Then this product will be packaged in single use plastics that are their own terrifying set of wasted resources and travel for thousands of miles more to warehouses, grocery stores, and finally to your home or restaurant where it will be consumed quickly, and the packaging thrown straight in the bin where it will decay for decades or more. While still a better alternative to meat, in terms of emissions, the energy and resources taken to make, sell, and consume, and throw away a product that we associate as "good" for the environment, tofu provides a wider perspective to how we consume goods and good products in general. There is hardly a thought given about resource consumption when it comes to most of the food we consume and how the food miles it takes to land on our doorsteps impacts the environment. Worse even is when we have these products and the recipe calls for only 150g of the 250g package of tofu, and even more is wasted.

Applying a more circular model to tofu we can find ways to reduce waste and maybe even learn something new along the way – for example, did you know you can make alternative tofu out of pantry staples and most legumes using a blender and water? Making tofu at home would solve a lot of the areas of waste and harm during the process of obtaining tofu while also helping to feed your own backyard with compost scraps; however, changes at every level of the of the linear model can help start to bend the line into the circular model we strive for. So, what would that look like?

1. Growing the soybeans
   a. Regenerative farming – using regenerative farming practices (see Le et al., 2021) that integrate local biodiversity and livestock to maintain soil health, reinvigorate the land, and sequester carbon by avoid practices that routinely till the land and release chemicals while drying out soil is one way to reduce the amount of resources, like water and chemical fertilisers, needed to maintain the crop – these types of farming not only absorb carbon and help balance the scales but also help the surrounding environment by limiting outside influence

Responsibility and Sustainability   141

    b.   Vertical farming – recent advancements in technology have developed vertical farming (see Birkby, 2016) for major crops like soy which require significantly less water, no pesticides, and increase the yield per growing area. Vertical farms are also indoors and can help reduce food miles when utilised in areas closer to the processing plants and consumers! All of which limits emissions and help create a more carbon neutral process

    c.   Growing different crops – diversifying the crops in the field and crops that go into the tofu product is another way to increase biodiversity and create a better balance of product coming from the same resources. Mixing lentils or chickpeas which require less resources to grow is a great way to do this

2. Food miles

    a.   Electric vehicles – switching to electric vehicles wherever possible is one way to reduce emissions from transporting food from farm to processing and packaging facility to warehouse to grocery store to table to landfill.

    b.   Optimisation – upgrading existing vehicles to run more efficiently and pass an emissions test can help reduce harmful gases emitted during food travel without costing a lot and without creating the need to introduce new products into the supply chain

3. Packaging

    a.   Biodegradable – changing packaging to more easily biodegradable ones can eliminate the plastics that currently hold tofu and help the entire degrading process of packaging that ends up in the landfill by speeding it up. Or even better by becoming compost that can feed your backyard, the organisms in it, or the vegetables in it that may be your next meal

    b.   None at all – making homemade tofu using legumes easily available to you reduces the need for new packaging and is a tasty way to use up inexpensive pantry items that may have been otherwise tossed away

This is only the start of some of the changes to one product that would help the environment, and these are just a few levels to think about consumption. Applying the linear model to products we use every day and noting all the areas where we or the industry can make changes is a great way to think critically and understand the background of our consumption habits – and where we can make changes to it. Notably, while all these changes help, it can become the same problem as beef to tofu, each having their own faults. For instance, switching to electric vehicles means increased mining for battery resources which come with their own set of consequences and impacts. Moreover, this is just one example of millions that could benefit from adapting the linear model of consumption. Looking around our home, business, and life is the first step in helping the planet. Think of where you produce the most, or even least, amount of waste and see how you can improve it through available changes, or lobby to upgrade the industries that impact you and the planet. It could start with the car you drive, the shirts you wear, or even the meat alternative that you choose.

The key is not eliminating our impacts and waste all at once but slowly integrating practices and becoming carbon negative wherever possible. So that may mean that right now we switch toward reducing the impact of products we already use, but in the future should be switching to products with a better effect on the planet. Coastal seaweed, for example, sequesters carbon while taking up little resources, provides stormwater surge protection, and requires minimal processing to be a food source (Gimlet Media, 2021). However, making the switch to kelp and other regenerative products in our everyday diets is never easy, but it is essential if the outcome of our home is important to us.

Historical and cultural practices that emphasise locally sourced food and resources will become more important as we move forward and accessing those products in a sustainable way is something we need to focus on as leaders of industry. One group that has carried on many of these traditions is the indigenous tribes in North America, where foraging, hunting, and preserving food in the same way their ancestors did for hundreds of years help to maintain ecosystems and avoid overconsumption by taking only what they need.

Rethink the Circular Model

Everything in the loop is food for something else and finding ways to feed each stage of the products we use, the environment we live in, and one another, will be our generation's greatest challenge. There are examples and answers all around us. Looking to nature and history for this circular model of living is the cheat sheet to rejuvenating our planet.

Our world has lived by the linear model for centuries and we will need to go back to find solutions to these modern issues we have found ourselves in. Moreover, we need to be considerate of all the changes in our world population and look to diversity as the best way to help the planet. Overproducing any one product, like soybean tofu in place of beef, will just cause strain in different areas and excess resources to meet demand. The avocado has created the same issue. As demand for avocados increased, supply had to keep up. And in order to supply more, land needed to be cleared for more avocados to be grown and then shipped around the world to satisfy the growing need for the aptly labelled 'superfood'. Although genetically modified organisms (GMO) can be beneficial in some circumstances to address these concerns, operating within nature's equilibrium is a better way to implement a circular model of consumption – since we can work with the environment and allow each process to feed each other, from the soil health to the natural pesticide measures and harvesting to the natural decay that feeds the soil again.

By understanding that the planet is a living, breathing organism we can see that the lungs, heart, and even waste system of the earth needs our attention and

Responsibility and Sustainability 143

some love. By using harm reduction methods and therapy through regenerative practices can we begin to do this.

For centuries civilisations and communities have been living in this circular, zero-waste way (see Kellogg, 2019). Indigenous communities in Canada, for example, are putting forth an ethos of interconnectedness when it comes to people, planet, and profit, in ways that many Eurocentric ethos' fail to consider when sustainability is brought up. Looking to the 4 pillars framework by the Cree and Stoney communities, an addition to UNESCO's 3 pillars of sustainable development (social, environment, and economic), which add "beauty" we can see how these historical perspectives are a key to rejuvenating the planet (Amber, 2017). This pillar of sustainable development both encompasses the aesthetic beauty of the environment we are trying to preserve in the original 3 UNESCO pillars and is the glue to bringing cultural perspectives to the circular sustainability framework that aims to regenerate the planet from the effects of centuries of industrialisation.

Looking to the traditional practices included in the Inuit food system, we can see this indigenous knowledge applied. It relies on hunting and foraging skills used for thousands of years, with a self-sustaining practice that takes only what they need and avoids the type of overconsumption and waste seen in western practices. Seals being a main source of food, the Inuit peoples will hunt in teams during winter and spring when the seal populations are peaking and hunt using handheld, handmade, traditional tools – this helps to limit the number of seals harvested and limits waste (Kuhnlein & Humphries, 2017). Next, they jointly prepare and preserve nearly every part of the seal to consume and use in other products; at this stage there is virtually no waste since even the bones can be used for new tools. With no waste, very limited processing, and practices that help control the seal population, the Inuit people found a way to harvest meat in ways vastly different than western livestock practices. This tradition both invigorates the Inuit people's environment and makes them an active part of its web. It connects people to the community around them, the environment and historic practices that encapsulate the sustainable development. By linking their livelihood to that in their immediate surroundings, we can take notes from cultural practices like Inuit seal hunting and learn how to connect with our immediate surroundings and act in ways that benefit the people around us, the environment and the economy without losing the beauty of the historical practices that came before us and the planet that ought to thrive after us.

So going back to considering circular ways of thinking, here is where we need to reimagine everything. What we now see as waste was seen as food for something else. Once used we reused. Then if it didn't work it was refurbished, if it couldn't be refurbished it was upcycled into something else. If that couldn't be done it was taken apart and used for various things. And as a last resort it was recycled or rehomed to someone else to make use of it.

The industrial revolution changed all of that. In developed countries (with those emerging countries now following suit) we have become the era of two cultures. One that we call 'the instant culture' and the other 'the throwaway culture'. We no longer know what it means to wait for something to grow, for something to be nurtured and for something to be lovingly handmade. As we sit in a restaurant or order something online, we get impatient and question why it is taking so long. And in the same breath we are happy to discard things. Don't want something any more? Doesn't look right? Doesn't fit in? Not working properly? That's OK, we will discard it and replace it.

Planet Conscious

There's a term mentioned earlier in the chapter and that is 'planet conscious'. What does it mean to be planet conscious? It means to be aware and connect with nature and everything within it. The planet is continuously flourishing, we just don't see it that way. The planet is seen as volatile and moving but never alive and breathing on a macro scale; we only think about small bits of the environment being alive like forests and not as a whole, where that forest provides oxygen and moves around energy to bring moisture in the air which follows our oceans and so on. Everything you do impacts the living being that is earth, so how can we get more planet conscious in our decision making?

Figures around sustainability and emissions can greatly vary depending on the source. We are only just learning about various ways to measure our carbon emissions and even then, it is difficult to know how accurate it is. As technology continues to advance, it is likely that we will continue to find more accurate ways to measure our environmental impact. Imagine being able to track the entire life cycle and emissions created from getting a single banana from farm to table, measuring each piece of packaging and insulation, temperature-controlled warehouse, gas emissions, etc. just to find out that that was the banana that ripened too quickly to eat and ended up in the bin untouched.

So, what is the big issue here? Is it plastic pollution? Should we all reduce how much plastic we use? Is it transportation? Should we be taking less flights? Is jumping on a plane submitting more carbon emissions than what you decide to eat? Most figures only show CO_2 emissions for direct agriculture. However, those figures do not include the other gases such as methane which are produced in huge quantities within agriculture and contribute more to the warming up of the planet than all the world's flights and ships put together. Before, we cleared land to build homes and now, we clear land to grow food, just like the example of the avocados.

Food Waste and Food Shortage – Two Extremes

Food waste and food shortage. Two extreme ends of the scale, yet both still exist in today's advanced world. Although have we even advanced? During the last two years as a pandemic took over, many people have fallen below the poverty line. A 2020 TEDx talk highlights the subject and that was just at the beginning of lockdown. Things have changed hugely since. Those who were readily able to find whatever rare and exotic foods they wanted found themselves in short

Responsibility and Sustainability 145

supply of staples such as rice. According to The United Nations Sustainable Development (2020) 17% of consumer-level food and one third of all food grown is wasted. The United Nations goal 12.3 aims to reduce food waste at both the retail and consumer level and reduce food loss across supply chains by 2030.

A UNEP (United Nations Environment Programme) food waste index report 2021 highlighted some major key findings (Forbes et al., 2021). It has been difficult to measure global food waste as some governments do not measure or monitor and figures are not always accurate. But you don't have to look far to know that this is a huge issue. The report showed that: if food waste and loss were a country it would be the third biggest source of greenhouse gas emissions. Reasons for food waste on the consumer level are often a result of excess demand, inappropriate "best before" dates, and limited portion options – consumers are forced to buy more food, more frequently, and avoiding waste isn't always possible. It's difficult to create demand for products that are difficult to find or do not exist yet, so on a business level getting consumer feedback and enacting those changes are essential in addressing some of the challenges associated with waste. Businesses have got to step up. And yes, many are making a change and offering choices to consumers. Supermarkets now stock what they call imperfect carrots or not so perfect potatoes that would have otherwise gone to waste. But hold on a moment. Read that sentence again. Imperfect carrots? Not so perfect potatoes? That is a concern. How have we moved from judging people on their skin colour or their size to judging and discriminating what a vegetable looks like! So, what would you find if you decided to purchase this bag of not so perfect potatoes? Potatoes that look exactly like potatoes that were supposed to be perfect! It just does not make sense. If we are throwing away food before it has even made it into the food consumption cycle, then we are now talking about food waste on a completely different level. This is now food waste that is born out of a demand for perfect-looking food. So, what needs to change here?

Is Plastic the Real Enemy?

Talking to clients daily means we hear what organisations' missions and values are in relation to their Environmental, Social and Governance goals to be more sustainable. For some it is a tick box exercise. Fair enough. If they are actually doing something. However, this leaves them open to fuelling green-washing and still adding to a linear model. In most cases there is education around the subject. One client said that their mission was to eliminate plastic by the year 2025. Great! However, innovative companies out there are taking the plastic that has already caused the damage and remaking it into some-thing else. Hence, not needing new raw materials and thus not creating more damage. Just like the example above about tofu, we can look at the creation of the plastic bag. The plastic bag was invented to save the planet. Yep. You heard that correct. Save the planet. Its creator, Swedish engineer Sten Gustaf Thulin,

146 *Divya Vaghela and Ulpa Chauhan*

invented the plastic bag in 1959 to help save the trees. Ironic really when you think about it. He intended each bag to be used over and over again until it could be used no more. No one, including Sten, would ever have known that 50 years later the world was looking to ban plastic bags as they were ending up in oceans and harming our marine life (Sustainability Illustrated, 2021). We stopped reusing the plastic bag and saw it as a single use item to be used the once and thrown away.

So, what does this teach us? It shows again another example of a linear model. Again, we need to think circular. Think about eating a meal in India. Instead of a disposable plate you may be served your meal on a banana leaf which is returned to the earth when you're done; no additional processing, chemicals or waste required. Now this is circular.

Plastic plays a huge role in food and beverage as most items are packaged or wrapped in plastic. But plastic isn't necessarily the issue. It's only an issue when it is single use. Single use of anything is not a great idea. We need to rethink how we use plastic. What if we reused this plastic waste and made it into something else? How can we keep plastics in the circular system rather than it end up in land fill? So many products already exist and keeping planet-conscious principles in mind means using what we already have and reusing it until it can be upcycled or transformed to its next life like the reincarnation principles we looked at earlier.

There has been a huge increase in biodegradable and compostable packaging. But it doesn't help to throw your biodegradable packaging in with your normal waste for it to then end up underneath a pile of rubbish and landfill that then doesn't allow it to biodegrade. There needs to be a system that supports businesses to do as much as they can to help them be planet conscious and to do this easily. However, as a business you don't need to wait for this to happen before you make changes in what you do. There will always be a "but" when making changes; however, as long as we continue to move forward and use missions and planet conscious thinking to guide us towards better alternatives we can continue to adapt and become more efficient and helpful to the planet.

Changing our food system is, according to the Ellen McArthur Foundation (2022), "one of the most impactful things we can do to address climate change, create healthy cities and rebuild biodiversity".

Conclusion

How Do We Make the Change?

Eliminating plastic waste is half the battle. What to do about food waste. Well, during the last couple of years forward-thinking companies got innovative and used their ideas to make sure things didn't go to waste. Beer being made into vinegar, pasta and bread off-cuts being made into beer. How about using banana skins to make another dish? Or using imperfect legumes and bread to make miso? The list is endless.

Responsibility and Sustainability   147

Keeping products in a circular model where the thing you started with and your next purchase are just a hop and a skip apart keeps businesses running and each item becoming useful even if its original life is over; reincarnation isn't just for Hindus and Buddhists. The end of an imperfect piece of food shouldn't be a landfill. Instead we need to look to honour food and the life it took on to get to each next step, continuing its path as far as we can take it before we return it to the earth. Otherwise, we risk wasting resources. Taking pieces and practices from nature, religion, and people, everything around us is just the start – the answers are there, we just need to start looking.

So, where to start? The one thing that you can guarantee is that we are all always learning. Knowledge is power. But to share that knowledge is empowering. Read, watch, listen, question and be curious. Only then can you make an informed decision about what it is that you want to do to make a change and take responsibility for your part.

We all have our part to play in the story that is unfolding in front of us, and we can decide what that part is that we want to play. Some more significant than others. But just like any movie, play or book, there are lead roles and there are supporting roles. But without all those various parts, there would be no story. We each have a responsibility for our contribution to the whole. Taking responsibility is not about blame or pointing fingers at who is not doing enough or anything at all but about understanding the part we are playing. And just like anything else you read, watch, and participate in, you have a choice.

Technology has helped us advance in so many ways. We just need to know how we can do better so that technology and innovation becomes circular too. So, what can you reduce? Think about your day-to-day activities. What do you use and consume? Beyond packaging, what can you change that can now be circular? Think about the products you may put straight in the bin? What is the one thing in your bin right now that you can add to the circular sustainable economy? Take an everyday item and see ways that it can be made circular. Think about the raw materials, the production, end of life of the product. Can you make it more circular?

What are you going to do right now, today, tomorrow, next week, next month and next year to make a change? The answer: something.

Food for Thought

- Being a lifelong learner is the key to bringing creative solutions to difficult problems. What are 3 ways you engage with your community and environment every day? It could be listening to a podcast, going for a walk, asking your local grocery store for more package-free options, and more!
- Take an everyday item and see ways that it can be made circular. Think about the raw materials, the production, end of life of the product. Can you make it more circular?
- What did you eat for lunch today? Considering the life cycle of the main 3 elements from farm to grocery store to processing and table. What did

148 *Divya Vaghela and Ulpa Chauhan*

this process look like 200 years ago? What are the impacts on your body and the environment as a result of those changes? What are some ways you could reduce the impact of that lunch – whether it be home-growing the tomatoes, buying from a local farmer, or even switching to a reusable container?

References

Amber, C. A. (2017). *Sustainability and indigenous worldviews: a circle of beauty and wisdom from Mother Earth's Children's Charter School*. University of British Columbia.

Birkby, J. (2016). Vertical farming. *ATTRA Sustainable Agriculture, 2*, 1–12.

Ellen McArthur Foundation (2022). Let's build a circular economy. Retrieved from https://ellenmacarthurfoundation.org/

Forbes, H. Quested, T. & O'Connor, C. (2021). Food Waste Index – Report 2021. United Nations Environment Programme.

Fournier, C. (2017). 10 Of The Most Popular Foods Are Also Among The Worst For The Environment. Retrieved from https://youmatter.world/en/10-worst-popular-foods/

Gimlet Media (2021). Kelp Farming, for the Climate - How to save a planet. Retrieved from https://gimletmedia.com/shows/howtosaveaplanet/94h3rvm

Hickman, L. (2010). Is tofu bad for the environment?. Retrieved from www.theguardian.com/environment/green-living-blog/2010/feb/15/ask-leo-tofu-bad-for-environment

Horler, M. (2021). Growing soy in CEA and Vertical Farming (VF) – The Soya Project. Retrieved from www.soyaproject.org/cea-soy#:~:text=The%20Potential%20Of%20Vertically%20Farming,be%20sited%20pretty%20much%20anywhere

Kellogg, K. (2019). *101 ways to go zero waste*. The Countryman Press.

Kuhnlein, H. V. & Humphries, M. M. (2017). Traditional Animal Foods of Indigenous Peoples of Northern North America – Seals. Retrieved from http://traditionalanimalfoods.org/mammals/seals-sealions-walrus/page.aspx?id=6392#:~:text=Inuit%20also%20used%20nets%20to,techniques%20suited%20to%20the%20season

Le, Q.V., Cowal, S., Jovanovic, G. & Le, D.T. (2021). A Study of Regenerative Farming Practices and Sustainable Coffee of Ethnic Minorities Farmers in the Central Highlands of Vietnam. *Frontiers in Sustainable Food Systems, 5*(26), 118–143.

Masi, D., Kumar, V., Garza-Reyes, J. A. & Godsell, J. (2018). Towards a more circular economy: exploring the awareness, practices, and barriers from a focal firm perspective. *Production Planning & Control, 29*(6), 539–550.

Sustainability Illustrated (2021). 6 dumbest reasons why there is so much plastic in the ocean. Retrieved from https://sustainabilityillustrated.com/en/

Taşnadi, A., Alexandru, I. E., Ustinescu, G. & Bradu, P. C. (2018). Consumerism and exclusion in a throw-away culture. *Theoretical & Applied Economics, 25*(3), 101–112.

United Nations Sustainable Development (2020). *UNDP*. Retrieved from www.undp.org/

Witjes, S. & Lozano, R. (2016). Towards a more Circular Economy: Proposing a framework linking sustainable public procurement and sustainable business models. *Resources, Conservation and Recycling, 112*, 37–44.

11 Culinary Culture, Co-Creation and the Sharing Economy

Elisabeth Kastenholz, Mariana Carvalho and Luís Souza

Introduction

Mausbach (2017) refers in a UNWTO report that food and wine tourism has grown 245% over the last decade. Indeed, gastronomy tourism has been gaining interest from visitors, the tourism sector and from academia (Robinson & Getz, 2014; Stone et al., 2018). Costa (2012) points out that, in Europe, 600.000 tourists are primarily motivated by food and wine to travel every year and around 20 million tourists assume this as a secondary motivation.

In the field of gastronomy tourism, new trends are emerging. According to the Euromonitor (2014), travellers increasingly seek enjoyable meals with local communities, as they appreciate the authenticity of such experiences, specifically when tasting local food (Williamson & Hassanli, 2022). This trend highlights the potential of the sharing economy in diverse domains of the tourism sector, specifically in cultural and food tourism, while research in this field is still limited (Atsız, Cifci & Law, 2022; Lin et al., 2021a).

Visitors are willing to get to know local food products and the culinary culture, when they are exploring a tourist destination, often also to take these products home as a valued extension of the experience (Kastenholz et al., 2016) and increasingly looking for perceived authentic and involving food-sharing opportunities (Cifci et al., 2021; Lin et al., 2021a; Taş Gürsoy, 2021). Tourists' intention to get immersed in the destinations' culture comprises tasting local food and understanding the local cuisine and its associated traditions (Taş Gürsoy, 2021), going beyond sustenance (Richards, 2021), reflecting a strong cultural, but also social motivation and meaning (Carvalho et al., 2021b; Lin et al., 2021a; Taş Gürsoy, 2021; Williamson & Hassanli, 2022). A diversity of food-related experiences have accordingly emerged (Carvalho et al., 2016; Carvalho et al., 2021b; Cifci et al., 2021; Lin et al., 2021b; Taş Gürsoy, 2021). Gastronomy tourism fosters experiences beyond food and wine tasting, comprising suppliers' sharing of historical and cultural aspects in home-dining experiences with locals, cooking classes and culinary workshops, food market visits, food events and food tours (Cifci et al., 2021; Lin et al., 2021a; Dixit, 2020). Besides, these experiences also contribute to increased visitor expenditures in local food (Chang et al., 2021).

DOI: 10.4324/9781003282532-15

In this context, meal-sharing economy platforms are emerging, comprising experiences that are delivered by locals who prepare typical meals for tourists in their private homes or in restaurants (Cifci et al., 2021; Lin et al., 2021a; Privitera & Abushena, 2019), where knowledge transfer about food products, ingredients and culinary practices also stand out. Besides, these experiences are highly immersive and contribute to memorability (Atsız, Cifci & Rasoolimanesh, 2022). Another key driver of gastronomy tourism is visitors' interest in participative experiences, being an active part of the food production and enjoying a meal with more awareness of particular processes, historical features and local lifestyle. Co-creation emerges in this interactive context, promoting more meaningful, immersive and distinctive experiences (Carvalho et al., 2021a, b).

In their study, Lin et al. (2021a) highlight the emergence of peer-to-peer dining as a new food tourism product, requiring deeper understanding. Atsız, Cifci and Rasoolimanesh (2022) point at a lack of research regarding the 'meal-sharing economy' in terms of experiential tourism, while also the co-creation lens of the tourist experience might improve understanding of the phenomenon for both tourists and local communities. Hence, this chapter reflects on the pertinence of co-creation in meal-sharing economy experiences, where host–guest interaction, experience and knowledge exchange and the cultural dimension of food, wine and culinary habits significantly contribute to value-creation in the tourist experience.

Sharing Economy

Sharing is an ancient practice, present in rituals of primitive communities and still relevant in contemporary relationships in modern societies. The traditional forms of sharing and collaboration between individuals are being redrawn through the emergence of several peer-to-peer (P2P) Internet-based businesses models, which enable closer interactions between people and provide new value to shareable products and services (Dredge & Gyimóthy, 2015; Guttentag, 2015). In these business models, value is created on the basis of relationship-building between individuals and encompass trust, reputation, collaboration, equality (horizontal relations between individuals), reciprocity and openness (Vallat, 2015).

The online marketplace of sharing is developed, essentially, by the encounters between common individuals (re)positioned as both producers/ suppliers and/ or consumers. Moreover, this marketplace is framed by relations of mutualism, sharing and reciprocity, furthering acts of hospitality and exchange. The marketplace of P2P Internet-based businesses is formed by (i) technology-based enterprises, which are responsible for intermediating the sharing action and (ii) by individuals providing and consuming the shareable goods or services (Botsman & Rogers, 2010; John, 2012). Frequently, this marketplace is identified by the term 'sharing economy' which refers to "forms of exchange facilitated through online platforms, encompassing a diversity of activities for-profit and

Culinary Culture, Co-Creation and the Sharing Economy   151

non-profit that aim to open access to under-utilised resources" (Richardson, 2015: 121).

The origins of sharing economy date from the late 1990s and early-mid 2000 when online platforms emerged enabling individuals to evolve P2P businesses at a previously unprecedented scale (Martin, 2016). Since then, business models based on sharing have been growing in popularity, changing and even disrupting diverse markets, such as tourism, hospitality, goods exchanges, car rental services, finance, staffing, music and video markets (Guttentag, 2015). The growing popularity of the sharing economy results from multiple factors, such as: (i) consumers' motivations related to sustainability issues, social appeal, psychological effects and economic value (Botsman & Rogers, 2010); (ii) the financial crises, driving entrepreneurial action, enabling individuals to earn extra money (Ranchordás, 2015); (iii) Low barriers of entry: the low investments required and the lack of regulation allow entrepreneurs to go online quickly and easily (Dredge & Gyimóthy, 2015; Sigala, 2017) and to grow through viral exposure (Sigala, 2017); (iv) technology: social media and interactivity tools available on Web 2.0 and the dissemination of mobile devices, like smartphones and tablets, have contributed to the spread of the sharing economy worldwide (Dredge & Gyimóthy, 2015; Sigala, 2017).

In tourism, new sharing business initiatives have developed in many fields, such as hospitality; travel guidance; food and beverage provision; transportation; tour operations (Dredge & Gyimóthy, 2015). Similar to other economic sectors, these initiatives are creating new core business value for tourism. They are changing the way travellers autonomously organise their tailor-made holidays (Guttentag, 2015), experience the destination by immersing in local culture (Forno & Garibaldi, 2015), and co-create value through meaningful social encounters with locals (Tussyadiah & Zach, 2016). Additionally, sharing economy creates value for locals, tourists, and other tourism service providers, since it incrementally helps visitors have access to a wide range of products and services at destinations, at more affordable prices, and facilitates authentic encounters between tourists and residents (Cheng, 2016). This exchange contributes to employment and income of many locals, because tourists participating in sharing-economy initiatives are likely to spend money also in non-tourist areas, peripheral localities, outside the tourist bubble (Guttentag, 2015).

As sharing economy gains attention and popularity, scholars have attempted to understand other factors motivating individuals' involvement in shared production and consumption such as: (i) sustainability concerns; (ii) utilitarian motives; (iii) psychological motives; (iv) the social appeal of the sharing economy.

Sustainability Concerns

Many scholars (Belk, 2010; Bucher et al., 2016; Lamberton, 2016) argue that individuals are attracted to a sharing economy because they are engaged in a less resource-intensive consumption. While a sharing economy may, indeed, help prevent unnecessary use of resources by reducing new purchases and promoting reuse in private arrangements (Piscicelli et al., 2015), the biased perception of sustainability in a sharing economy (also designed as 'sustainability bias') has been criticised. Most concerns are related to (i) an unregulated marketplace, since P2P platforms, in particular Airbnb and Uber, are criticised for unfair competition with conventional operators and for promoting tax avoidance (Martin, 2016). Additionally, a sharing economy leads to decentralised labour practices, opening up unregulated spaces of (under) employment that might be exploited by sharing-economy start-ups (Richardson, 2015), possibly eroding workers' rights (Martin, 2016); (ii) adverse social impacts: mainly related to shared accommodation, such as gentrification, disturbance in residential areas caused by tourists, issues with renting/selling properties (Guttentag, 2015); (iii) exclusivity and inequity: providers of sharing-economy options are mostly those who possess economic capital like properties, cars, other assets, etc. (Martin, 2016). Hence, a sharing economy is discussed as increasing inequalities rather than social justice. Still, these arguments may be less relevant for 'sharing meals' initiatives, although also here competition with traditional restaurants (and the corresponding value, tax and employment generation) may be an issue.

Utilitarian Motives

In many cases, earning and saving money are key drivers for the sharing economy. The sharing economy has become more popular during the economic crisis in the United States and in some European countries in 2008 (Vallat, 2015), with evidence confirming such utilitarian reasons (Botsman & Rogers, 2010). Thus, consumers participating in sharing-economy initiatives are largely motivated by self-interest, due to economic gains in the sharing process (Lamberton, 2016; Tussyadiah & Pesonen, 2016). This may be true for food-sharing initiatives, as well.

Psychological Motives

Altruism and generosity form the "ethos" of sharing, and individuals get involved in sharing because it is viewed as pro-social and voluntary (Belk, 2010; Bucher et al., 2016). When individuals share for altruistic reasons, they are motivated by convenience, courtesy, or kindness, and feel positive emotions, such as mutual respect, compassion, sympathy, or simply joy and fun when sharing. These motives may result in non-monetized or fair-cost sharing, while the main concern lies in the value of the shared experience.

The Social Appeal of Sharing Economy

The sharing economy relies on social relations to mobilise and allocate resources. In this sense, sharing attitudes are driven by social appeal motivations (Bucher et al., 2016; Martin et al., 2015; Tussyadiah & Pesonen, 2016).

Culinary Culture, Co-Creation and the Sharing Economy 153

The potential role of social interaction as a value proposition and motivating factor for engaging in the sharing economy is stressed by Botsman and Rogers (2010), who highlight the individuals' wish to return to old models of consumption, buying directly from each other, like in the old bazaars, trying to reconnect to local and personalised exchange, which were lost in mass or hyper consumption. Similarly, Bucher et al. (2016) recognise that the sharing economy is driven by the wish to establish new social ties, to be part of a community, and to find companionship, with sociability standing out as the strongest driver of overall sharing motivations in an empirical study, as corroborated by Tussyadiah and Pesonen (2016).

The social relationships developed through sharing-economy initiatives allow tourists to get closer to a place's real life through direct contact with locals in their habitual residential areas, permitting more authentic experiences and genuine cross-cultural encounters. As authenticity plays a key role in perceived value of travel experiences (Paulauskaite et al., 2017), it is vital to understand how tourists may connect to destinations' everyday life. Amongst sharing-economy initiatives, food sharing may be considered as a prominent opportunity for tourists to meaningfully and intimately engage with local residents in authentic daily-life contexts (Sidali et al., 2015), thus enhancing the value of their experience of travel, as discussed next.

Meal-Sharing Initiatives

Tourists are especially interested in tasting local food during their travels since it provides a closer contact with local culture and values (Agapito et al., 2017; Zago et al., 2013). Dinneer, EatWith, Withlocals, Feastly, VizEat are examples of meal-sharing-economy platforms that allow tourists to dine with locals in their home or at a local restaurant (Atzis & Cifci, 2022; Ketter, 2019). The meal-sharing platforms present opportunities for tourists to socialize with locals, to learn about gastronomic habits and local culture (Demir, 2020), permitting access to locals' real life through direct contacts in daily living contexts, thus furthering immersion in local culture and enhancing perception of authenticity, as found in previous studies on sharing-economy experiences (Souza et al., 2020).

The social appeal is recognized as a central factor pushing tourists towards meal sharing (Ketter, 2019). By visiting hosts' homes and joining a private group meal, tourists engage in authentic connections and accept the tasks associated to face-to-face sharing initiatives. Food- and meal-sharing initiatives expose tourists to a distinct form of hospitality, not found in traditional restaurants, involving social relationships between tourists, the host and companions participating in the shared dinner event (Ketter, 2019; Lin et al., 2021b). The social aspect of the meal-sharing experience also benefits the hosts, who apart from obtaining economic gains, obtain social success by impressing their guests (Ketter, 2019).

According to Ketter (2019), tourists participating in meal sharing are likely to spend money in non-tourist areas, since many meal-sharing hosts live in peripheral localities, outside the tourist bubble. Dredge and Gyimóthy (2015) stress the quest for local identity and authentic narratives, provided by encounters with local destination culture, as core motivation for sharing-economy users. By recognizing the relevance of genuine cross-cultural encounters around food, tourists frequently increase value ratings of their hosts, when they perceive authenticity in meal-sharing initiatives (Mhlanga, 2020). According to these perspectives, meal sharing may be considered an innovative business model as well as a true cross-cultural sharing opportunity, involving tourists and hosts, even sometimes chefs in genuine, spontaneous and intimate cross-cultural encounters, providing a favourable environment for value co-creation in gastronomy tourism, as will be explored next.

The Co-creation of Culinary Tourism in the Sharing-Economy Paradigm

Gastronomy Tourist Experiences and the Sharing Economy

The culinary culture is a distinctive element of the destination's attractiveness, perceived by tourists as a vehicle to understanding territories' singular culture, allowing their immersion in the local lifestyle and giving them the opportunity to experience something new (Atsız, Cifci & Law, 2022; Ketter, 2019). The diversity of tourist experiences related to local cuisine is increasing and so is visitors' interest to try local delicacies while travelling (Richards, 2021).

Culinary is part of the wider concept of gastronomy, related to local dishes, local food products and food preparation techniques (Kivela & Crotts, 2006). According to the UNWTO (2019: 44), gastronomy tourism refers to the "visitors' experience linked with food and related products and activities while travelling", comprising "authentic, traditional, and/or innovative culinary experiences ... and related activities such as visiting the local producers, participating in food festivals and attending cooking classes". This definition highlights gastronomy experiences beyond food and culinary specificities, embracing territories' unique culture and lifestyle. Gastronomy fosters pleasurable social encounters, allowing visitors to get immersed in the destination, its community and culture while and through tasting local delicacies (Dixit, 2020). Besides, gastronomy allows multisensory, engaging and thus more memorable experiences (Kivela & Crotts, 2006).

Interactive and culturally enriching food experiences are increasingly offered on meal-sharing economy platforms, permitting tourists close contact with locals, through affordable food experiences, that reveal culinary practices, specificities about ingredients and historical aspects related to food (Atsız, Cifci & Law, 2022). For example, 'EatWith' and 'Withlocals' are two online platforms for meal-sharing experiences. 'Eatwith' comprises over 5000 culinary

Culinary Culture, Co-Creation and the Sharing Economy   155

experiences (delivered in person and online), led by locals. With the motto "Unforgettable, immersive culinary experiences", 'EatWith' is "the world's largest community for authentic culinary experiences with locals, available in over 130 countries" (Eatwith, 2022). The unique experiences that 'Eatwith' promotes rely on the involvement of several hand-selected local hosts, who provide immersive experiences in private homes. 'Withlocals' is another emergent platform, created in 2013 in the Netherlands and later expanded worldwide (Cifci et al., 2021), inspired by "connecting people with cultures by breaking down barriers between travellers and locals worldwide" (Withlocals, 2022). The here promoted food-sharing experiences include food walking tours and multiple food-sharing encounters in daily living contexts, fostering meaningful and engaging host–guest interaction involving food.

According to Lin et al.'s study (2021a), the factors making tourists look for peer-to-peer dining experiences are related to three push dimensions: "seeking variety" (of quality food and catering experiences), "gaining authentic experience" (regarding local lifestyle, food culture and the host), and "enhancing social circle" (socializing with both other visitors and hosts). The latter dimension seems to be less relevant for visitors in foreign peer-to-peer dining experiences, where tourists apparently value the genuine opportunity to try local food at a local ambience (a private home or a typical restaurant) over socializing (Lin et al., 2021a). The authors underline the importance of comfortable and authentic home atmosphere sought by visitors (Lin et al., 2021a). Cifci et al. (2021) stress the importance of food authenticity for visitors experiencing food tours in Thailand with local guides, also involving contact with vending areas (street food market) and getting to know about local ingredients and ways of cooking.

Through local gastronomy, visitors seek the authenticity of places that makes destinations truly distinctive. Through content analysis of tourists' meal-sharing experience reviews from Istanbul (via the platforms EatWith and Withlocals), Atsız, Cifci and Law (2022: 140) identified key motivational dimensions, contributing to tourists' satisfaction and memorability: "knowledge" (learning about local food culture, cooking methods and traditions), "authenticity" (tourists' interest in traditional, genuine local culture and habits), "local hospitality" (tourists feeling welcome), and "social interaction".

Richards (2021) underlines that the second generation of gastronomic experiences considers tourists' central role in experience co-creation and suggests the third generation increasingly focuses on an integrated experience of immersion in foodscape and the destination's culture. Indeed, culinary experiences foster tourists' active participation in culinary processes, with value-creation results from their involvement with their hosts and the experiencescape (Prayag et al., 2020). The meal-sharing economy in culinary tourism is therefore shaped by value-co-creation between hosts and guests, within a particular (social and physical) context of local culture (Atsız, Cifci & Rasoolimanesh, 2022), as detailed next.

Co-creation Experiences in the Meal-Sharing Economy

Against this background, the concept and principles of co-creation seem particularly adequate for gastronomy tourism. Co-creation has developed from the ideas of the service-dominant logic (Vargo & Lusch, 2004), considering consumers as co-producers of their experiences, getting involved in the value-creation process together with supply agents, who should facilitate the consumers' active role in the experience (Binkhorst & Den Dekker, 2009; Vargo & Lusch, 2004). Indeed, the active and central role increasingly sought by consumers is of particular importance, permitting self-expression and promoting unique, subjectively meaningful experiences (Binkhorst & Den Dekker, 2009). In tourism studies, co-creation research is relatively recent, enhancing our understanding of the dimensions and requirements of optimal value-co-creation (Carvalho et al., 2021a). Co-creation has been analyzed in different tourism contexts, namely in cultural tourism (e.g. Minkiewicz et al., 2014), peer-to-peer accommodation (e.g. Schuckert et al., 2018), smart tourism (e.g. Buhalis & Sinarta, 2019) and, more recently food & wine tourism (Carvalho et al., 2021a; Rachão et al., 2020). Based on a literature review, Carvalho et al. (2021a) suggest that co-creation in food & wine tourism is successfully experienced by tourists when interaction (with others and the environment), active participation, engagement (cognitive and emotional) and personalization are fostered.

Co-creation in meal-sharing experiences is an understudied, yet promising field of research. When analyzing these private and intimate food experiences, several features stand out that fall within these co-creation dimensions, contributing to a tourist experience that goes beyond enjoying a meal. Figure 11.1

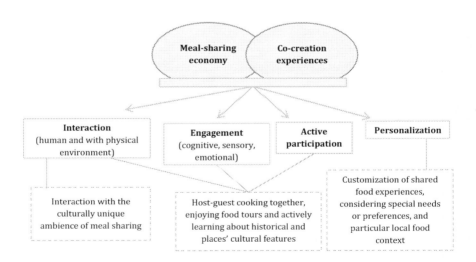

Figure 11.1 Dimensions of co-creation in meal-sharing experiences

suggests the analytical lens of co-creation for the meal-sharing economy context, inspired by Carvalho et al. (2021a).

The co-creation of culinary experiences is hence promoted when value-creation results from the hosts–guests' social interaction and cognitive engagement, as well as from cultural knowledge transfer, not only to visitors, who immerse in a different food culture, but also to hosts, who learn from interacting with tourists, in rich cross-cultural encounters (Atsız, Cifci & Rasoolimanesh, 2022; Lin et al., 2021a; Privitera & Abushena, 2019). Atsız, Cifci and Rasoolimanesh (2022) stress the role of social interaction (between tourists and hosts), triggering a feeling of local hospitality (hosts make tourists feel at home, care), and fostering emotional involvement, which seems highly appreciated by visitors in unfamiliar environments (Karlsson & Dolnicar, 2016). Hosts assume the role of cultural brokers and facilitators of an informal atmosphere that is required to involve guests in meal preparation and enjoyment, together with historical and cultural aspects complementing the experience (Atsız, Cifci & Rasoolimanesh, 2022; Binkhorst & Den Dekker, 2009). Lin et al. (2021a) studied peer-to-peer dining experiences, with meal sharing in a private home, hosted by locals who share knowledge about local food and culinary habits, presenting such (emotionally and cognitively) engaging opportunities of interaction, in an informal and pleasant atmosphere, perceived as authentic and memorable (Atsız, Cifci & Rasoolimanesh, 2022). Additionally, interaction with the service/ experiencescape (the ambiance of the place), with references to local culture (regarding elements of local lifestyles, historical facts, cooking techniques) that trigger the highly valued perception of 'authenticity' as well as of 'novelty', increase cognitive and emotional engagement (Privitera & Abushena, 2019; Sthapit et al., 2019). Visitors are also more active in such personalized sharing contexts than in the commercial setting of consumption at a restaurant. In their study on food and wine experiences, Rachão et al. (2020) highlight the contribution of hands-on gastronomic experiences in co-creative contexts, stimulating visitors' cognitive involvement and learning. Some authors stress that more interactive and participative visitors tend to live more memorable experiences (Sthapit et al., 2019; Dixit, 2020). Personalized co-creative meal-sharing experiences may also increase tourist satisfaction, considering, for example, food diets, like veganism and macrobiotics, or food restrictions, due to allergies to specific ingredients (Cifci et al., 2021). Although this adaptation may be difficult for some hosts, also the preservation of authenticity of local food is a challenge, even when attending to dietary restrictions/preferences.

However, there are other challenges of meal sharing, since the private context where such experiences occur may set pressure on the hosts' privacy, if not managed carefully (Pivitera & Abushena, 2019). This requires, on the one hand, preservation of a genuine living ambience of sharing food experiences and culture, while, on the other hand, the private family context also deserves preservation. The risk of evolving into a commoditized experience should be recognized, as standardized approaches imply the loss of genuineness, harmful to both hosts and guests. Lin et al. (2021a) also call for care not to over-decorate the meal-sharing settings, resulting in lack of authenticity. Co-creation in home-dining experiences may require limits in numbers of both visitors and meals provided (in a certain time frame), to avoid 'serial reproduction of culture' (Richards, 2011). Sharing meals in small groups allows visitors' co-production, in a relaxing ambience, where guests' immersion in a local way of life through true cross-cultural encounters, may foster genuine connection between both parts. High expectations regarding authentic meal sharing also require visitors' trust in who provides home-dining experiences, which is promoted through other visitors' reviews on the digital platforms (Pivitera & Abushena, 2019; Veen, 2019). Still, tourists assume risks when seeking a meal in a private home, due to the lack of regulation in this domain, which may even jeopardize health and safety (Lin et al., 2021a; Mhlanga, 2020). Hence, it is important to understand how the social, cultural and sensorial experience quality of home-dining may be preserved, as it offers great opportunities to enhance meaningful tourist–community encounters, and increase destinations' appeal and visitors' place attachment through unique and memorable culinary experiences.

Conclusion

The unique features of destinations' culinary culture have become more prominent in the tourism sector. Gastronomy is undoubtedly central to most travel experiences. Tourists' interest in tasting new delicacies and being involved in different food-related experiences, such as meal sharing in diverse local living contexts, has become a trend (Williamson & Hassanli, 2022).

This chapter reflects on the role and potential of the sharing economy in gastronomy tourism, the main tourist motivations underlying its appeal and the pertinence of considering the co-creation lens for a better understanding of the essence and power of meal sharing and for the potential to add value to these experiences as well as to preserve, thereby contributing to a destination's competitiveness and sustainability. Specifically, the increasing interest visitors show in local food, as central to unique place experiences, suggests the positive role that co-creative meal sharing may play in distinctive, appealing and memorable travel experiences.

As pointed out by Atsız, Cifci and Rasoolimanesh (2022), the continuous growth of meal-sharing economy platforms calls for an improved comprehension of this particular, culturally and socially meaningful sharing experience in tourism, while the phenomenon should also be carefully monitorized to avoid any negative impacts of this recent sharing sector (Mhlanga, 2020), similar to what is criticized in the literature about accommodation and car-sharing (Martin, 2016). Still, given the apparently powerful positive effects of meal-sharing opportunities reported in several studies, regarding satisfaction with the destination experience, possibly enhancing place attachment, while permitting preservation of local food and traditions, in a context of respectful cross-cultural exchange (Atsız, Cifci & Rasoolimanesh, 2022; Ketter, 2019; Lin et al., 2021a), these offers may enhance local pride and identity, maintain local

Culinary Culture, Co-Creation and the Sharing Economy 159

agro-production and community well-being, i.e. sustainable destination development (Fusté-Forné & Jamal, 2020).

Hence, it is relevant to understand the nature, opportunities and limits of co-creation in meal-sharing experiences that local service providers and DMOs may strategically use to foster their competitiveness. Local hosts play an important role in facilitating unique, genuine hospitality, through culinary experiences, possibly shared in private homes or in community contexts. DMOs have a strategic role in providing local hosts with tools and guidelines that may help them engage in such co-creative meal-sharing experiences in a way that adds value to all involved.

Food for Thought

- What are visitors' main motivations when engaging in meal-sharing experiences?
- Considering the features of the sharing economy and co-creation of value, how can elements of these two fields contribute to fostering memorable culinary experiences?
- What are possible positive and negative impacts of meal-sharing experiences at a destination, determining this offering's contribution to sustainable development?

Acknowledgements

This chapter was partially developed in the scope of the research project TWINE-PTDC/GES-GCE/32259/2017-POCI-01-0145-FEDER-032259, funded by the ERDF through the COMPETE 2020 - Operational Programme Competitiveness and Internationalization (POCI), and national funds (OPTDC/GES-GCE/32259/2017-E), through the FCT/MCTES.

References

Agapito, D., Pinto, P., & Mendes, J. (2017). Tourists' memories, sensory impressions and loyalty: In loco and post-visit study in Southwest Portugal. *Tourism Management, 58,* 108–118. https://doi.org/10.1016/j.tourman.2016.10.015

Atsız, O., & Cifci, I. (2022). Exploring the motives for entrepreneurship in the meal-sharing economy. *Current Issues in Tourism, 25*(6), 864–873. https://doi.org/10.1080/13683500.2021.1908239

Atsız, O., Cifci, I., & Law, R. (2022). Understanding food experience in sharing-economy platforms: insights from Eatwith and Withlocals. *Journal of Tourism and Cultural Change, 20*(1–2), 131–156. https://doi.org/10.1080/14766825.2021.1880419

Atsız, O., Cifci, I., & Rasoolimanesh, S. (2022). Exploring the components of meal-sharing experiences with local foods: a netnography approach. *Current Issues in Tourism, 25*(6), 919–936. https://doi.org/10.1080/13683500.2021.1905619

Belk, R. (2010). Sharing. *Journal of Consumer Research, 36*(5), 715–734. https://doi.org/10.1086/612649

160 Elisabeth Kastenholz, Mariana Carvalho and Luís Souza

Binkhorst, E., & Den Dekker, T. (2009). Agenda for co-creation tourism experience research. *Journal of Hospitality Marketing & Management, 18*(2–3), 311–327. https://doi.org/10.1080/19368620802594193

Botsman, R., & Rogers, R. (2010). *What's mine is yours: The rise of collaborative consumption.* New York: Harper Collins.

Bucher, E., Fieseler, C., & Lutz, C. (2016). What's mine is yours (for a nominal fee) – Exploring the spectrum of utilitarian to altruistic motives for Internet-mediated sharing. *Computers in Human Behavior, 62*, 316–326. https://doi.org/10.1016/j.chb.2016.04.002

Buhalis, D., & Sinarta, Y. (2019). Real-time co-creation and nowness service: lessons from tourism and hospitality. *Journal of Travel and Tourism Marketing, 36*(5), 563–582.

Carvalho, M., Kastenholz, E., & Carneiro, M. J. (2021a). Co-creative tourism experiences—a conceptual framework and its application to food & wine tourism. *Tourism Recreation Research.* https://doi.org.10.1080/02508281.2021.1948719

Carvalho, M., Kastenholz, E., & Carneiro, M. J. (2021b). Interaction as a central element of co-creative wine tourism experiences—Evidence from *Bairrada*, a Portuguese wine-producing region. *Sustainability, 13*(16), 9374. https://doi.org/10.3390/su13169374

Carvalho, M., Lima, J., Kastenholz, E., & Sousa, A. (2016). Co-creative rural tourism experiences: Connecting tourists, community and local resources. In E. Kastenholz, M. J. Carneiro, C. Eusébio & E. Figueiredo (Eds.), *Meeting Challenges for Rural Tourism through Co-Creation of Sustainable Tourist Experiences* (pp. 79–101). Newcastle upon Tyne, UK: Cambridge Scholars Publishing.

Chang, J., Okumus, B., Wang, C.-H., & Chiu, C.-Y. (2021). Food tourism: cooking holiday experiences in East Asia. *Tourism Review, 76*(5), 1067–1083. https://doi.org/10.1108/TR-09-2019-0399

Cheng, M. (2016). Current sharing economy media discourse in tourism. *Annals of Tourism Research, 60*(c), 111–114. https://doi.org/10.1016/j.annals.2016.07.001

Cifci, I., Atsız, O., & Gupta, V. (2021). The street food experiences of the local-guided tour in the meal-sharing economy: the case of Bangkok. *British Food Journal, 123*(12), 4030–4048. https://doi.org/10.1108/BFJ-01-2021-0069

Costa, A. (2012). Food & wine tourism: Challenges and Opportunities. In UNWTO, *Global Report on Food Tourism* (pp. 4849). Spain: UNWTO.

Demir, Y. (2020). Analysis of food sharing sites in context of sharing economy. *Güncel Turizm Araştırmaları Dergisi, 4*(1), 54–69.

Dixit, S. K. (2020). Marketing gastronomic tourism experiences. In S. K. Dixit (Ed.), *The Routledge handbook of tourism experience management and marketing* (pp. 323–336). Routledge.

Dredge, D., & Gyimóthy, S. (2015). The collaborative economy and tourism: Critical perspectives, questionable claims and silenced voices. *Tourism Recreation Research, 40*(3) 286–302. https://doi.org/10.1080/02508281.2015.1086076

Eatwith (2022). *About us.* Retrieved from www.eatwith.com/about-us.

Euromonitor International. (2014). *World travel market: Global trends report 2014.* Retrieved from http://go.euromonitor.com/rs/euromonitorinternational/images/WTM-2014.pdf.

Forno, F., & Garibaldi, R. (2015). Sharing economy in travel and tourism: The case of home-swapping in Italy. *Journal of Quality Assurance in Hospitality & Tourism, 16*(2), 202–220. https://doi.org/10.1080/1528008X.2015.1013409

Fusté-Forné, F., & Jamal, T. (2020). Slow food tourism: An ethical microtrend for the anthropocene. *Journal of Tourism Futures*, *6*(3), 227–232. https://doi.org/10.1108/JTF-10-2019-0120

Guttentag, D. (2015). Airbnb: disruptive innovation and the rise of an informal tourism accommodation sector. *Current Issues in Tourism*, *18*(12), 1192–1217. https://doi.org/10.1080/13683500.2013.827159

John, N. A. (2012). Sharing and Web 2.0: The emergence of a keyword. *New Media & Society*, *15*(2), 167–182. https://doi.org/10.1177/1461444812450684

Karlsson, L., & Dolnicar, S. (2016). Someone's been sleeping in my bed. *Annals of Tourism Research*, *58*, 159–162. https://doi.org/10.1016/j.annals.2016.02.006

Kastenholz, E., Eusébio, C. & Carneiro, M. J. (2016). Purchase of local products within the rural tourist experience context. *Tourism Economics*, *22*(4), 729–748. https://doi.org/10.1177/1354816616654245

Ketter, E. (2019) Eating with EatWith: analysing tourism-sharing economy consumers. *Current Issues in Tourism*, *22*(9), 1062–1075. https://doi.org/10.1080/13683500.2017.1357682

Kivela, J., & Crotts, J. (2006). Tourism and Gastronomy: Gastronomy's influence on how tourists experience a destination. *Journal of Hospitality & Tourism Research*, *30*(3), 354–377. https://doi.org/10.1177/1096348006286797

Lamberton, C. (2016). Collaborative consumption: A goal-based framework. *Current Opinion in Psychology*, *10*, 55–59. https://doi.org/10.1016/j.copsyc.2015.12.004

Lin, P., Ok, C., & Au, W. (2021a). Peer-to-Peer Dining: A Motivation Study. *Journal of Hospitality and Tourism Research*. https://doi.org/10.1177/1096348021990709

Lin, P., Ok, C., & Au, W. (2021b). Tourists' private social dining experiences. *Tourist Studies*, *21*(2) 278–299. https://doi.org/10.1177/1468797620986088

Martin, C. J. (2016). The sharing economy: A pathway to sustainability or a nightmarish form of neoliberal capitalism? *Ecological Economics*, *121*, 149–159. https://doi.org/10.1016/j.ecolecon.2015.11.027

Martin, C. J., Upham, P., & Budd, L. (2015). Commercial orientation in grassroots social innovation: Insights from the sharing economy. *Ecological Economics*, *118*, 240–251. https://doi.org/10.1016/j.ecolecon.2015.08.001

Mausbach, V. (2017). *Mendoza: Creation and Evolution of a Gastronomy Destination.* In UNWTO, *Affiliate Members Report, Volume sixteen – Second Global Report on Gastronomy Tourism* (pp. 54–55). Madrid: UNWTO.

Mhlanga, O. (2022). 'Meal-sharing' platforms: a boon or bane for restaurants? *Current Issues in Tourism*, *25*(20), 3291–3308.

Minkiewicz, J., Evans, J., & Bridson, K. (2014). How do consumers co-create their experiences? An exploration in the heritage sector. *Journal of Marketing Management*, *30*(1–2), 30–59.

Paulauskaite, D., Morrison, A., Powell, R., & Stefaniak, J. (2017). Living like a local: Authentic tourism experiences and the sharing economy. *International Journal of Tourism Research*, *19*(6), 619–628. https://doi.org/10.1002/jtr.2134

Piscicelli, L., Cooper, T., & Fisher, T. (2015). The role of values in collaborative consumption: Insights from a product-service system for lending and borrowing in the UK. *Journal of Cleaner Production*, *97*, 21–29. https://doi.org/10.1016/j.jclepro.2014.07.032

Prayag, G., Gannon, M., Muskat, B., & Taheri, B. (2020). A serious leisure perspective of culinary tourism co-creation: The influence of prior knowledge, physical

162 *Elisabeth Kastenholz, Mariana Carvalho and Luís Souza*

environment and service quality. *International Journal of Contemporary Hospitality Management, 32*(7), 2453–2472.

Privitera, D., & Abushena, R. (2019). The home as a consumption space: Promoting social eating. In J. Byrom, & D. Medway (Eds.), *Case studies in food retailing and distribution* (pp. 69–86). Cambridge: Woodhead Publishing.

Rachão, S., Breda, Z., Fernandes, C. & Joukes, V. (2020). Cocreation of tourism experiences: are food-related activities being explored? *British Food Journal, 122*(3), 910–928. https://doi.org/10.1108/BFJ-10-2019-0769

Ranchordás, S. (2015). Does sharing mean caring? Regulating innovation in the sharing economy. *Minnesota Journal of Law, Science & Technology, 16*(1), 413–475. Retrieved from http://ssrn.com/abstract=2492798%5Cnhttp://conservancy.umn.edu/bitstream/handle/11299/172061/Ranchordás.pdf?sequence=1&isAllowed=y

Richards, G. (2011). Creativity and tourism: The state of the art. *Annals of Tourism Research, 38*, 1225–1253. https://doi.org/10.1016/j.annals.2011.07.008

Richards, G. (2021). Evolving research perspectives on food and gastronomic experiences in tourism. *International Journal of Contemporary Hospitality Management, 33*(3), 1037–1058.

Richardson, L. (2015). Performing the sharing economy. *Geoforum, 67*, 121–129. https://doi.org/10.1016/j.geoforum.2015.11.004

Robinson, R., & Getz, D. (2014). Profiling potential food tourists: an Australian study. *British Food Journal, 116*(4), 690–706. https://doi.org/10.1108/BFJ-02-2012-0030

Schuckert, M., Peters, M., & Pilz, G. (2018). The co-creation of host–guest relationships via couchsurfing: A qualitative study. *Tourism Recreation Research, 43*(2), 220–234. https://doi.org/10.1080/02508281.2017.1384127

Sidali, K., Kastenholz, E., & Bianchi, R. (2015). Food tourism, niche markets and products in rural tourism: combining the intimacy model and the experience economy as a rural development strategy. *Journal of Sustainable Tourism, 23*(8–9), 1179–1197. https://doi.org/10.1080/09669582.2013.836210

Sigala, M. (2017). Collaborative commerce in tourism: implications for research and industry. *Current Issues in Tourism, 20*(4), 346–355. https://doi.org/10.1080/13683500.2014.982522

Souza, L., Kastenholz, E., Barbosa, L., & Carvalho, M. (2020). Tourist experience, perceived authenticity, place attachment and loyalty when staying in a peer-to-peer accommodation. *International Journal of Tourist Cities, 6*(1), 27–52. https://doi.org/10.1108/IJTC-03-2019-0042

Sthapit, R., Coudounaris, D., & Björk, P. (2019). Extending the memorable tourism experience construct: An investigation of memories of local food experiences. *Scandinavian Journal of Hospitality and Tourism, 19*(4–5), 333–353. https://doi.org/10.1080/15022250.2019.1689530

Stone, M., Soulard, J., Migacz, S., Wolf, E. (2018). Elements of Memorable Food, Drink, and Culinary Tourism Experiences. *Journal of Travel Research, 57*(8) 1121–1132. https://doi.org/10.1177/0047287517729758

Taş Gürsoy, İ. (2021). Slow food justice and tourism: Tracing karakılçık bread in seferihisar, Turkey. *Journal of Sustainable Tourism, 29*(2–3), 466–486. https://doi.org/10.1080/09669582.2020.1770772

Tussyadiah, I., & Pesonen, J. (2016). Drivers and barriers of peer-to-peer accommodation stay – an exploratory study with American and Finnish travellers. *Current Issues in Tourism, 21*(06), 703–720. https://doi.org/10.1080/13683500.2016.1141180

Tussyadiah, I. P., & Zach, F. (2016). Identifying salient attributes of peer-to-peer accommodation experience. *Journal of Travel & Tourism Marketing, 34*(5), 636–652. https://doi.org/10.1080/10548408.2016.1209153

UNWTO (2019). UNWTO Tourism Definitions. Retrieved from https://doi.org/10.18111/9789284420858

Vallat, D. (2015). Une alternative au dualisme État-Marché: l'économie collaborative, questions pratiques et épistémologiques, 1–21. Retrieved from https://halshs.archives-ouvertes.fr/halshs-01249308/

Vargo, S. L., & Lusch, R. F. (2004). Evolving to a new dominant logic. *Journal of Marketing, 68*(1), 1–17. https://doi.org/10.1509/jmkg.68.1.1.24036

Veen, E. J. (2019). Fostering community values through meal sharing with strangers. *Sustainability, 11*(7), 2121.

Williamson, J., & Hassanli, N. (2022). Sharing, caring, learning: Role of local food in domestic trips. *Tourism Analysis, 27*(1), 107–111. https://doi.org/10.3727/108354220X15987151867890

Withlocals (2022). *About Withlocals*. Retrieved from www.withlocals.com/info/about-withlocals.

Zago, A., Sales. G., & Oliveira, P. (2013). Eventos Culturais e Stakeholders: A Gastronomia Como Fator Promocional do Turismo no Festival Revelando São Paulo. *Rosa dos Ventos, 5*(2), 333–348.

12 Health and Safety Issues in Food and Beverage Tourism

Alicia Orea-Giner

Introduction

The tourism sector has seen the current trends among travellers eager to spend more time and money on distinctive food and beverage experiences (Okumus, 2021). In previous research, food experiences have also been demonstrated to impact travel satisfaction, vacation well-being, and inclination to return to a place (Andersson et al., 2017; Kim et al., 2011; Tsai & Wang, 2017).

Tourism is concerned about actual and perceived safety and health risks (Pendergast, 2021). Food safety is one of the most significant aspects of the gastronomic experience, and it is an important consideration in potential consumers' decision-making process (Lee et al., 2019; Maclaurin, 2004; Yeung & Yee, 2013). The individual's impression of the existence of safety in food and the likelihood and severity of health repercussions of eating it is known as food safety risk perception (Machado Nardi et al., 2020; Schroeder et al., 2007).

The worldwide epidemic has raised awareness of the risk of transmission via surfaces in food establishments and human closeness (Pendergast, 2021). According to Bae and Chang (2021), the magnitude of the effect and risks associated with COVID-19 is unprecedented in human history. Due to the impact, travel risk perception and anxiety have grown (Pendergast, 2021). Management should address the fear of COVID-19 since it lowers consumer satisfaction and behavioural intention (Rehman et al., 2021). Customer satisfaction is critical in sustaining long-term connections between restaurants and consumers (Rehman et al., 2021).

This chapter aims to analyse the process of change that the providers of food services have undergone due to the pandemic and the influence of safety rules, and allergen and cross-contamination control protocols, on the experience in food and beverage tourism. To this end, academic articles and COVID-19, allergen and cross-contamination control protocols are analysed, as well as qualitative online interviews with restaurants applying these protocols.

DOI: 10.4324/9781003282532-16

Food Safety and Health Issues in Food Tourism Services

The hospitality catering industry is part of the catering sector, and the most important and delicate point is the health of the guests in this sector (Garcia et al., 2020). Okumus (2021) highlights that one of the key themes linked to food tourism is food safety challenges.

The implications of food safety issues in travel and tourism research have been examined in several studies (Cui et al., 2016; Fuchs & Reichel, 2011). To acquire the most helpful, trustworthy information, consumers are likely to assess the significance, quality and reliability of the information offered by each information source (Gursoy, 2019).

Food safety is very important in the hospitality industry, as failure to follow the rules can contaminate food and cause illness to visitors. In the food service industry, organisational food safety culture has been identified as an essential risk factor for predicting foodborne disease outbreaks (Clayton & Griffith, 2008). Non-compliance with food safety strategies at every stage of the food supply chain, such as poor food handling practices, wrong manufacturing process, unfair agricultural practices, inefficient transportation system, inefficient marketing practices, and poor hygiene, lead to food contamination with microbes (Carrasco et al., 2012; Legnani et al., 2004). Foodservice staff's crucial roles and duties in avoiding foodborne disease outbreaks have been documented (Roberts et al., 2008). Poor personal hygiene, time and temperature abuse, and cross-contamination are the most critical variables linked to foodborne infections (Abidin et al., 2013).

The World Health Organization (WHO) is committed to contributing to the global prevention, detection and response to public health threats posed by unsafe food. The ISO 22000 Food Safety System (ISO, 2018) is an effective and essential food safety practice that actively eliminates microbiological, physical and chemical hazards in the food and beverage industry. Regulation EU 1169/2011 establishes the framework for consumer protection around food information at the European Union level. National and international authorities must monitor compliance with these rules (European Union, 2011).

Food Consumers' Approach

Food and drinks produced by established sanitary standards are critical to the health and satisfaction of consumers at food and beverage establishments. Good health and safety practices are not only crucial for the protection of people in the hospitality industry, but they are also an essential aspect of good customer service: those who work in restaurants, bars or pubs have an additional responsibility to ensure that the food is safe to eat and prepared hygienically. International travellers sometimes become ill because of ingesting contaminated food or food prepared under questionable sanitary conditions (Lee et al., 2019). One place that has been implicated in these foodborne illnesses is food service establishments (Medus et al., 2010).

166 *Alicia Orea-Giner*

Some dietary requirements related to food consumption are linked to cultural or religious aspects. Considering that food taboos are common in all human societies, context is vital when it comes to the acceptance of food. Ethical consumption deals with people making consumption decisions based on moral beliefs (Kittler & Sucher, 2004; Makäniemi et al., 2011; Meyer-Rochow, 2009), and considering this aspect we can identify halal food or kosher food.

Consumers also encounter a high degree of performance risk related to tourism services in the case of suffering from illnesses related to food (Fuentes-Moraleda et al., 2022; Muñoz-Mazón et al., 2021). For those travellers with dietary requirements linked to food allergies, intolerances, chronic illnesses, and other dietary requirements, food safety is a crucial concern (Getz & Robinson, 2014). Travelling overseas is challenging for these individuals, who must prepare carefully and adhere to self-imposed limitations to minimise danger (Barnett et al., 2012). There are five risk characteristics that individuals with specific food requirements need to face when planning a trip: dread, control over risk, framing effects, willingness to take risk and tolerance level of exposure (Yeung & Yee, 2020).

Another important aspect related to the consumer perspective is that COVID-19 has generated in some people travel anxiety, which will need behavioural changes (Bratić et al., 2021). COVID-19 causes an adverse emotional condition that captures depression and stress due to the awareness of possible outcomes (Ahorsu et al., 2020; Rehman et al., 2021). Even tourists satisfied with local food can be afraid of COVID-19. It damages the relationship between tourists' satisfaction and behavioural intention (Luo & Lam, 2020). Because of this fact, COVID-19 food safety measures must be considered. These actions can also avoid other types of food risks because these measures are based on high hygienic practices and control of food processing.

COVID-19 Food Safety Measures in Food Tourism Services

COVID-19 has had a significant influence on health and food systems. The pandemic has highlighted our current food safety and handling standards and educated the public about the necessary safety measures. The COVID-19 pandemic has affected how we produce, manage and sell food to ensure future human health. The development and implementation of adequate surveillance systems that can be used to evaluate and quantify the impact of COVID-19-related changes in food safety and public health practices will accurately assess the positive and negative effects of changes in our food security systems in connection with the COVID-19 pandemic (Trmcic et al., 2021).

Regarding COVID-19 control in food services, there is no indication that the virus is spread by food nor that it can be reproduced in food. COVID-19, on the other hand, is transmitted by respiratory droplets that develop while coughing or sneezing and settle on objects and surfaces (Jayaweera et al.,

Health and Safety Issues in Food and Beverage Tourism   167

2020). Because of the virus's persistence, food safety and hygiene demand extra attention regarding COVID-19 transmission. As a result, good cleaning and hygiene measures are essential for preventing the virus from spreading through culinary venues and experiences (Pendergast, 2021).

The worldwide pandemic may have boosted awareness of purposeful efforts to prevent the undesirable pandemic virus transmissions, such as improving food safety and cleanliness. Wiping down surfaces, providing hand sanitisers, wearing gloves, and having food workers wash and sanitise their hands more frequently would enhance food safety and prevent foodborne diseases (Pendergast, 2021).

Health agencies have developed various techniques and preventative measures to avoid the spread of COVID-19. When suffering from COVID-19 symptoms, it is critical to maintain a good diet and keep active. Online nutrition education treatments that attempt to influence behaviour might be beneficial (Mumena, 2021). Because consuming fruits and vegetables can help people prevent health problems, including heart disease, obesity and cancer (Slavin & Lloyd, 2012), tourists request more fruits and vegetables in local recipes (Bansah et al., 2021).

Considering all these aspects, it is possible to analyse the changes that have occurred in food service providers due to the COVID-19 pandemic, as well as to relate all the safety measures that have been implemented to other aspects such as allergen control and cross-contamination.

Methodology

This book chapter is based on a literature review and qualitative methods. The first part of this research consists of developing a literature review based on academic articles published about food safety in tourism services, considering the most relevant papers as well as recent publications. The second part of this research is based on a deductive approach by conducting 10 online surveys with staff from restaurants specialised in allergen and cross-contamination control. These restaurants apply strict protocols and serve as a good practice example.

Design and Qualitative Approach

The study adopts a qualitative approach through an online qualitative structured survey with open questions. Previous research about restaurant services used online surveys (Liu & Tse, 2018; Sung et al., 2021). Qualitative surveys can give detailed accounts of the context that qualitative researchers are focused on (Braun et al., 2021). They are self-administered, with all participants receiving the same set of questions in the same sequence. Instead of picking from predetermined response alternatives, participants type their comments in their own words (Braun & Clarke, 2013). Even if individual replies are brief, qualitative survey datasets can give richness and depth when considered in their totality (Braun et al., 2021).

Online Qualitative Survey Design and Distribution

The online qualitative survey was divided into the following blocks: (1) COVID-19 protocols and food safety (Bansah et al., 2021; Bratić et al., 2021; Jayaweera et al., 2020; Mumena, 2021; Pendergast, 2021; Sung et al., 2021; Trmcic et al., 2021); (2) allergens and cross-contamination control (Abidin et al., 2013; Carrasco et al., 2012; Cui et al., 2016; Fuentes-Moraleda et al., 2022; Garcia et al., 2020; Legnani et al., 2004; Machado Nardi et al., 2020; Roberts et al., 2008; Schroeder et al., 2007; Yeung & Yee, 2013; Yeung & Yee, 2020).

This research is based on purposive sampling. Purposive sampling should maximise the breadth and variety of ideas (Rossiter, 2011). The researcher made a list of restaurants by searching restaurants on Instagram using different keywords (allergens, gluten-free and vegan) to make a list of restaurants specialised in allergens and cross-contamination control (Spain). The researcher compiled 142 names and contacted all of them. These restaurants were contacted to participate by using Instagram.

Participants

The final sample comprises ten restaurant staff specialised in allergens and cross-contamination control (Spain). Each restaurant has been assigned a code to preserve their anonymity and facilitate identifying their opinion and contribution during the qualitative analysis. For instance, the code for the first restaurant participating is R1.

Analysis

The protocols and the qualitative data were analysed manually using a deductive approach (Bingham & Witkowsky, 2021). The results are contrasted with previous studies and protocols about COVID-19 avoidance, and allergen and cross-contamination control, included considering their worldwide application, focusing our attention on WHO, FAO and UNWTO publications.

Results

The following section presents the principal points regarding COVID-19, allergens and cross-contamination control protocols for restaurants considering the results obtained.

COVID-19 Protocols and Food Safety

The COVID-19 protocols applied to catering were developed considering the fundamental safety measures to prevent the transmission of COVID-19 both in the kitchen and in serving the public. These protocols considered the WHO and FAO guidelines (2020), and each country published their catering protocols

Health and Safety Issues in Food and Beverage Tourism 169

considering these basic guidelines. The catering services had the following basic recommendations (WHO & FAO, 2020):

- Training the staff on food hygiene principles.
- Staff who are feeling unwell should stay at home.
- Staff must use personal protective equipment (mask and gloves).
- Frequent use of alcohol-based hand sanitisers.
- Handwashing and sanitation at all food processing, production and marketing stages. It means following strict hygiene and sanitation procedures. Frequent cleaning and disinfection of work surfaces and touchpoints. Alcohol-based sanitisers disinfectants must be used in concentrations of 70–80%.
- Physical separation with respect to the staff. Maintaining distance at workstations, restricting the number of employees in the food preparation area, and dividing employees into working groups to allow less interaction.
- Physical separation between consumers, and hand sanitisers available for consumers.
- Delivery service measures. Drivers must be aware of maintaining a good level of personal cleanliness and wearing clean protective equipment. Food must be kept safe from contamination and isolated from other items that might cause contamination. Drivers must also keep all transportation containers clean and disinfected.

FAO published an updated guide in 2021, highlighting that food safety practices in food premises should continue to adhere consistently to all applicable food hygiene standards.

Considering other protocols to prevent the spread of COVID-19, the Inter-American Development Bank published a complete document considering the principal risk aspects. This publication counts with the support of the World Tourism Organization (UNWTO). The parts contemplated in this document that add more information are (IDB, 2021):

- Air renewal should be ensured in all the spaces.
- The importance of waste management.
- The need to control and monitor workers' common areas.
- Buffet services should be given totally or partially in outside areas.
- Maintaining the safety distance and using contactless payment methods.

The most interesting aspect highlighted in this document is the identification of the central COVID-19 infection risk nodes at restaurants and their level of coverage (low, medium and high). These nodes are represented in Figure 12.1 (IBD, 2021):

Implementing these protocols to prevent the spread of COVID-19 in catering services was preceded by a period of assessment and adaptation. During strict containment in March 2020, restaurants were not allowed to offer their services. Subsequently, delivery services started to be activated strictly following

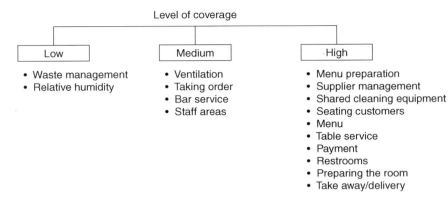

Figure 12.1 COVID-19 infection risk nodes at restaurants considering the level of coverage with the application of COVID-19 protocols
Source: Elaborated by the authors based on IBD (2021)

the protocol. In the following narrative, it is possible to see how in these uncertain times, catering services have been adapted to the new situation beyond the application of COVID-19 protocols:

> During the first few months of uncertainty, we had to make do, and we implemented the delivery service early on to be able to invoice in some way. In addition, we reinvented ourselves with deliveries to remote areas ... We had to start cutting costs of suppliers that were not optimal. It was not all bad because it helped us avoid waste.
>
> (R3)

> COVID-19 forced us to reinvent our previous business, and our restaurant was born because of that. In the beginning, it was 100% delivery and take-away services.
>
> (R6)

The application of these measures has changed according to the socio-sanitary situation, with a reduction or increase in capacity and the use of masks by diners except for eating food or non-use due to non-complete use inside the establishment. However, food safety measures in the kitchen are still in place. Although it is possible to remove the mask altogether, its use is recommended in case of symptoms of any kind of illness by kitchen staff. The following statement shows how in catering services, this is a fundamental aspect:

> We have followed the recommendations of the health authorities.
>
> (R6)

Our staff continue to wear face masks and will do so until we deem it safe for our employees and customers.

(R3)

We believe that masks and hand gel remain as measures until the end of the pandemic. COVID-19 measures are a barrier against the spread of other respiratory transmitted diseases.

(R10)

According to the participants, these measures will remain stable and will continue to be used by the restaurants, even if the masks are removed. These are measures that ensure the safety of staff and customers, as can be seen from the following statements:

COVID-19 has changed us a lot. We think about protecting ourselves, and especially about taking care to maintain maximum hygiene in food handling and how vulnerable we are to infecting each other with life-threatening diseases. We must all take care of each other.

(R2)

Eliminating gloves in food handling is essential to increase hygiene as in many cases workers wearing gloves relax food safety measures. However, constant hand cleaning minimises the risk of contamination.

(R3)

I think it is a good idea to drop the measures for general hygiene and to avoid bacteria.

(R5)

Allergens and Cross-Contamination Protocols

Practitioners, customers, the restaurant business and the government, through laws, are all important participants in reducing food-allergic reactions in restaurants (Carter et al., 2020). WHO and FAO adopted the Code of Practice on food allergen management for food business operators in 2020. This document highlights that the most common food allergies are provoked by a variety of proteins presented in the following foods and derived products: cereals containing gluten, crustaceans, eggs, fish, milk, peanuts, soybeans and tree nuts.

The possible cross-contamination sources include the following steps (WHO & FAO, 2020): (1) during food processing, (2) during the point of purchase, (3) during food preparation, and (4) food placement. Concerning restaurants, the ingredients and products used must be carefully selected and stored. Products and food together present a higher risk of cross-contamination (WHO & FAO, 2020). The following quote explains how the purchase process works in these types of restaurants:

172   *Alicia Orea-Giner*

> In our establishment, the entire menu is gluten-free. We shop as if it were for our own home. We take a good look at every ingredient, and if we have any doubts, we don't buy the product.
>
> (R2)

Some strategies used by restaurants to reduce the presence of allergens such as gluten include the use of spreadsheets to keep up to date with the products used in the kitchen and their allergens. Moreover, the most followed way to avoid allergens and cross-contamination is to stop buying products that contain those ingredients and the use of separate cooking tools and areas. The following sentences summarise the techniques used during this process in restaurants to offer allergen and cross-contamination free options:

> The use of datasheets, certified ingredients, general hygiene and separate areas for different types of food are essential.
>
> (R5)

> We purchase certified ingredients that are susceptible to gluten. We reduce the purchase of gluten-containing products and isolate these products. In addition, we have separate fryers, steamers and utensils.
>
> (R10)

Considering that allergen-free restaurants have to follow a strict protocol to control the presence of allergens and guarantee that the food is free of cross-contamination, some restaurants can opt to hire people suffering from allergies because it simplifies the training of the staff due to their previous knowledge and concern about these illnesses. The following quote is a good example of this type of strategy:

> Our protocol is rigorous. We always hire empathic staff and even sufferers from allergies so that they understand it perfectly.
>
> (R7)

Some restaurants highlight the role of associations focused on these illnesses. For example, coeliac disease associations work a lot to offer training and information to the restaurants. Moreover, these associations can certify with a label that the restaurant is supported by the association, as the following quote says:

> As always, we are a restaurant that complies with allergen control regulations from the start of production to the end of service, which is why we are certified gluten-free by the celiac association.
>
> (R8)

One type of restaurant that focuses on offering a high allergen and cross-contamination control system is those restaurants that offer gluten-free options or have an entirely gluten-free menu. In the case of the former, it is more challenging to control cross-contamination, and, in many cases, they have two separate kitchens. In addition, these types of establishments often offer other allergen-free options and vegetarian and vegan options. The following sentences show an interest in providing a high-quality service and following a rigorous allergen and cross-contamination control protocol:

> Regarding gluten, we have no cross-contamination because we are 100% gluten-free. Until now, we have not had any type of cross-contamination about dairy products, but with the souffle cake that we have incorporated, and which does contain dairy products, we have had to take extreme precautions. One of the measures we have taken is that on the day we bake this cake, no other sweet is baked, or if it is, it is the last one to be baked. Regarding the handling, knives and kitchen palettes are cleaned with every cut of cake to avoid risks of contamination for those allergic to milk protein.
>
> (R3)

> In the buffets, food can easily become contaminated because other dishes may be nearby. We give personalised attention to people who indicate that they are allergic or suffer from coeliac disease.
>
> (R7)

> The allergen information is always up to date. Controlling cross-contamination is relatively simple, I only have one product containing gluten, the bread, which is at the opposite end of the kitchen and from there it is only moved to the table, always considering that it must not cross any other food. We always prepare and serve the celiac tables or diners first.
>
> (R9)

This offer focused on allergen and cross-contamination control attracts a type of tourist who needs a high level of food safety and carefully plans his holidays considering the appropriate catering service. This means that the search for information on allergen-free restaurants and establishments is essential, as this is the first thing they do before starting to organise other aspects of the trip. In the following sentence, it is possible to see how this type of tourist carries out an exhaustive search for information:

> The allergic tourist plans his holidays according to his allergies ... almost before the accommodation.
>
> (R1)

> We certainly believe that being gluten-free and practically dairy-free makes national and international tourists seek us out. In addition, the addition of vegan dishes to our menu has also contributed (which I haven't mentioned

but was another of the improvements that COVID-19 has given us in terms of reinventing ourselves). One of the owners is celiac, and from her own experience, she knows that when you go to a new destination, one of the first things a celiac or food-allergic person does is look for places where they can eat safely. In addition, our offer is unique, and we believe it will be of interest to many people who have never been able to try Gyozas or Takoyaki before, for example.

(R3)

To attract tourists and offer a quality service, it is necessary to follow a strict protocol and, in addition, to have quality seals for allergen control. This provides the potential customer with greater security. In addition, this type of customer plans their trips conscientiously, so it is recommended to give them as much information as possible about the food preparation process and the updated menu on social networks and the restaurant's website. The following sentence shows an example of making information available on the establishment's website:

In our case, we put every ingredient of the product in bold on the website, although it is not mandatory. We also answer all queries from customers regarding allergens and cross-contamination.

(R8)

Conclusion

Managers might customise their efforts to foster a favourable food safety culture to the demographics of their workforce (Abidin et al., 2013). COVID-19 protocols applied to restaurants are based on social distancing and food, hand, respiratory, surface and ventilation hygiene (Pendergast, 2021). COVID-19 protocols implemented in restaurants are fundamental to avoid its dissemination and its application is linked with improving cleanliness and, consequently, reducing other disease transmission. Ensuring food safety is closely linked to hygiene in the restaurant, being one of the fundamental aspects of avoiding other diseases transmitted through food. This strict cleaning protocol is also related to greater cross-contamination control in the case of allergens and material hygiene and staff concern for keeping their hands and uniforms clean.

In the case of allergens and cross-contamination, following a strict and specific protocol on an allergen-by-allergen basis is necessary. However, general guidelines are presented in the Figure 12.2, combined with the measures to prevent the transmission of COVID-19.

Customers continue having food allergy episodes despite warning servers, cooks and chefs about their allergies, implying underlying issues with the line of communication among restaurant personnel or employees' lack of knowledge about ingredients (Kwon & Lee, 2012).

Health and Safety Issues in Food and Beverage Tourism   175

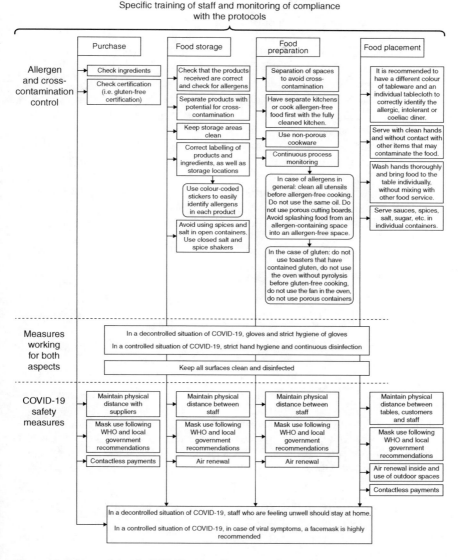

Figure 12.2 A model of COVID-19, allergen and cross-contamination avoidance protocols in food tourism services

Providing restaurant workers with food allergen management resources, such as ingredient lists, specialised kitchen equipment, documented plans, and food allergy training, is critical to creating good attitudes about tolerating food allergies (McAdams et al., 2018). Allergens' management requires a continuous

176 *Alicia Orea-Giner*

training process for staff, so it is necessary to invest in this aspect and review the process from food purchasing through storage, food preparation, and food placement. Previous research identified a general lack of access to critical food allergy risk management materials and training, considering that there are differences between restaurant styles of operation (McAdams et al., 2018).

In case of offering gluten-free options, it is recommended to obtain a gluten-free certificate to reduce the uncertainty and increase food safety. It includes four different aspects: food legislation, food safety procedure compliance, cross-contamination management, and restaurant and foodservice training (Muñoz-Mazón et al., 2021). These certificates are provided by coeliac and non-coeliac gluten sensitivity associations, which offer training and subsequently include the restaurant in the list of eligible restaurants (Muñoz-Mazón et al., 2021).

Food safety is essential in the hospitality sector, as failing to follow the protocols might cause serious health issues for the tourists. Organizational food safety culture concerning food tourism services must consider all the aspects mentioned above to guarantee the good condition of the food on tourism services.

Food for Thought

- How can COVID-19 protocols ensure food safety from other viral diseases?
- What advantages can restaurants have when implementing allergen and cross-contamination protocols?
- Imagine you are the manager of a restaurant. How do you think you could ensure that these protocols are followed at all times?

References

Abidin, Ungku Fatimah Ungku Zainal, Arendt, S. W., & Strohbehn, C. H. (2013). Exploring the Culture of Food Safety: The Role of Organizational Influencers in Motivating Employees' Safe Food-Handling Practices. *Journal of Quality Assurance in Hospitality & Tourism, 14*(4), 321–343. http://doi.org/10.1080/15280 08X.2013.802587

Ahorsu, D. K., Lin, C., Imani, V., Saffari, M., Griffiths, M. D., & Pakpour, A. H. (2020). The Fear of COVID-19 Scale: Development and Initial Validation. *International Journal of Mental Health and Addiction.* http://doi.org/10.1007/s11469-020-00270-8

Andersson, T. D., Mossberg, L., & Therkelsen, A. (2017). Food and tourism synergies: perspectives on consumption, production and destination development. *Scandinavian Journal of Hospitality and Tourism, 17*(1), 1–8. https://doi.org/10.1080/15022250.2016.1275290

Bae, S. Y., & Chang, P. (2021). The effect of coronavirus disease-19 (COVID-19) risk perception on behavioural intention towards 'untact' tourism in South Korea during the first wave of the pandemic (March 2020). *Current Issues in Tourism, 24*(7), 1017–1035. https://doi.org/10.1080/13683500.2020.1798895

Bansah, A. K., Adam, I., & Hiamey, S. E. (2021). Segments of cognitive responses towards local food safety concerns amongst international students in Ghana: Segments of cognitive responses towards local food safety concerns amongst international students in Ghana. *African Journal of Hospitality and Tourism Management, 3*(1), 20–43. https://doi.org/10.47963/ajthm.v3i1.252

Barnett, J., Botting, N., Gowland, M. H., & Lucas, J. S. (2012). The strategies that peanut and nut-allergic consumers employ to remain safe when travelling abroad. *Clinical and Translational Allergy, 2*(1), 12. https://doi.org/10.1186/2045-7022-2-12

Bingham, A. J., & Witkowsky, P. (2021). Deductive and inductive approaches to qualitative data analysis. In C. Vanover, P. Mihas & J. Saldana (Eds.), *Analyzing and interpreting qualitative data: After the interview* (pp. 133–146). Sage.

Bratić, M., Radivojević, A., Stojiljković, N., Simović, O., Juvan, E., Lesjak, M., & Podovšovnik, E. (2021). *Should I Stay or Should I Go? Tourists' COVID-19 Risk Perception and Vacation Behavior Shift.* https://doi.org/10.3390/su13063573

Braun, V., & Clarke, V. (2013). *Successful qualitative research: A practical guide for beginners.* Sage.

Braun, V., Clarke, V., Boulton, E., Davey, L., & McEvoy, C. (2021). The online survey as a qualitative research tool. *International Journal of Social Research Methodology, 24*(6), 641–654.

Carrasco, E., Morales-Rueda, A., & García-Gimeno, R. M. (2012). Cross-contamination and recontamination by Salmonella in foods: A review. *Food Research International, 45*(2), 545–556. https://doi.org/10.1016/j.foodres.2011.11.004

Carter, C. A., Pistiner, M., Wang, J., & Sharma, H. P. (2020). Food Allergy in Restaurants Work Group Report. *The Journal of Allergy and Clinical Immunology: In Practice, 8*(1), 70–74. https://doi.org/10.1016/j.jaip.2019.09.013

Clayton, D. A., & Griffith, C. J. (2008). Efficacy of an extended theory of planned behaviour model for predicting caterers' hand hygiene practices. *International Journal of Environmental Health Research, 18*(2), 83–98. 10.1080/09603120701358424

Cui, F., Liu, Y., Chang, Y., Duan, J., & Li, J. (2016). An overview of tourism risk perception. *Natural Hazards, 82*(1), 643–658. 10.1007/s11069-016-2208-1

European Union. (2011). European Union No 1169/2011 of the European Parliament and of the Council of 25 October 2011 on the provision of food information to consumers, http://data.europa.eu/eli/reg/2011/1169/oj

FAO. (2021). COVID-19: Guidance for preventing transmission of COVID-19 within food businesses. Rome: https://doi.org/10.4060/cb6030en

Fuchs, G., & Reichel, A. (2011). An exploratory inquiry into destination risk perceptions and risk reduction strategies of first time vs. repeat visitors to a highly volatile destination. *Tourism Management, 32*(2), 266–276. https://doi.org/10.1016/j.tourman.2010.01.012

Fuentes-Moraleda, L., Muñoz-Mazón, A., Santiago-Rincón, C., & Orea-Giner, A. (2022). Defining risk reduction strategies for tourists with specific food needs: a qualitative approach. *British Food Journal, 124*(2), 590–612. https://doi.org/10.1108/BFJ-04-2021-0398

Garcia, S. N., Osburn, B. I., & Jay-Russell, M. (2020). One Health for Food Safety, Food Security, and Sustainable Food Production. *Frontiers in Sustainable Food Systems, 4.* www.frontiersin.org/article/10.3389/fsufs.2020.00001

Getz, D., & Robinson, R. N. S. (2014). Foodies and Food Events. *Scandinavian Journal of Hospitality and Tourism, 14*(3), 315–330. https://doi.org/10.1080/15022250.2014.946227

Gursoy, D. (2019). A critical review of determinants of information search behavior and utilization of online reviews in decision making process (invited paper for 'luminaries' special issue of International Journal of Hospitality Management).

178 *Alicia Orea-Giner*

International Journal of Hospitality Management, 76, 53–60. https://doi.org/10.1016/j.ijhm.2018.06.003

IDB. (2021). *Recommendations to Minimize COVID-19 Transmission in Restaurants.* http://dx.doi.org/10.18235/0003526

ISO. (2018). ISO 22000:2018 Food safety management systems—Requirements for any organization in the food chain. www.iso.org/standard/65464.html

Jayaweera, M., Perera, H., Gunawardana, B., & Manatunge, J. (2020). Transmission of COVID-19 virus by droplets and aerosols: A critical review on the unresolved dichotomy. *Environmental Research, 188*, 109819. https://doi.org/10.1016/j.envres.2020.109819

Kim, Y. H., Kim, M., & Goh, B. K. (2011). An examination of food tourist's behavior: Using the modified theory of reasoned action. *Tourism Management, 32*(5), 1159–1165. https://doi.org/10.1016/j.tourman.2010.10.006

Kittler, P. G., & Sucher, K. P. (2004). Accent on Taste: An Applied Approach to Multicultural Competency. *Diabetes Spectrum, 17*(4), 200–204. https://doi.org/10.2337/diaspect.17.4.200

Kwon, J. H., & Lee, Y. M. (2012). Exploration of past experiences, attitudes and preventive behaviors of consumers with food allergies about dining out: a focus group study. *Food Protection Trends, 32*(12), 736–746.

Lee, Y., Pennington-Gray, L., & Kim, J. (2019). Does location matter? Exploring the spatial patterns of food safety in a tourism destination. *Tourism Management, 71*, 18–33. https://doi.org/10.1016/j.tourman.2018.09.016

Legnani, P., Leoni, E., Berveglieri, M., Mirolo, G., & Alvaro, N. (2004). Hygienic control of mass catering establishments, microbiological monitoring of food and equipment. *Food Control, 15*(3), 205–211. https://doi.org/10.1016/S0956-7135(03)00048-3

Liu, P., & Tse, E. C. (2018). Exploring factors on customers' restaurant choice: an analysis of restaurant attributes. *British Food Journal, 120*(10), 2289–2303. https://doi.org/10.1108/BFJ-10-2017-0561

Luo, J. M., & Lam, C. F. (2020). Travel Anxiety, Risk Attitude and Travel Intentions towards "Travel Bubble" Destinations in Hong Kong: Effect of the Fear of COVID-https://doi.org/1910.3390/ijerph17217859

Machado Nardi, V. A., Teixeira, R., Ladeira, W. J., & de Oliveira Santini, F. (2020). A meta-analytic review of food safety risk perception. *Food Control, 112*, 107089. https://doi.org/10.1016/j.foodcont.2020.107089

Maclaurin, T. L. (2004). The Importance of Food Safety in Travel Planning and Destination Selection. *Journal of Travel & Tourism Marketing, 15*(4), 233–257. 10.1300/J073v15n04_02

Mäkiniemi, J., Pirttilä-Backman, A., & Pieri, M. (2011). Ethical and unethical food. Social representations among Finnish, Danish and Italian students. *Appetite, 56*(2), 495–502. https://doi.org/10.1016/j.appet.2011.01.023

McAdams, B., Deng, A., & MacLaurin, T. (2018). Food allergy knowledge, attitudes, and resources of restaurant employees. *British Food Journal, 120*(11), 2681–2694. https://doi.org/10.1108/BFJ-01-2018-0028

Medus, C., Smith, K. E., Bender, J. B., Leano, F., & Hedberg, C. W. (2010). Salmonella infections in food workers identified through routine public health surveillance in Minnesota: impact on outbreak recognition. *Journal of Food Protection, 73*(11), 2053–2058.

Meyer-Rochow, V. (2009). Food taboos: their origins and purposes. *Journal of Ethnobiology and Ethnomedicine, 5*(1), 18. https://doi.org/10.1186/1746-4269-5-18

Mumena, W. (2021). Impact of COVID-19 curfew on eating habits, eating frequency, and weight according to food security status in Saudi Arabia: a retrospective study. *Prog.Nutr, 22*, e2020075. https://doi.org/10.23751/pn.v22i3.9315

Muñoz-Mazón, A., Orea-Giner, A., Fernández Muñoz, J. J., Santiago, C., & Fuentes-Moraleda, L. (2021). Risk perception before travelling: solutions for consumers with vulnerabilities. *Journal of Services Marketing, 35(6)*, 791–806. https://doi.org/10.1108/JSM-07-2020-0304

Okumus, B. (2021). Food tourism research: a perspective article. *Tourism Review, 76*(1), 38–42. https://doi.org/10.1108/TR-11-2019-0450

Pendergast, D. (2021). Food Safety and Hygiene. In J.Wilks, D. Pendergast, P.A. Leggat & D. Morgan (Eds.), *Tourist Health, Safety and Wellbeing in the New Normal* (pp. 145–165). Singapore: Springer. https://doi.org/10.1007/978-981-16-5415-2_6

Rehman, U., Shahnawaz, M. G., Khan, N. H., Kharshiing, K. D., Khursheed, M., Gupta, K., Kashyap, D., & Uniyal, R. (2021). Depression, anxiety and stress among Indians in times of COVID-19 lockdown. *Community Mental Health Journal, 57*(1), 42–48. https://doi.org/10.1007/s10597-020-00664-x

Roberts, K. R., Barrett, B. B., Howells, A. D., Shanklin, C. W., Pilling, V. K., & Brannon, L. A. (2008). Food safety training and foodservice employees' knowledge and behavior. *Food Protection Trends, 28*(4), 252–260. http://hdl.handle.net/2097/806

Rossiter, J. R. (2011). Qualitative Research from a C-OAR-SE Perspective. *Measurement for the Social Sciences* (pp. 115–139). Springer. https://doi.org/10.1007/978-1-4419-7158-6_8

Schroeder, T. C., Tonsor, G. T., Pennings, J. M. E., & Mintert, J. (2007). Consumer Food Safety Risk Perceptions and Attitudes: Impacts on Beef Consumption across Countries. *The B. E. Journal of Economic Analysis & Policy, 7*(1). https://doi.org/10.2202/1935-1682.1848

Slavin, J. L., & Lloyd, B. (2012). Health Benefits of Fruits and Vegetables. *Advances in Nutrition, 3*(4), 506–516. https://doi.org/10.3945/an.112.002154

Sung, Y.-K., Hu, H.-H., & King, B. (2021). Restaurant behaviors preventive and the role of media during a pandemic. *International Journal of Hospitality Management, 95*, 102906. https://doi.org/10.1016/j.ijhm.2021.102906

Trmcic, A., Demmings, E., Kniel, K., Wiedmann, M., & Alcaine, S. (2021). Food Safety and Employee Health Implications of COVID-19: A Review. *Journal of Food Protection, 84*(11), 1973–1989. https://doi.org/10.4315/JFP-21-201

Tsai, C., & Wang, Y. (2017). Experiential value in branding food tourism. *Journal of Destination Marketing & Management, 6*(1), 56–65. https://doi.org/10.1016/j.jdmm.2016.02.003

WHO & FAO. (2020). COVID-19 and food safety: guidance for food businesses. www.who.int/publications/i/item/covid-19-and-food-safety-guidance-for-food-businesses

Yeung, R. M. W., & Yee, W. M. S. (2013). Risk measurement framework. *British Food Journal, 115*(8), 1073–1089. https://doi.org/10.1108/BFJ-03-2011-0071

Yeung, R. M. W., & Yee, W. M. S. (2020). Travel destination choice: does perception of food safety risk matter? *British Food Journal, 122*(6), 1919–1934. https://doi.org/10.1108/BFJ-09-2018-0631

Part IV
Looking towards the Future

13 The Changing Face of Gourmet Tourism

Matthew J. Stone

Introduction

There are many connections between luxury experiences and travel, as travel was once an exclusive act for a moneyed class. Early food travel researchers (Hall & Sharples, 2003) proposed that those traveling with the primary motive to visit a specific restaurant, market or winery were participating in "gourmet (gastronomic) tourism." They categorized "culinary tourism" as tourism where food and drink was of more moderate interest to consumers.

However, these definitions (in which gourmet tourism was defined by motivation) did not catch on. World Food Travel Association (WFTA) research found that 80% of travelers have been motivated to take a trip or to visit a particular destination because of a culinary activity or attraction (Stone & Migacz, 2016), so using the term gourmet tourism to refer to food-motivated tourists no longer makes sense. Today, food travel, food tourism, gastronomic tourism, and culinary tourism are considered to be nearly synonymous, and gourmet tourism can be considered as a subset of food tourism.

While food travel may once have focused on fine-dining or gourmet experiences, today, "culinary tourism does not have to mean gourmet food. It is increasingly about unique and memorable experiences" (Gozzoli, 2012: 23). Stone et al. (2020) cautioned that "destinations that continue (or wish to) focus exclusively on gourmet experiences should think twice, as the size of the gourmet food-loving travel market is considerably smaller than the mainstream food travel market" (p. 173).

This chapter investigates the importance of *gourmet* in food tourism. First, the chapter explains how the definition of *gourmet* has changed. Then, using data from an international WFTA study of food travelers, psychographic segmentation is presented to better explain who identifies as a gourmet food traveler. Next is explored the popularity of fine-dining (gourmet) restaurant experiences among travelers, including the demographic attributes of fine-dining travelers and their other activities while traveling. Finally, a case study addresses the marketing of a destination (Houston, Texas) and how destinations can market gourmet experiences as part of a complete destination offering.

DOI: 10.4324/9781003282532-18

How Is Gourmet Defined?

When considering the gourmet food travel market segment, it is important to define *gourmet*. Traditionally, gourmet dining was an exclusive and expensive activity. The food magazine *Gourmet* focused on an upscale market segment and often featured travel stories focusing on food. American restaurant advertisements and hotel brochures from the 1950s to 1970s reflected well-dressed white couples dressed in suits and skirts being served by tuxedoed servers at white tablecloth restaurants. In these times, fine dining and gourmet could be considered synonymous, as (with some exceptions) high-quality food could not often be found at lower-priced establishments.

In recent decades, the farm-to-table movement and chef-driven restaurants have introduced quality food at lower price points, opening "gourmet" dining to a greater population of consumers. This suggests that all gourmet restaurants are not necessarily expensive, fine-dining establishments. The exclusivity of the term *gourmet* is further weakened by its overuse. American casual and quick service restaurant chains (which are definitely not fine-dining or chef-driven experiences) use the word *gourmet*. For example, there is a burger chain called Red Robin Gourmet Burgers and Brew, and Jimmy John's Sandwiches holds trademarks including the terms "World's greatest gourmet sandwiches."

Just as the availability of gourmet food in restaurants has changed through the years, the dictionary definition of *gourmet* has also changed. A 1963 dictionary (World Book, 1963) defined *gourmet* as "a person who is expert at judging and choosing fine foods, wines, etc.; epicure." This reflects a way of thinking that gourmet relates to luxury, upscale consumption.

Today, Merriam-Webster (2022) gives *gourmet* two definitions: 1) "a connoisseur of food and drink" (where *connoisseur* is defined as "an expert"); and 2) "of, relating to, or being high quality, expensive, or specialty food typically requiring elaborate and expert preparation." Breaking down this definition, it implies that a gourmet is a food and drink expert, although it is unclear exactly what makes one an expert. The traveler whose television is set to the Food Network may qualify as a gourmet, as may someone who loves dining out. When it comes to the dining experience, definition 2 expressly mentions three different features: high quality, and/or, expensive, and/or specialty. Based on this, gourmet would include not just fine dining (as it did in 1963), but also farm-to-table, and even specialty ethnic restaurants. Individuals may even have their own perceptions of *gourmet*—from their own identity as gourmets, from an aspiration to consume expensive meals.

While a full exploration of the connotations of *gourmet* is beyond this article, it can be concluded that a *gourmet* has changed from exclusively upscale experiences to also include high-quality and specialty dining. To avoid confusion, this paper uses "fine dining" to define upscale, high-quality, and expensive dining experiences. The word "gourmet" will be used to refer to a psychographic category of food travelers.

Who Identifies as a "Gourmet" Food Traveler?

WFTA research determined there are thirteen psychographic profiles of food travelers, called Psychoculinary® profiles (see Stone & Migacz, 2016). These include profiles such as *trendy* (for those who seek trendy, hip, and cool food and drink experiences), *social* (seeking social food and drink experiences), *innovative* (seeking to experiment and try new things), and *gourmet* (seeking fine dining and gourmet dining).

These profiles were explored in the WFTA's *2020 Food Travel Monitor* report (Stone et al., 2020). In late 2019, 4,554 travelers from six countries were surveyed using an international survey panel research company. Respondents were at least 18 years old and had taken an overnight trip or a trip of at least 80 km (50 miles) from home in the past year. The survey was conducted online with a sample of travelers which was balanced by generation (age) and gender.

Respondents were asked to identify the three Pscychoculinary profiles they most closely aligned with, acknowledging that individuals may identify as more than one psychographic profile. Results showed that "gourmet" ranked eighth in popularity among the thirteen Psychoculinary profiles. Travelers were much more likely to identify in other ways. In particular: 43% identified as eclectic (seeking a wide variety of experiences), 40% identified as authentic (seeking local food and drink prepared according to the recipes and traditions of the region), and 29% identified as localist (seeking locally-owned and operated restaurants and bars) (Stone et al., 2020). Only in France did gourmet travelers make up more than 25% of the respondents, where gourmet ranked behind only authentic and localist. In the United States, only 14.7% identified as gourmet travelers (see Table 13.1).

Table 13.1 Attributes of travelers related to gourmet food tourism

	All travelers	*Canada*	*Mexico*	*USA*	*France*	*United Kingdom*	*China*
Sample size (N=)	**4,554**	897	530	1,542	530	499	556
Identify as "gourmet" Psychoculinary profile	**19.1%**	18.1%	20.8%	14.7%	30.4%	16.0%	23.9%
Consider themselves knowledgeable about food and drink in general	**71.4%**	67.0%	79.2%	69.2%	73.4%	63.9%	82.2%
Visited a fine-dining (gourmet) restaurant in the past two years	**44.1%**	46.5%	48.5%	46.1%	42.3%	34.9%	40.5%

As previously mentioned, survey respondents selected three Psychoculinary profiles that best described them, so it could be determined what else interests gourmet travelers, besides just upscale, fine dining. Those identifying as gourmet food travelers were most likely to also identify as: authentic, eclectic, and innovative. This data is useful for marketing to gourmet food travelers. Showcasing experiences that connect travelers to the food and drink traditions of a region *(authentic) is* important. Likewise, gourmet travelers like a variety of different things *(eclectic)*. While Michelin-starred restaurants serving local cuisine can attract travelers, they are also looking to experiment with new cuisines, new restaurants, and unexpected experiences *(innovative)*. Here, destinations can focus on experiences other than just fine dining.

Do gourmet diners also identify as experts (or *connoisseurs,* based on the dictionary definition)? Eighty percent (80%) of gourmet travelers considered themselves to be knowledgeable about food and drink in general. However, results showed that over two-thirds (71.4%) of all travelers considered themselves knowledgeable about food and drink in general. Despite the fact that many travelers do not identify as gourmet, they still may be gourmets (based on the recent dictionary definition). Therefore, we cannot conclude that self-identified gourmets make up all or most of the food-passionate or food-educated market segment.

This leads us to a few conclusions. Being a gourmet is not central to the identity of many food travelers. Overall, travelers felt it was more important to seek out a variety of authentic experiences at locally-owned restaurants. A majority of travelers consider themselves knowledgeable about food and drink. However, less than a third consider themselves to be gourmet. Therefore, there seems to be a population of food-knowledgeable travelers who do not identify as gourmet. Based on the definitions and the data, it is troublesome to use the term *gourmet,* as there are many interpretations.

How Important Are Fine-Dining Restaurants to the Visitor Experience?

Many activities can typically be considered to be gourmet food travel activities, including wine tastings, gourmet food tours, and cooking classes. However, the most common gourmet experience may be to eat at fine-dining (often called gourmet) restaurants.

Gourmet restaurants can contribute greatly to attracting visitors. Batat (2021) studied Michelin-starred restaurants and found that they contribute to the "gastronomication" of rural destinations. They can also help to build destination brand awareness, contribute to media capital, and enhance the attractiveness of a destination. The destination brand was not build solely through gourmet local dining experiences, but also through staging and storytelling.

While fine-dining restaurants can attract travelers to a destination, it can also be said that travelers are vital to the financial health of fine-dining restaurants. The National Restaurant Association's (2020) research shows that in a typical pre-COVID year, an average of 41% of American fine-dining revenue is from travelers and visitors to the area. For about one-fourth of fine-dining restaurants, at least 60% of pre-COVID sales came from travelers and visitors. (It is important to note that many of these sales came from business travelers on expense accounts, not just leisure travelers). It does not seem possible that gourmet food travelers (who number less than 15% of American travelers) can account for all of these revenues.

Daries et al. (2018) found that there were two major segments of tourists visiting top-level restaurants. The first segment considered the culinary experience at the Michelin-starred restaurant as the main reason for visiting the destination, and the other segment considered their visit to the destination as the main reason for their trip. A major difference between the segments is that the Michelin-motivated travelers felt that a visit to a Michelin-starred restaurant could provide them with higher social status and social acceptance.

To investigate *gourmet* food tourism experiences, it may be most appropriate to use activity-based segmentation. This eliminates any confusion based on self-definition. Therefore, the study also asked if travelers have eaten at a fine-dining (gourmet) restaurant while traveling in the past two years. In this chapter, these individuals are called *fine-dining travelers*.

Stone et al. (2020) found that nearly half (46.2%) of American travelers had eaten at a fine-dining restaurant while traveling in the past two years. Less than one-fourth (22.6%) of these identified a gourmet Psychoculinary profile as one of their top three profiles. Details for other countries are listed in Table 13.1. Among gourmet food travelers, nearly two-thirds (65.5%) had eaten at a fine-dining restaurant. While this confirms that gourmets enjoy fine dining, it also shows that gourmet food travelers and fine-dining travelers are not the same.

Those identifying as gourmet travelers cannot be considered to be the same population as those eating at fine-dining restaurants, as a majority of travelers from all six countries who eat at fine-dining restaurants do not identify as gourmet. Clearly there are a lot more travelers visiting fine-dining restaurants than those identifying as gourmet travelers. This suggests that destinations should not focus solely on those who identify as gourmet.

What Are the Attributes of Travelers Who Dine at Fine-Dining Restaurants?

When considering the importance of gourmet restaurants to a destination, it seems better to investigate those who eat at fine-dining restaurants instead of just those who identify as gourmet. I consider the sample of American travelers who have eaten at a fine-dining (gourmet) restaurant when traveling in the past two years. Data show there are very few unique attributes based on demographics (see Table 13.2). The percentage of each generation who has recently eaten at a fine-dining restaurant is consistent across generations, and gender, age, and family status reveal little difference. This follows Barrère et al. (2014), which

188   *Matthew J. Stone*

Table 13.2 Percentage of American travelers in each category

	Sample size	Percentage who have eaten at a fine-dining restaurant while traveling in past two years	Percentage who are comfortable spending a significant amount of money on gourmet meals
U.S. travelers (total)	**N=1,542**	**46.1**	**47.4**
Female	N=825	47.6	46.1
Male	N=710	44.5	49.4
Have children under 18 at home	N=589	45.3	53.3
No children under 18 at home	N=953	46.6	43.8
Single	N=509	45.6	45.2
Married	N=865	48.2	49.9
In a relationship, but not married	N=150	38.7	42.7
Not a college graduate	N=475	39.6	44.8
College graduate	N=1062	49.0	48.7
By generation			
Boomers (born 1946–64)	N=296	48.0	31.1
Generation X (born 1965–80)	N=521	46.3	48.3
Millennials (born 1981–96)	N=595	45.2	52.6
Generation Z (born 1997–2001)★	N=130	45.4	56.9
By income level			
<$50,000	N=331	34.7	42.6
$50,000–99,999	N=572	42.3	50.3
$100,000–149,999	N=303	52.1	43.5
$150,000 & up	N=246	64.2	56.9

Note: For each category, sample size may differ because other/prefer not to say results are omitted.

★ Gen Z is a small sample because of the smaller population of this generation at the time of the survey

acknowledged the growth of a mass luxury segment in gastronomic tourism, in which upscale or luxury experiences are available to a larger range of travelers.

The demographic profile with the greatest difference is not surprising. American travelers with higher income and higher education (which is correlated with income) are more likely to have eaten at a fine-dining restaurant while traveling in the past two years (see Table 13.2). However, travelers from all income levels frequently participated in fine dining while traveling, providing further evidence to support Barrère et al.'s (2014) statement that the middle classes have regular or occasional access to the upper segments of tourism and gastronomy more than before.

To learn more about behavior, the survey asked if respondents are "comfortable spending a significant amount of money on gourmet meals" (see Table 13.2). Younger generations were more comfortable spending on gourmet meals. This may be because these generations are more interested in food overall

The Changing Face of Gourmet Tourism   189

(Stone et al., 2020). At all income levels, at least 40% of American travelers were comfortable spending a lot on gourmet meals. This indicates that gourmet dining is a preference for a broad range of travelers—not focused solely on income. It could be argued that these may be the passionate gourmets, rather than those who identify as gourmet (psychographic profile). Among all traveler types, there is a population in which fine (gourmet) dining appears to be an experience worth splurging on. There are certainly a large number of travelers participating in fine-dining and gourmet experiences, but it is difficult to define this as a homogeneous market segment.

What Other Food and Drink Activities Are Fine-Dining Travelers Doing While Traveling?

Travelers eat many meals in a day, and it is unlikely that all of their experiences are fine dining. Learning about what other activities that target markets participate in can help a destination to market effectively to these market segments. This shows what other food and drink activities fine-dining travelers participate in while traveling. This data can help destination marketers to understand a larger spectrum of activities that may entice gourmet and upscale travelers. Travelers were asked if they have participated in many different food and drink activities while traveling in the past two years. Table 13.3 shows the results.

Table 13.3 Participation in food/beverage/culinary activities on recent trips. Percentage of respondents who have participated in the following activities while traveling in the past two years

	Fine-dining travelers (N=2,008)	Other travelers (N=2,546)
Went to a restaurant for a memorable experience	71.4	49.8
Ate at a food truck, food cart, or food stall	44.7	37.5
Ate at a fine-dining (gourmet) restaurant	100.0	0
Ate or drank at a famous or landmark restaurant or bar	45.9	28.7
Took cooking classes	10.6	9.6
Participated in a food or beverage tour of a destination	21.9	16.2
Attended a food festival	30.3	21.8
Attended a beer festival	23.4	19.2
Attended a wine festival	21.2	12.0
Visited a winery or wine trail	27.6	15.5
Visited a brewery, taproom, or beer trail	20.2	14.3
Went to a distillery or a beverage trail (such as a whiskey trail)	18.5	11.0
Visited a farmers' market or agricultural fair	34.1	25.0
Visited a farm or orchard	26.9	18.2
Visited a food production facility or factory	20.3	12.0

190 *Matthew J. Stone*

One clear finding is that these fine-dining travelers are seeking memories when they travel. Over two-thirds have eaten at a restaurant for a memorable experience, compared with less than half of other travelers. It seems obvious that travelers want to make memories when they travel, but it is notable that they want to make their memories through food and drink. They are also eating at landmark restaurants. These findings imply that fine-dining travelers are planning ahead and learning about food and drink offerings prior to departure. To confirm this, a question asked: "Prior to traveling to a destination, I seek out detailed information about where to eat and drink." 73.0% of American fine-dining travelers agreed with this statement.

This data shows the variety of food and drink activities that destinations can market to supplement the fine-dining experience for travelers. In particular, these diners enjoy beverages (wine, beer, and distilleries) more than other travelers. They also enjoy events and festivals. When seeking to attract upscale food travelers, it seems to be essential to promote a collection of experiences—a varied assortment of passive and active.

Travelers who participate in fine-dining (gourmet) food and drink experiences enjoy a greater variety of food and drink experiences than other travelers. Therefore, the term *cultural omnivore* can be used for those who engage in fine dining. The term *cultural omnivore* originated in musicology. Musical tastes have been used to determine class distinctions (upper- versus lower-class), and it was often assumed there were "highbrow" and "lowbrow" segments. Peterson and Simkus (1992) found that those who participated in highbrow activities actually had a broad range of tastes and activities, and called these people cultural omnivores (in contrast to univores). A follow-up study (Peterson & Kern, 1996) found that omnivores had broadened their tastes. Even though not everything appeals to them, cultural omnivores are open to a great variety of activities.

This study shows that fine-dining travelers do not simply participate in upscale food and drink travel experiences. While some activities (such as winery visits and food tours) may be associated with highbrow consumption, others (such as eating at food trucks or visiting a brewery) may not be. The finding that fine-dining visitors are cultural omnivores shows their value to destinations beyond the smaller segment of self-identified gourmet travelers. Not only are fine-dining travelers spending money at upscale restaurants, they are participating in many food and drink travel activities. This suggests that, with a few possible exceptions, destinations should focus on a variety of experiences rather than focusing solely on fine dining.

Case Study: Houston (Texas), Culinary Capital of the South

Houston (Texas) is the fourth-largest city in the USA. Its evolution from oil city to foodie destination showcases how cities can capitalize on marketing of diverse cuisines which are attractive to food travelers. In the 1980s, Houston (like most cities of its size) had many restaurant experiences, but it was not

The Changing Face of Gourmet Tourism   191

well-known as a destination for food. Houston's identity nationwide was as the center for the United States' oil and gas (now "energy") industry. Venerated travel writer Jan Morris called Houston "a bit of a dump, I suppose" (Morris, 1984: 64), mentioning its traffic, crime, and adult bookstores. She wrote of "cattle-people [coming] into town for dinner or convention, paunchy with their generations of beer and prime steaks" (p. 64). Not known as a leisure travel destination, Houston relied on these business travelers.

While visiting, the focus of dining was often stereotypical Texas foods like steaks and barbeque, with perhaps a foray into fine dining. Texas is known for its beef, and one of the area's most famous steakhouses, Taste of Texas, was opened in 1977 near Houston's Energy Corridor, home to many energy companies and their expense-account visitors. The influx of oil money to Houston in the 1970s and 1980s (before the famous oil bust of the early to mid-80s) also helped build up its fine-dining scene. Aside from fancy steakhouses, Houston's fine-dining restaurants included Tony's (founded by local legend Tony Vallone), Americas, and Café Annie.

From a business traveler perspective, the focus was on gourmet dining, but Houston was quietly developing a casual dining scene. In 1977, Jim Goode took over a failing barbeque restaurant and renamed it Goode's B-B-Q, and it remains open today. Houston's restaurant scene also featured some quirky local haunts. The only restaurant mentioned in Morris' essay was the Hobbit Hole Café (now Hobbit Café), which opened in an old house in 1972, serving only vegetarian food. It has moved to a different location, still in a converted house, and continues with a vegetarian-friendly (but not exclusively vegetarian) menu.

At the same time, ethnic cuisines began to emerge as popular spots for locals. Houston has large immigrant communities, in particular Mexican-American, Vietnamese-American, and Chinese-American, which have contributed to its restaurant diversity. Fajitas, today a staple of Tex-Mex Cuisine, were said to have been invented at Mama Ninfa's restaurant, opened by Mexican immigrant "Mama" Ninfa Laurenzo in 1973. In 1982, Vietnamese immigrant Kim Su Tran La ("Mama La") opened a casual dining restaurant named Kim Son in Chinatown, just outside downtown, which featured Chinese and Vietnamese dishes. It emerged as a local favorite. As Vietnamese cuisine was on the rise in the 1990s, Kim Son was showcased in *Bon Appetit* magazine in 1995 for its ability to "entice adventurous eaters ... to try a cuisine unknown to most" (Criswell, 1995).

Aside from occasional national accolades like this article and Robert Del Grande (Café Annie) being named Best Chef Southwest in the James Beard Awards in 1992, Houston was considered to be a business city, not a culinary destination. In the 1990's Houston's destination marketing organization (DMO) advertised Houston as "Space City," due to its connection to space exploration and the home of NASA's Johnson Space Center. When I arrived in Houston in 1995, it seemed that locals appreciated the diversity of the local restaurant scene, but the city remained outside the spotlight national travel and food media, and the DMO did not focus on food as a key point of differentiation.

192 *Matthew J. Stone*

In the early 1980s Jan Morris (1984: 74) acknowledged that "nobody can be altogether immune to the blazing promise of [Houston]" (Morris, 1984: 74), but it took until the 2010s for this promise, in terms of its national food identity, to arrive. Visit Houston (Houston's DMO), has branded Houston as the "Cultural and Culinary Capital of the South." They have a website *Taste Houston* dedicated to telling food stories and giving visitors ideas for food exploration (from vegan and veg dining in H-Town to where to eat during Houston LGBT+ Pride). Rather than focusing on only fine-dining restaurants, of which Houston has many, they focus on the diversity of international cuisines and experiences at all price points, knowing that food travelers, including gourmet food travelers, will be enticed to visit. In 2013, the *New York Times* named Houston as one of the top 10 places to visit and noted its efforts to become "the state's cultural and culinary capital." In *Food & Wine* magazine, James Beard Award winner David Chang pronounced Houston "the most exciting food city in America" (Sugar, 2018) because of its diversity and that it was not bound by tradition.

Houston has recently been recognized for its gourmet experiences. In a four-year period, three Houston chefs won the James Beard Award for Best Chef Southwest (2014, Chris Shepherd; 2016, Justin Yu; 2017, Hugo Ortega). Fine dining in Houston (as with much of the country) has become more casual, welcoming a broader range of diners. Houston is still a fine-dining city, but that is only part of its appeal. The Culture Trip noted that Houston's appeal as a culinary capital was "all about diversity" (Choi, 2017), and a *New York Times* feature on Chris Shepherd focused on the Houston's restaurant diversity (Anderson, 2020). Visit Houston stresses the city's appeal to those seeking eclectic cuisines (from Vietnamese to Tex-Mex to Cajun), and it also showcases its immigrant communities, ethnic cuisines, and innovations. In one example, renowned chef Marcus Samuelson focused on West African cuisine for the Houston episode of his show *No Passport Required* in 2020. This balance between international, national, and local restaurants has been proposed as a key element in success as a food travel destination (Kalenjuk, et al., 2015).

The increased attention to food and the birth of the "foodie" movement have led to the growth of more culinary attractions. In 2021, the *Houston Chronicle* named the 100-vendor Urban Harvest's Saturday Farmers' Market as the best local farmers' market. This is remarkable because it started in 2004 with only seven vendors (Balter, 2021. Today, Houston also features several food halls, including POST Houston, which opened in 2021 with 30 vendors in the former central post office. Houston's own foodie residents are responsible for patronizing and promoting new restaurants, food halls, and markets, which are also appealing to travelers.

In 2020, the Houston Texans, a professional NFL (American football) team, announced they will feature more local restaurants at their stadium, to celebrate "the culinary capital of the South." When the TV show *Top Chef* announced that Season 19 would be filmed in Houston, it wasn't just the DMO which led the promotion. Mayor Sylvester Turner said, "We are proud of the diverse community and unique heritage that makes our city such a hot culinary destination — from classics like Tex-Mex and barbecue to local inventions like Viet-Cajun and Japanese Tapas" (Gonzalez, 2021).

On the DMO website, dining information is the biggest factor (other than general categories of "attractions" and "calendar of events") in enticing visitors or encouraging them to stay longer. "Food is always in the top three drivers overall and always No. 1 when it comes to specific topic," according to Visit Houston chief marketing officer Holly Clapham-Rosenow (Cook & Marago, 2019). If these quality restaurants and diverse cuisines have been in Houston for decades, what changed that led Houston to focus on its culinary diversity? How did they build into a foodie culture? Houston's DMO determined that one of its unique value propositions to visitors was its varied (and comparatively affordable) restaurants. According to branding expert Bill Baker, too many cities try to be all things to all people or to be something they are not. Houston followed Baker's destination branding observations. Every place "has its own stories, character, style, history, people, and culture that reflects the distinctiveness of the place. When these can be preserved, and are shareable, they can establish an edge over places that are contrived and convey an all too familiar sameness" (Baker, 2019; 46).

What can be learned from Houston's success?

- Local residents helped to build the scene, and the DMO helped to market it. Capitalize on what makes your destination special.
- Rather than focusing on only fine dining, find diverse cuisines and experiences to attract gourmet travelers.
- Tell your own unique story, including the stories of minority and immigrant communities.
- Showcase the individual stories of the chefs and restaurateurs.
- Create and encourage development of markets, food halls, and restaurants.
- Encourage your local foodies and local media to become brand ambassadors.
- Promote food experiences for visitors with food-focused content on your websites, rather than just a list of restaurants.
- Make food (including food tourism) a part of your DNA. Political leaders and business leaders should help to create this gourmet identity among all citizens—which spreads to visitors.

Conclusion and Strategic Implications

Early definitions implied that gourmet food tourism was the most essential aspect of food tourism motivation. Today, it is clear that there is more to culinary tourism than gourmet experiences. There is no clear common connotation of the word gourmet, and destinations should be careful when using the word *gourmet,* as its definition has changed over time from exclusively "fine dining" to incorporate high-quality and specialty foods. Additionally, it may have different connotations among different travelers. Culinary travelers may identify as "foodies" or "adventurers" or "localists," and they may associate

194   *Matthew J. Stone*

gourmet with their grandparents' generation of stuffy, formal dining. Destinations are recommended to use the word *gourmet* carefully in marketing, as there are many definitions of the word, and so-called "gourmet" experiences may turn off those who perceive *gourmet* as expensive or stuffy. The term *gourmet* may also not reach food-passionate and food-educated travelers who may technically be "gourmets" (in its definition as food-educated connoisseurs), but may not identify as such.

Self-identified gourmet travelers make up only a small portion of the food travel market segment. Travelers are more likely to identify as seeking eclectic, authentic, or local experiences. These "gourmet travelers" are not the only ones who engage in fine-dining (gourmet) experiences while traveling. Because of the small percentage of those identifying as gourmet, this article focused on understanding those who participate in fine-dining (gourmet) restaurants while traveling.

Travelers are important to fine-dining restaurants. Additionally, fine-dining experiences are important to the food travel experience. Fine dining should be a part of a destination's food tourism offerings and marketing, but it may be risky to make it the heart of destination branding and messaging. A focus on luxury experiences and high-end dining may turn off potential visitors, and even those who seek out fine-dining experiences are unlikely to eat gourmet at every meal. Marketing of fine-dining (gourmet) restaurants should also capitalize on local and authentic experiences when possible.

Fine-dining travelers are a diverse group of individuals—from gender to generation to family status. One finding is quite obvious: a larger percentage of those in higher income levels eat at fine-dining restaurants while traveling. However, just because high-income individuals are more likely to eat at a fine-dining restaurant does not mean that these restaurants are their exclusive domain. With the exception of those making less than US$50,000 per year, at least 40% of each income level had eaten at a fine-dining (gourmet) restaurant on a recent trip. At all income levels, American travelers were comfortable spending a lot on gourmet meals—and this was especially pronounced among younger generations. Marketing fine-dining restaurants to only high-income market segments is likely to turn off many younger and less- affluent diners who see a trip as the occasion to splurge on high-end restaurants.

Gourmet experiences alone do not seem to be enough to satisfy fine-dining travelers. They are cultural omnivores who take part in a great variety of food and drink experiences. By focusing only on top-tier experiences, such as Michelin-starred restaurants, destinations may actually repel food travelers who are seeking variety. While there are a few worldwide destinations, such as Napa Valley and Basque Country, that may successfully focus on high-end culinary experiences, this is not the case for many destinations. Best practices include determining the unique attributes of a destination and focusing on that, rather than a gourmet identity. Fine-dining experiences can be part of this destination food and drink mix. Destinations like Houston, which identify a unique and

The Changing Face of Gourmet Tourism   195

varied mix of restaurants, cuisines, and experiences, may be best positioned to attract food travelers.

Food for Thought

- After reading this chapter, how would you define "gourmet" when applied to food tourism?
- If you were designing a weekend at your destination, how would you recommend that visitors balance fine-dining, gourmet, and other local dining experiences (both high-end and casual) to ensure that they had the best local experience possible?
- Younger generations are more willing to splurge on gourmet meals, yet many fine-dining or gourmet experiences seem to be tailored to older generations. How can you ensure these experiences are also appealing to younger visitors?

References

Anderson, B. (2020, March 17). The face of Houston's diverse dining scene is a white guy from Nebraska. *New York Times*. www.nytimes.com/2020/03/17/dining/chris-shepherd-houston-restaurants.html

Baker, B. (2019). *Place Branding for Small Cities, Regions & Downtowns: The Essentials for Successful Destinations*.

Balter, E. (2021, July 6). Your definitive guide to Houston's farmers markets. *Houston Chronicle*. www.houstonchronicle.com/food-culture/article/houston-farmers-market-guide-fruit-veggies-16281384.php

Barrère, C., Bonnard, Q., & Chossat, V. (2014). Tourisme de luxe et gastronomie de luxe: une nouvelle Sainte Alliance sur fond de patrimoines?. *Territoire en mouvement Revue de géographie et aménagement. Territory in Movement Journal of Geography and Planning, 21*, 6–26.

Batat, W. (2021). The role of luxury gastronomy in culinary tourism: An ethnographic study of Michelin-Starred restaurants in France. *International Journal of Tourism Research, 23*(2), 150–163.

Choi, M. (2017, August 9). Houston Is the Next Culinary Capital and It's All About Diversity. *Culture Trip*. https://theculturetrip.com/north-america/usa/texas/articles/houston-is-the-next-culinary-capital-and-its-all-about-diversity

Cook, A. & Morago, G. (2019, March 26). From Space City to Food City: In 2019, Houston's brand is all about delicious diversity. *Houston Chronicle*. www.houstonchronicle.com/entertainment/restaurants-bars/article/From-Space-City-to-Food-City-In-2019-13718519.php

Criswell, A. (1995, August 30). Two hums up for Mideast chickpea dip. *Houston Chronicle*. https://web.archive.org/web/20100127040114/https://www.chron.com/CDA/archives/archive.mpl?id=1995_1294189

Daries, N., Cristobal-Fransi, E., Ferrer-Rosell, B., Marine-Roig, E. (2018). Behaviour of culinary tourists: A segmentation study of diners at top-level restaurants. *Intangible Capital, 14*(2). Accessed from: www.intangiblecapital.org/index.php/ic/article/view/1090

Gonzalez, A. (2021, September 21). Houston selected as next Bravo's 'Top Chef' culinary destination for season 19. Click2Houston (NBC News Houston). www.click2hous ton.com/features/2021/09/21/houston-is-selected-as-next-culinary-destination-for-season-19-of-bravos-top-chef

Gozzoli, C. (2012). Foda. In *Global Report on Food Tourism* (pp. 22–23). Madrid: UNWTO (United Nations World Tourism Organization).

Hall, C. M., & Sharples, L. (2003). The consumption of experiences or the experience of consumption? In C. M. Hall, L. Sharples, R. Mitchell, N. Macionis, B. Cambourne (Eds.) *Food tourism around the world* (pp. 1–24). Routledge.

Kalenjuk, B., Tešanović, D., Gagić, S., Erdeji, I., & Banjac, M. (2015). Offer of authentic food as a condition for gastronomic tourism development. *The European Journal of Applied Economics*, *12*(2), 27–34.

Merriam-Webster. (2022). Gourmet. In *merriamwebster.com dictionary*. Merriam-Webster, Incorporated. Accessed from: www.merriam-webster.com/dictionary/gourmet

Morris, J. (1984). Boomtown. In *Journeys*, pp. 63–75. Oxford University Press.

National Restaurant Association (2020). Tourism-related spending in restaurants fell sharply in recent months. Accessed from: https://restaurant.org/education-and-resources/resource-library/tourism-related-spending-in-restaurants-fell-sharply-in-recent-months

Peterson, R. A., and Kern, R. M. (1996). Changing highbrow taste: From snob to omnivore. *American Sociological Review*, *64*(5), 900–907.

Peterson, R. A., & Simkus, A. (1992). How musical taste groups mark occupational status groups. In M. Lamont and M. Fournier (eds.), *Cultivating Differences: Symbolic Boundaries and the Making of Inequality*, pp. 152–168. Chicago: University of Chicago Press.

Stone, M. J., & Migacz, S. (2016). *2016 Food Travel Monitor*. World Food Travel Association.

Stone, M. J., Migacz, S., Garibaldi, R., & Wolf, E. (2020). *2020 Food Travel Monitor*. World Food Travel Association.

Sugar, R. (2018, February 16). Why David Chang thinks Houston is the most exciting food city in America. *Food & Wine*. www.foodandwine.com/news/david-chang-ugly-delicious-houston

World Book. (1963). Gourmet. In *World Book Encyclopedia Dictionary* (Vol. *1*, p. 859). Doubleday & Company.

14 Elevating Gastrodiplomacy's Role in Marketing Identity

Johanna Mendelson Forman and Kathiana LeJeune

Introduction

Today the old refrain "you are what you eat" (Brillat-Savarin, 2011) may need a reframing. In a world where food choices have become so international, what you eat may no longer convey identity but rather may become a gateway to a greater understanding of other cultures. What do we mean? Precisely this. Our palates are often the point of entry for learning about different cultures. When we consume foods from different countries, we immediately achieve a physical sense of what it's like to consume part of a culture's identity. Moreover, with all the challenges faced around the world and defining identity or acknowledging various cultural identities, food is a catalyst that brings individuals together and our palates bring us closer because of the appreciation or misappreciation of a dish or flavor (Mendelson Forman, 2016).

Furthermore, our senses all contribute to the memories that we have of places that we travel, people that we meet, events we attend, and so much more. In these moments, we are then able to connect with others. The emotional quotient, intelligence, and empathic moment that comes from sharing a meal allow for connections to be made and bridges to be formed. This experience is confirmed by many psychological studies that demonstrate how trust is increased by sharing a meal with another person (Woolley & Fishbach, 2017).

This chapter will explore how food has become the new internet. Just as we built a smaller world through real-time communications and access to knowledge, food has become the medium through which we connect to others globally (Musk, 2015). Through sharing a meal, or by recreating a recipe, or through dining in a distant land, or just eating at a local restaurant whose owners are part of the large global diaspora, we have all been transformed into citizen food diplomats.

Specifically, we will examine the evolution of gastrodiplomacy, and what distinguishes it from culinary diplomacy. We will then review how in the last decade gastrodiplomacy has created a form of soft power that has allowed many nations to stand out by promoting their gastronomic specialties. This form of diplomacy also has an important commercial dimension since countries promote their cuisines by marketing local products which they export. Research

DOI: 10.4324/9781003282532-19

198 *Johanna Mendelson Forman and Kathiana LeJeune*

about gastrodiplomacy has also confirmed its power to attract new tourists to destinations because of what is now known as "nation-branding" through food (World Food Travel Association, 2022).

Gastrodiplomacy: The Power of Citizen Food Ambassadors

Before we discuss gastrodiplomacy it is important that we get our terminology straight. Gastrodiplomacy is often confused with culinary diplomacy. Both are forms of public diplomacy, but they are substantially different.[1] Their common bond is food. They are both forms of soft power (Nye, 2004).

Culinary diplomacy is a very specific form of engagement used by governments as a tool of statecraft. Think state dinners and private meetings between diplomats during negotiations about sensitive matters (Stelzer, 2013). It uses cuisine as a medium to enhance formal diplomacy in official diplomatic functions such as visits by heads of state, ambassadors, and other dignitaries. Culinary diplomacy seeks to increase bilateral ties by strengthening relationships through the use of food and dining experiences as a means to engage visiting dignitaries (Rockower, 2014).

Culinary diplomacy is a tricky subject because it is often used to describe other types of activities in the food space. Part of the confusion arises from an article about culinary diplomacy that conflated the terms, thus causing confusion between the use of food by the state as a form of soft power, and gastrodiplomacy being a sub-set of this concept since often national and local governments promote food to brand regions, products or both (Chapple-Sokol, 2013). Culinary diplomacy is a tool of statecraft and a form of soft power. It is the use of food for diplomatic pursuits, including the proper use of cuisine amidst the overall formal diplomatic procedures (Hickey, 2019).

Gastrodiplomacy is its own thing, meaning that it is really about engaging the public around food. By eating the cuisines of other cultures, we are also becoming individual diplomats who are learning to appreciate and also recreate components of different cultures (Rockower, 2014). There is an old refrain about immigrants that the first thing the new generation loses is their native language; the last thing that gets lost is their food traditions. Taste memory is very much a part of gastrodiplomacy, and it is this memory that drives people to seek a taste of home in an ethnic restaurant or journey to other lands to enjoy a recreation of a dish.

Gastrodiplomacy more generally "revolves around the people-to-people role … and the manner in which food is used to shape and expand perceptions and understanding" (Rockower, 2012). For example, Michael Rakowitz, a conceptual artist, created Enemy Kitchen, a cooking course that taught students his mother's Iraqi recipes "as a new route through which Iraq can be discussed." His goal was to make visible another dimension of Iraqi culture by expanding the political space and using food to promote local culture (Rakowitz, n.d).

Gastrodiplomacy is also a public relations tool of both governments and the private sector in the promotion of national cuisines and local products.

The practice of gastrodiplomacy has evolved to include an expansive list of activities starting with the earlier concept of ethnic food restaurants serving as cultural bridges to understanding others through the use of food. Moreover, as public diplomacy in the age of globalization transcends state-to-public relations and increasingly includes people-to-people engagement, gastrodiplomacy also transcends the realm of state-to-public communication and can also be found in forms of citizen diplomacy. In recent times, the term has come to include the use of food to promote awareness of different foodways and cultures (Rockower, 2014: 11). Today gastrodiplomacy includes the work of both government agencies and the private sector using food as a tool to promote national dishes or local products. In addition, using food to promote tourism, while not new, has embraced the use of the term gastrodiplomacy to distinguish how food can draw travelers to visit new places and taste unique local cuisines.

Today, gastrodiplomacy is practiced by a wide range of actors—public and private. The term has also included activities beyond just eating new cuisines, to marketing different regional and local foods, to acts of tourism focused primarily on seeking out new cuisines. More than any other means, television programs have highlighted the connections between food as a bridge to understanding culture. Pioneering work by the late Anthony Bourdain opened a window on a hidden world of cooking, especially in places unfamiliar to many Western audiences. More recent efforts by actor Stanley Tucci underscore the way food defines a person's heritage, while also showing audiences the variety of cuisines in a country like Italy.

Maybe you have heard of Kimchi Diplomacy, a reference to Korea's promotion of its foods and export products. Or, maybe you wonder why you have seen so many Thai restaurants in different countries around the world. These are forms of Middle Power diplomacy.

It's not by chance that these countries use gastrodiplomacy as a way to go beyond the ancient concept of breaking bread. They are doing this to promote their culture, market their country's finest dishes, and connect with others around the globe who either relate to their identity or would like to connect with the culture in a deeper way. In 2017, a non-profit company named *Global Gastros* did a study on how food plays a role in human culture and connection. They also analyzed humanity through the lenses of food. Global Gastros wrote an article, "The Role of Food in Human Culture," and mentions how:

> our minds have allowed us to develop civilization, create incredible technology, and literally change the face of our planet. With all the advances of the human race, we often forget that our uniqueness throughout earth goes back even further and deeper, back to the very roots of our existence and to one of our most basic needs—food.
>
> (Global Gastros, 2017)

In the article, they also expressed how we as individuals have an emotional connection with food before having an instinctive need for food—meaning that it goes beyond being hungry sometimes, for food can be love, memory, connection, and understanding and that is what strengthens us as people, no matter your cultural background.

Emotional Intelligence and connections are made through sharing food. Many millennials and Gen Zs use the terminology "foodie" on social media platforms to connect with their viewers as a place to introduce new food spots or culinary dishes. Several have become culinary influencers, encouraging everyone from all parts of the world to connect by means of food. Eating with the eyes reflects the evolution of technology with global "foodies" who are educating their audiences and sharing various dishes from around the world (Turow, 2015).

Standing Out in a Crowd: Middle Power Food Diplomacy

In the last decade, a growing literature has featured research about nation-branding, including governments using cuisine to promote tourism. It has also demonstrated its use by middle powers.

Food has become a powerful means of building a national brand. Paul Rockower explains that using something as basic as cuisine can be a way for a middle power to stand out in the crowd. States that pursue gastrodiplomacy through nation-branding hope to promote increased tourism and export of indigenous foods. A related component of nation-branding occurs when countries seek international recognition of their unique culinary contributions to the world by soliciting UNESCO to designate a certain dish or food preparation part of the world's intangible cultural heritage (Rockower, 2014).

Nation-branding has become a vital part of public diplomacy (Anholt, 2007). According to J. E. Peterson "Branding has emerged as a state asset to rival geo-politics and traditional considerations of power. Assertive branding is necessary for states as well as companies to stand out in the crowd since they offer similar products" (Peterson, 2006).

What is NEW is branding as "a strategic, policy-making approach, designed to help places build on the strengths that will earn them a better reputa-tion." There is a phenomenon known as the "brand state." A "brand state" comprises the outside world's ideas about a particular country (Peterson, 2006; Rockower, 2014).

In 2015, the University of Southern California Center on Public Diplomacy highlighted ten countries that used the opportunity of public diplomacy to not only share but also promote their nation's dishes, fresh ingredients, and expertise in dining styles. The ten countries that were the top practitioners of gastrodiplomacy at the time were: Thailand, Demark, Sweden, Norway, Japan, Malaysia, Peru, South Korea, Taiwan, and Australia.

The story of the Global Thai program is the poster child for what has become a growing form of food nationalism as nations compete for foreign audiences by using their kitchens as a draw. When the government of Thailand introduced

Elevating Gastrodiplomacy's Role in Marketing Identity   201

their Global Thai Campaign in 2002 "their objective was to both increase the number of Thai restaurants around the world and to make dishes like Pad Thai and Pad See internationally recognizable" (Rockower, 2014). Additionally, "the campaign sought to raise Thailand's profile abroad, branding the country not just as a culinary destination, but also to cultivate economic opportunities and partnerships for Thai chefs, food products, and culture" (USC Center on Public Diplomacy, 2015).

Similarly, other Asian countries like Malaysia, Taiwan, and Japan kickstarted their culinary diplomacy and marketing programs later in the 2000s (Lipscomb, 2019). In 2010,

> the Malaysian External Trade Development Corporation (MATRADE) launched "Malaysia Kitchen for the World" in five key markets: the United States, the U.K, Australia, New Zealand, and China. This campaign brought top Malaysian chefs to food festivals and events, invested in international Malaysian restaurants and restaurateurs, and opened night markets [in] major global cities including London, Los Angeles, and New York, all in an effort to showcase Malaysian food and culture and brand the country through its cuisine.
>
> (USC Center on Public Diplomacy, 2015)

Taiwan launched their gastrodiplomacy campaign "All in Good Taste: Savor the Flavors of Taiwan" in 2010 and was sponsored by its Ministry of Economic Affairs. Known colloquially as "Dim Sum diplomacy," this campaign invested $34.2 million over four years in an effort to raise Taiwan's international brand, including its culinary, cultural, and commercial offerings (Booth, 2010). To that end, Taiwan has hosted international food festivals and competitions and sent its chefs to culinary schools and events overseas. The government has invested funds in a Taiwanese food foundation which seeks to both develop and promote Taiwanese restaurants, coffee shops and ingredients to an international clientele" (USC Center on Public Diplomacy, 2015).

In 2009 South Korea launched a $77-million initiative that has become known internationally as "Kimchi Diplomacy" to kickstart South Korea's gastrodiplomacy debut.

> With the express goal of quadrupling the number of Korean restaurants overseas and establishing Korean food as a major global cuisine by 2017, funds from this initiative have sponsored culinary classes at Le Cordon Bleu and the Culinary Institute of America, and supported Korean students with grants and scholarships to attend international culinary schools and food festivals. The government also helped fund a team of "Bibimbap Backpackers," a quintet of backpackers who dished out bowls of the spicy Korean beef and rice dish to more than 8,000 people across 30 countries during their 8-month international tour.
>
> (Pham, 2013; USC Center on Public Diplomacy, 2015)

202 *Johanna Mendelson Forman and Kathiana LeJeune*

In addition, the Japan Brand Working Group, launched in 2005, is the country's gastrodiplomacy initiative, "Shoku-bunka kenkyū suishin kondankai" (Food Research Promotion Discussion Group), a public diplomacy fusion of Japanese culinary history and state strategy. Subsequently, the non-profit organization "Japanese Restaurants Overseas" was created to invest in and develop restaurants showcasing traditional Japanese ingredients, culinary techniques, and design/cultural aesthetics. In 2008, the JRO [Japanese Restaurant Overseas] opened offices in Bangkok, Shanghai, Taipei, Amsterdam, London, Los Angeles and Paris. Soon after, Japan established Sozai, the first Japanese cooking school in the U.K., held a series of sake seminars in London and Paris, and sponsored Japanese chefs to attend cooking schools and workshops all over the world (USC Center on Public Diplomacy, 2015).

The Northern European countries also made the list as the Nordic Food Movement began in 2004 as a way to promote locally sourced ingredients, traditional dishes, and modern culinary techniques from the region. In November of that year, Nordic chefs and food professionals met in Copenhagen to discuss "the potential for developing a new Nordic food culture." The objectives of the movement were to promote the Nordic countries as a culinary destination, preserve traditional cuisines and practices, and bolster the economy through tourism, trade, and development. In 2011, the Council recognized the public diplomacy value of the "Nordic Food Programme" and launched "Nordic Food Diplomacy" (USC Center on Public Diplomacy, 2015; Morris, 2020).

The sum total of our food-related activities, what scholars have termed "foodways," form a sort of culinary identity that serves to both define and to differentiate: those who eat similar foods are deemed trustworthy and safe, while those whose foods differ are viewed with suspicion and revulsion.

Multilateral Institutions and Branding

UNESCO's Convention on Intangible Cultural Heritage adopted in 2003 changed the game for nation-branding, especially among those countries seeking to set themselves apart with their cuisine. Using this designation provided a formal way to help a nation preserve culinary traditions and other unique elements of national culture. France was the first to receive UNESCO's designation as a cuisine that was a part of the nation's intangible cultural heritage. Since 2003 there have been many more countries who have applied for this brand and have been successful (UNESCO, 2022).

The process of achieving UNESCO recognition starts with a formal application that a country submits. It can take several years to receive a final decision. Applications are reviewed by a panel of experts to determine whether or not the cuisine is unique to that culture. And this is where the conflict begins. Often more than one country can apply and claim a certain food as a national dish. Resolving these disputes is not easy and often requires diplomatic interventions. For example, in 2016 Morocco, Algeria, Mauritania, and Tunisia all claimed couscous, the semolina grain dish, as their own. Each country made

Elevating Gastrodiplomacy's Role in Marketing Identity   203

an application to UNESCO. None were successful as the judges felt that couscous was eaten throughout the region, and was not limited to one country. This last one was also mired in political tensions as all three countries claimed ownership to couscous, but thanks to the Solomonic wisdom of the UNESCO team a solution to their ownership claims was resolved by a multi-national application. UNESCO asked that all four countries reapply as a unified regional dish. But it was not that easy given the difficult relations between Morocco and Algeria. In the end, diplomacy held sway. It created a space for diplomacy that opened up important political space between Morocco and Algeria, a major achievement. Tunisia served as a mediator. The end result was a success. All four countries agreed to make a joint application and by 2019 were successful in making couscous a regional delicacy special to these Maghreb countries (McCabe, 2019).

A similar dispute is currently underway as Ukraine and Russia are at war. It is about who owns borsch. Ukraine has claimed this beet, cabbage, and potato soup as its own, but Russia also thinks that it is theirs. As this paper goes to press Ukraine's application to designate borsch as a unique culinary heritage has been expedited due to the ongoing war. In July 2022 UNESCO declared that borsch was indeed part of Ukraine's unique culinary tradition. The decision underscored how culinary nationalism's deep roots even surface in times of conflict (Kassam, 2022).

Food-Washing

One of the interesting elements of gastrodiplomacy is the way countries that once were considered off-limits for travel because of wars, or criminal activities that impacted tourists, have used their cuisines as a means to bring back travelers.

Peru, with its *Mucho Gusto Peru*, was the first campaign that used its diverse cuisine and wonderful chefs to help attract visitors. A nation with incredible tourist sites such as Machu Picchu, the home of the ancient Incan civilization, was in dire straits as tourists could no longer visit there. An internal guerilla group, Sendero Luminoso, had managed to block access to the site, and also make travel there very dangerous. An urban guerilla group, operating in Lima and other cities, the Tupac Amaru, contributed to the insecurity. In the early 1990s, when the leader of the Sendero Luminoso group, Anibal Guzman, was finally captured and the urban guerillas subdued, the government began the reinvention of its image. Food became the centerpiece of its campaign to bring back visitors, using the culinary skills of Chef Gaston Acuria, to entice visitors to sample his cuisine, a fusion of indigenous products, the region's ample seafood, and the use of new cooking techniques to bring these flavors to diners (Perez, 2011; Perú, 2020).

Other examples of food-washing include efforts by Mexico, Colombia, and Rwanda. Mexico's campaign, *Ven a Comer* (Let's Eat), was geared toward elevating what is an incredible and diverse cuisine to international recognition.

204 Johanna Mendelson Forman and Kathiana LeJeune

Managed by the foreign ministry, the campaign's goal was to escape the stereotype of tacos and enchiladas, or other fast-food variations and introduce an international visitor to the variety of regional cooking and tastes that are part of the Mexican Kitchen. The campaign was also an example of gastronationalism as it used the cuisine to promote a respect for the originality of its foodways (Mexico Consular Affairs, 2020).

Colombia is another country that has emerged as a culinary destination after more than 60 years of civil war. After the Peace Accord was signed in 2016 the number of tourists increased 200 percent from 2007 (Orozco et al., 2016). In 2018 Colombia had more than three million visitors. While its branding campaign is not solely focused on food, it does recognize the nation as a home of diverse flora and fauna, with over 3000 species of birds. One of the other dimensions of Colombia's creative marketing is that it elevated its chefs to become food ambassadors, using many of them, like the late Alejandro Cuellar, to cook with locals in some of the nation's former war zones (Mzezewa, 2019).

In the case of Rwanda, a country that experienced one of the worst genocides of the 20th century, the government is at work to restore attention to returning to a place that enjoys some of the world's most wonderful natural resources: mountain gorillas. These animals have become central to the marketing of Rwanda as a place for eco-tourism, and also a way to sample the local cuisines and foodways of the nation. Rwandan coffee and tea have become international brands thanks to a successful export promotion campaign (Mzezewa, 2019).

This also influences how we continue our various cultures when moving to new cities, towns, or countries and trying to assimilate. Travel has a huge impact on our outlook on food introductions or culture appreciation moments. Part of why so many people travel is to try foods that they have dreamed of eating or have sampled at a local market but would like to have the real thing overseas or in another town. In other cases, the concept of trading foods to experience other flavors from around the world has sparked the "proud food source" brands we see in our stores today (Crowther, 2018).

Can a Nation Be a Brand? Practical Opportunities

Before people traveled abroad one way to learn about another culture was through the palate. Eating the foods of other cultures provided a gateway for people to appreciate the different types of world cuisines (Scranton, 2002). Today, international travel is the norm, with millions of people traveling to places near and far to sample the foods, enjoy the culture, and hopefully learn more about the unique contributions of a country. The COVID-19 pandemic, which began in early 2020 and is still with us, again returned people around the world to relying on their palates and their cooking skills to recreate the foods of other cultures.

In Kathiana LeJeune's *The Power of the Palate*, she encourages those who aren't ready to travel again to turn their homes into embassies and backyards into meeting people. Imagine what our world would look like if we opened our homes or backyards to family and friends to start small talk conversations that evolved into special moments.

She also mentions how we are ambassadors of our homes.

> So, if you think about it, we are all representatives of our own homes or "embassies." There's something special and impressive to guest[s] or friends when hosting a dinner party. Inviting others into your home, preparing a meal for them to eat, and preparing a space for them to be and enjoy their evening changes you.
>
> (LeJeune, 2020)

Breaking bread with others has been a heavily respected and practiced tradition since the beginning of time. Therefore, the upside to turning our homes into embassies is a practical example of an opportunity to share a different culture's food or for restaurants to promote nation-branding. It is also another way of silently telling a person that they are welcomed and accepted. Lejeune created a practical list on how to turn our homes into embassies when hosting friends, family, or guests for dinner parties.

Restaurant Food Kits

Similar to the recommendations shared previously, during the pandemic, in the United States, several restaurants and companies partnered with influencers to promote restaurant meal kits.

> Meal kits are packaged, pre-portioned food items shipped from a restaurant to a customer's doorstep. In most cases — like pizzas and desserts— the food is assembled for preparation, frozen to retain quality, and requires heating or baking to recreate the dish you love most. And when meats are involved, throwing [them] on the grill or using the stovetop is necessary to attain a delicious, savory taste.
>
> (The Daily Meal, 2020)

The purpose of these meal kits was also to bring various restaurants into people's homes and teach several others about their cultural backgrounds through the dishes (The Daily Meal, 2020).

Restaurant meal kits or food company-based meal kits may be a future outlet for gastrodiplomacy in the marketing space. According to a recent article by the market section of *Vertices Food Service*:

> While a number of businesses have been adversely impacted by the COVID-19 pandemic due to nationwide lockdowns and a general decline in consumer confidence and spending power, the meal kit industry has thrived. As a result of the pandemic, consumers are spending more time

than ever at home. This has drastically changed cooking and dining habits for many, not only because supermarket shopping now carries a much greater risk due to virus transmission, but also because restaurant and café closures have prevented eating out. Meal kits are also seen as a cheaper and healthier alternative to takeaways, given the emphasis on fresh, sustainable produce that companies such as Gousto promote ... Growing consumer demand for meal kit services during the pandemic is reflected by the boom in revenue seen by companies such as HelloFresh and Gousto in 2020. According to GlobalData, HelloFresh saw a 122.6% Y-o-Y revenue growth in Q2 of 2020, a trend that the company was positive would continue over the remainder of the year. Similarly, Gousto saw sales rise by 129% over the year and achieved "unicorn" status, following losses in the previous year. While market growth in the meal kit industry may not quite match the outstanding pace seen in 2020, it is likely to remain a lucrative sector in the years to come. According to a survey conducted by sustainable London-based meal kit company, Mindful Chef, 7 in 10 customers stated that they would continue using the service after the pandemic. This suggests that consumers' grocery shopping and cooking habits have been permanently altered.

(Market Line, 2022)

Refugee Kitchens

In a time when refugees and migrants have been forced from their homes due to wars and conflicts, it is important to consider the importance that newcomers have on local cuisines and tastes when they get settled in a different country (Anjari & Sit, 2018). A day does not go by that the refugee chefs and kitchens that appear in cities like Berlin and New York, Istanbul and Missoula, Montana, or New Haven, Connecticut all demonstrate how new tastes and cuisines can create demand for international cuisines (Cahill, 2019; Eat Offbeat, n.d.). The power of refugee cooking, especially arising from the Syrian civil war that led to a massive outpouring of humanity from the Middle East in 2015 to the Russian invasion of Ukraine in 2022, shines a light on the connection between migration and cooking (Medrano, 2019).

The power of food to help people who have left their native lands suggests that one way to survive has often come through the kitchen. Food entrepreneurship has created the means for those who often do not speak the language of the new home to still support themselves by cooking, introducing new flavors into their adopted homeland, and also counteract negative images of different groups. For example, in Turkey, Syrian refugee women worked alongside their Turkish counterparts learning food entrepreneurship, but also learning more about the similarities of Levantine cuisine. Realizing that your cuisine has many similar characteristics becomes a point of entry and a form of communication in the kitchen even when there is a language barrier (LIFE, 2017; Center for International Private Enterprise, 2019).

The Future of Gastrodiplomacy: Looking Forward

Since *The Economist* (2002) first used the term gastrodiplomacy in 2002 to describe the efforts of Thailand to promote its image through its cuisine, more than two decades have passed since we have seen the rise of food as a central component of promoting tourism and trade. The emergence of food as a central component of a nation's brand underscores the soft power of food to help build trust, dispel stereotypes of others, and provide a window into the vast world of food.

An excellent review of the elements of gastrodiplomacy's marketing techniques was compiled in 2015 by Juyan Zhang (2015). Writing in an academic journal he examined how different countries were able to market their cuisine. Among the factors he noted were interesting slogans and logos so people would associate them with a country's food. Messages and themes were also another way to get tourists to buy, including the promotion of food as healthy and nutritious, to exotic and natural. These elements and many more were essential to helping advance a national brand that focused on special elements of a cuisine (Zhang, 2015).

Among the other areas that carried weight in branding campaigns was a focus on environmentalism. A survey done by the World Food Travel Association showed that many millennials consider sustainable agriculture and food practices an important reason for patronizing a country's kitchens when they travel (World Food Travel Association, 2022).

Gastrodiplomacy has also morphed into a cluster of different "gastros" with such concepts as gastronationalism (DeSoucey, 2010) or gastroadvocacy (Turshen, 2017) and gastromediation (Avieli, 2016). The environmental movement has also contributed to a new vocabulary of food with the concept of gastroecology, the realization that food waste contributes to greenhouse gas emissions and plays a role in climate change.

There is also another related phenomenon which is bringing chefs out of the kitchen and onto the barricades (SDG2 Advocacy Hub, n.d.). Social gastronomy, the use of food as a means toward greater awareness of social inequalities, from wage disparities to lack of inclusion of people of color and women in the kitchen, has also become part of the growing world of good advocacy (Mendelson Forman, 2022a). Since the term was first introduced in 2015 at the World Economic Forum, the concept of using food as a way to achieve social impact, from job creation, to training refugees as entrepreneurs in the food space, to helping chefs reduce food waste, the movement has grown in number and relevance (Adams, 2017). Today it boasts a global membership that supports training, dialogue, and networking (King, 2018; Social Gastronomy Movement, n.d.).

The COVID-19 pandemic has changed the gastrodiplomatic space for the better. Chefs who were using their skills to introduce new cuisines quickly converted their kitchens to feeding centers. Because of food shortages due to supply chain issues many people who had not considered preparing their own meals were now looking for ways to feed themselves. This need gave rise to more home cooks looking for recipes and trying new cuisines and new products. Finally, the pandemic brought out the best in the culinary world as so many chefs and home cooks recognized the urgency of finding ways to prepare food for those who needed it. In New York City, Migrant Kitchen turned its kitchen into a feeding center for health workers, preparing meals they delivered to different hospitals as cafeterias had closed down (Migrant Kitchen, 2022).

School closures also produced a gap in feeding alternatives as children who had relied on getting breakfasts and lunches through school programs no longer had this option when classrooms were shuttered in March of 2020. In the city of Baltimore, one group, the Mera Kitchen Collective, a group of refugee chefs, came to the rescue preparing meals that could be picked up by parents outside school buildings (Mera Kitchen Collective, n.d.). Stories like these point to the way food connected diverse communities in the height of a global pandemic by using creative solutions to a basic need.

As the world emerges from the throes of a once in a century event, there are questions arising about whether COVID-19 has created a new conversation about the need for locally sourced foods. Disruptions in food supply chains underscored the need for industry to reassess the sourcing of basic goods. We also saw how the pandemic brought the role of chefs and others who prepare and deliver our food into focus as essential workers remained on the job to feed others. Their hard work has helped produce increased hourly pay and benefits at fast-food chains like McDonald's, and also at local eating establishments.

Finally, it is hard to ignore how tenuous our own food security is as we witness the global impact of a war in Ukraine on the cost of basic commodities that are essential for everyone, such as grains and oils. From the Middle East to sub-Saharan Africa, we are seeing how interdependent the world is when it comes to food supply (Mendelson Forman, 2022b). This conversation is at the center of deliberations at the United Nations and also in corporate boardrooms. A growing recognition of how all sectors, public and private, are linked is at the heart of a renewed attention to agricultural sustainability, climate change and sustainability practices.

Food for Thought

- Why has food become the new internet of the 21st century? How has it served to connect people by making them the new citizen ambassadors of gastrodiplomacy?
- Can you think of examples, other than the ones cited in this paper, where nations have used their cuisines as a brand that will attract tourism?
- Why is it important for UNESCO to support cuisine as part of a nation's intangible cultural heritage?

Note

1 There is no single definition of public diplomacy, but there is consensus that as a concept it is a key mechanism through which nations foster mutual trust and productive relationships and has become crucial to building a secure global environment. See USC Center on Public Diplomacy.

References

Adams, T. (2017). Massimo Bottura and His Global Movement to Feed the Hungry. *The Observer*. [online] 21 May 2017 www.theguardian.com/lifeandstyle/2017/may/21/massimo-bottura-feed-the-hungry-food-for-soul 20 Apr. 2020.

Anholt, S. (2007). *Competitive Identity: the new brand management for nations, cities and regions*. New York: Palgrave Macmillan.

Anjari, M. & Sit, J. (2018). *The Bread and Salt Between Us: Recipes and Stories from a Syrian Refugee's Kitchen*. New York: Lake Isle Press, Inc.

Avieli, N. (2016). The Hummus Wars Revisited: Israeli-Arab Food Politics and Gastromediation. *Gastronomica: The Journal of Critical Food Studies, 16*(3), 19–30.

Booth, R. (2010). Taiwan Launches "Gastro-Diplomacy" Drive. *The Guardian,* 8 August, available online at www.guardian.co.uk/world/2010/aug/08/taiwan-launches-gasto-diplomacy-drive, 5 September 2021

Brillat-Savarin, J. A. (2011). *The Physiology of Taste*. Edited and translated by M. K. F. Fisher. New York: Vintage Classics.

Cahill, T. (2019). Sanctuary Kitchen transforms refugees' lives through the power of food | Faith and Leadership. [online] Available at: https://faithandleadership.com/sanctuary-kitchen-transforms-refugees-lives-through-power-food [Accessed 18 Jul. 2020].

Center for International Private Enterprise (2019). *The Cuisine of LIFE: Recipes and Stories of the New Food Entrepreneurs of Turkey*. Center for International Private Enterprise.

Chapple-Sokol, S. (2013). Culinary Diplomacy: Breaking Bread to Win Hearts and Minds. *The Hague Journal of Diplomacy, 8*(2), 161–183.

Crowther, G. (2018). *Eating Culture: An Anthropological Guide to Food*, pp. 237–266. Toronto: University of Toronto Press.

The Daily Meal. (2020). Tasty Meal Kits You Can Get Shipped from Restaurants around the Country. *The Daily Meal*, May 26. www.thedailymeal.com/eat/restaurant-meal-kits-nationwide-delivery.

DeSoucey, M. (2010). "Gastronationalism: Food Tradition and Authenticity Politics in the European Union," *American Sociological Review, 75*(3), 432–455.

Eat Offbeat. (n.d.). EAT OFFBEAT. https://eatoffbeat.com/who-we-are July 18 2020

The Economist (2002). Thailand's Gastrodiplomacy. February 21, 2002, www.economist.com/asia/2002/02/21/thailands-gastro-diplomacy

Global Gastros. (2017). The Role of Food in Human Culture · Global Gastros. *Global Gastros*. https://globalgastros.com/food-culture/role-of-food-in-human-culture

Hickey, C. K. (2019). All the Presidents' Meals. *[online] Foreign Policy*. Available at: https://foreignpolicy.com/all-the-presidents-meals-state-dinners-white-house-infograp hic/ 18 Jul. 2020].

Kassam, A. (2022). Ukrainian borscht recognized by UNESCO with entry on to safeguarding list. 1 July 2022, *The Guardian*. www.theguardian.com/world/2022/jul/01/ukrainian-borscht-recognised-by-unesco-with-entry-onto-safeguarding-list

King, R. (2018). Social Gastronomy: Can Food Change Society? [online] Available at: www.finedininglovers.com/article/social-gastronomy-can-food-change-society [Accessed 2 Apr. 2020].

LeJeune, K. (2020). *The Power of the Palate: Through the Great Exchange*. New Degree Press.

LIFE. (2017). LIFE. [online] Available at: https://lifeforentrepreneurs.com/ [Accessed 18 Jul. 2020].

Lipscomb, A. (2019). Culinary Relations: Gastrodiplomacy in Thailand, South Korea, and Taiwan. *The Yale Review of International Studies*. http://yris.yira.org/essays/3080#_ftn13, 7 September 2021.

Market Line (2022). The Meal Kit Industry Boomed in 2020 and Will Continue to Thrive beyond the Pandemic. *Verdict Food Service*, March 31. www.verdictfoodservice.com/comment/meal-kit-boom-continue-beyond-pandemic/.

McCabe, C. (2019). The Diplomacy of Couscous in the Maghreb. *Morocco World News*, April 19, 2019, www.moroccoworldnews.com/2019/04/271122/the-diplomacy-of-couscous-morocco-tunisia-algeria

Medrano, K. (2019). Restaurants Around the World Will Host a Giant Food Festival Celebrating Refugees. [online] *Thrillist*. Available at: www.thrillist.com/travel/nation/refugee-food-festival-2019 [Accessed 26 Jul. 2020].

Mendelson Forman, J. (2016). Foreign Policy in the Kitchen. *E-IR*, www.e-ir.info2016/10/05/foreign-policy-in-the-kitchen/

Mendelson Forman, J. (2022a). *Is Social Gastronomy A Recipe for Peace?* In A. Borghini & P. Engisch (Eds.), *A philosophy of recipes: making, experiencing, and valuing*. London: Bloomsbury Publishing.

Mendelson Forman, J. (2022b). A Global Food Meltdown. *The Diplomatic Pouch*, April 14, 2022, https://medium.com/the-diplomatic-pouch/analysis-a-global-food-meltdown-4401bc303e1a

Mera Kitchen Collective. (n.d.). Mera Kitchen Collective. [online] Available at: www.mera.kitchen/ [Accessed 18 Jul. 2020].

Mexico Consular Affairs (2020). Ten Years Later: Mexico's Traditional Cuisine and Gastrodiplomacy Efforts. www.consulardiplomacy.com/home/ten-years-later-mexicos-traditional-cuisine-and-gastrodiplomacy-efforts November 17.

Migrant Kitchen, www.themigrantkitchennyc.com/our-philosophy/ July 2, 2022.

Morris, K. (2020). What Noma did next: how the "New Nordic" is reshaping the food world. *The Guardian*. [online] 28 Feb. Available at: www.theguardian.com/food/2020/feb/28/what-noma-did-next-new-nordic-food-rene-redzepi-claus-meyer-locavore-foraging 17 Mar. 2020.

Musk, K. TEDx Talks (2015). Fertile ground: why food is the new Internet | Kimbal Musk | TEDxMemphis. *YouTube*. Available at: www.youtube.com/watch?v=iUU1BffGon0 [Accessed 18 Jul. 2020].

Mzezewa, T. (2019). How to Re-Brand a Country. November 23, 2019. New York Times, www.nytimes.com/2019/11/23/travel/rebrandng-croatia-colombia.html

Nye, J. S. (2004). *Soft Power: The Means to Success in World Politics*, p. 5. New York: Public Affairs, London.

Orozco, T., De Mesa, J. L. & Rodríguez, E. (2016). Germán Montes and Prosperidad Social. *Cocina y Paz*. Medellín (Colombia) Cuellar Editores.

Perez, P. (2011). Mistura, El poder de la comida. Available online at: www.youtube.com/watch?v=fkSWgt-_SLM, accessed on 7 September 2021.

Perú Ministerio de Comercio Exterior y Turismo. (2020). Gastronomía Peruana | Perú Travel. [online] www.peru.travel/gastronomia/pe/ 18 July.

Peterson, J. E. (2006) Qatar and the World: Branding for a Micro-State. *The Middle East Journal, 60*(4), 732–748.

Pham, M. J. (2013). Food as Communication: A Case Study of South Korea's Gastrodiplomacy. *The Diplomatist: Online Home of American US Public and Cultural Diplomacy Forum, January 25.*

Rakowitz, M. (n.d.). Enemy Kitchen. [online] MICHAEL RAKOWITZ. Available at: www.michaelrakowitz.com/enemy-kitchen [Accessed 18 Jul. 2020].

Rockower, P. S. (2012). Recipes for Gastrodiplomacy. *Place Branding and Public Diplomacy, 8*(3), 235–246.

Rockower, P. S. (2014). The State of Gastrodiplomacy. *Journal of Public Diplomacy, Winter 2014,* 11.

Scranton, P. (2002). Introduction. In P. Scranton and W. Belasco (Eds.), *Food Nations: Selling Taste in Consumer Societies.* New York: Routledge.

SDG2 Advocacy Hub (n.d.). Chefs' Manifesto: Join our community today | SDG2 Advocacy Hub. [online] Available at: www.sdg2advocacyhub.org/chefmanifesto [Accessed 20 Apr. 2020].

Social Gastronomy Movement. (n.d.). Social Gastronomy Movement. [online] Available at: www.socialgastronomy.org/ [Accessed 20 Apr. 2020].

Stelzer, C. (2013). *Dinner with Churchill: Policy-Making at the Dinner Table.* New York; London: Pegasus Books.

Turow, E. (2015). *A Taste of Generation Yum: How the Millennial Generation's Love for Organic Fare, Celebrity Chefs and Microbrews Will Make or Break the Future of Food.* New York: Pronoun.

Turshen, J. (2017). *Feed the Resistance - Recipes +Ideas for Getting Involved.* San Francisco: Chronicle Books.

UNESCO.org. (2022). UNESCO - Intangible Heritage Home. [online] Available at: https://ich.unesco.org/en/home.

USC Center on Public Diplomacy. 2015. Eight Great Gastrodiplomacy Nations | USC Center on Public Diplomacy. USC Center on Public Diplomacy. https://uscpubl icdiplomacy.org/story/eight-great-gastrodiplomacy-nations.

Woolley, K. & Fishbach, A. (2017). A Recipe for Friendship: Similar food consumption promotes trust and cooperation. *Journal of Consumer Psychology, 27*(1), 1–10.

World Food Travel Association (2022). https// https://worldfoodtravel.org/what-is-food-tourism.

Zhang, J. (2015). The Foods of the World: Mapping and Comparing Contemporary Gastrodiplomacy Campaigns. *International Journal of Communication, 9,* 569.

15 The Double-Edged Role of Cuisine in Both Research and Practice

Hennie Fisher and Gerrie du Rand

Introduction

This chapter addresses the problem of the double-edged role of cuisine in both research and practice, focusing on the relationship between academia and the culinary tourism industry. A discussion of food as a specialty offering to the gastro-tourist is presented. The historical development of culinary tourism is given and how it has increased in popularity. The initial lack of attention given to culinary tourism in the broader spectrum of the tourism research is depicted. The power of the changing lifestyles of the consumer as a driver for food tourism in the future is presented and how it has led to the enhancement of food tourism experiences. The need for collaboration between academia and practitioners is stressed as the contribution it makes to the development of strategies and focused food tourism research. Culinary innovation is used to compare differences in the application of processes by practitioners and their analysis by academics. The lack of research in this area is highlighted and the process of innovation as applied by chefs as a creative process is presented. A brief outline of the methodology is offered by the identification of theoretical foundations identified from a variety of published content to provide a narrative overview of the double-edged development of gastro-tourism in South Africa. Special attention is paid to the food offerings in a contemporary South African context, with a specific focus on gastro-cultural heritage and the way it informs tourism development. The results exemplified similar innovation process being followed in the South African food service and restaurant industries. The growth in innovative offerings in the South African restaurant environment, providing authentic food tourism, is presented and the discussed. Finally, the need for deeper collaboration between academics and the practitioners regarding innovative authentic food tourism experiences is stated.

Food as a Specialty Offering to the Gastro-Tourist

Food is increasingly becoming the focus of various tourism products, where it is foregrounded as an important component by destination authorities, businesses in the tourism industry and as a marketing tool to attract tourists (Henderson,

DOI: 10.4324/9781003282532-20

2009). Culinary tourism only became an identifiable industry and research interest in the late 1990s (Mulcahy, 2019), although it developed as an informal interest long before any formal research focus was developed. This greater sense of awareness was facilitated by improved communication, transport networks and globalization, which increased people's familiarity with unknown and foreign foods (Gajic, 2015; Mulcahy, 2019). The focus on culinary heritage increased and served as a drawing card to lure gastro-tourists to have authentic culinary experiences, thereby generating another source of income for destinations (Mulcahy, 2019). Food tourism has become increasingly popular during the last two decades (Weinberger, 2020). Hall (2020) refers to this as the industrialization of the food, hospitality and tourism industry, as many initiatives have been specifically 'invented' to be used as tools in culinary tourism.

Food has increasingly become an important tourist attraction and plays both a primary and supporting role in tourist decision-making and the visitor experience (Henderson, 2009). The gastro-tourist has become a catalyst for the development of culinary tourism as they seek more opportunities to encounter gastronomic experiences, which stimulated an increased interest in studies and research in culinary tourism (Mulcahy, 2019). Studying food tourism and researching the tourism product, the destination, the tourist, tourist decision-making and their expectations, are essential and provide scientific support for tourism development.

Collaboration between industry and academia in the field of culinary tourism has contributed to improved destination marketing and culinary tourism development. Challenges experienced in the culinary tourism industry are addressed by doing appropriate research enabling the provision of tourism experiences expected by the gastro-tourist. Sustainable development of the culinary tourism product and destination is facilitated by combining practice and research. Limited information due to a lack of focused research in the field of culinary tourism led to the increased attention it received in the early 2000s. To address the proper development of culinary tourism, focused and dedicated research combined with support from practitioners is required to achieve a more engaged academic–practitioner discourse. Erik Wolf, the president of the World Food Travel Association presented a white paper on culinary tourism in 2001 that highlighted the significance of culinary tourism (Wolf, 2006). Further attention in the form of specific, focused studies and dedicated research on culinary tourism were undertaken globally by various institutions in Canada, Australia, the USA and Europe (Getz, Robinson & Vujicic, 2014). Although real growth in academic research only occurred in the mid 2000s when the largest academic study in culinary tourism was conducted (Getz et al., 2014), much uncertainty still prevails as the development of terminology and conceptualization of culinary tourism continue to receive attention.

The contribution of culinary tourism to a destination, its people and their combined sustainability is great. It is important to keep in mind that providing positive tourist experiences and assuring that the destination benefits in terms of tourism business is crucial (Hall, 2020). Hall (2020) suggests that research both

Food Tourism, the Underdog Niche of Tourism

Initially, food and culinary tourism did not receive much attention as a research focus area in the broader spectrum of tourism. It was not regarded as an integral part of the consumer experience of tourist services, and only became an area of study in its own right in recent years (Hall & Sharples, 2003). The reason for this could be the ubiquity of food as part of everyday life, causing it to be disregarded as a serious subject for research (Hall & Sharples, 2003). The rise of food tourism as a special niche area occurred as a result of an increased academic focus on tourism and its relationship to food. Gyimóthy and Mykletun (2009) ascribe this growing interest to the fact that cooking and culinary consumption became more important as an experience and component of leisure consumption.

The increased interest in local food products and the symbolism attached to them provided an opportunity for food tourism to come into its own as a developing niche for both practitioners and academic researchers (Cleave, 2013). Initial references to food and gastronomy in the body of tourism knowledge focused more on the ingredients and dishes that were available to the traveler (Cleave, 2013). Various references are made to the importance and value of gastronomy and the study thereof to support the connection between food and tourism (Hegarty & O'Mahony, 2001; Hjalager & Richards, 2002; Kivela & Crotts, 2009). In the early 2000s, gastronomy was regarded as an analysis of what is eaten by society, and gastronomic tourism was defined as a subset of food tourism (Hall & Mitchell, 2006). Gajic (2015) states that gastronomic tourism is evolving and that a new set of travelers is emerging; those that not only want to enjoy food and drink but are hungry for knowledge about the food, where it comes from and how it is prepared. Furthermore, media influence has made consumers increasingly aware of health, wellness and sustainability. Consumers are changing their lifestyles and food plays an important role in achieving these changes. These are the drivers that will play an important role in the growth and advancement of food tourism in the future.

Academia and Gastro-Tourism/Food Tourism

Within the academic world of gastro-tourism, the interest and concern are often about terminology and conceptualization, sustainability, authenticity, local stakeholders (recognition of indigenous cultures) and lastly food itself, as part of the traveling experience. Academia is often more concerned about the product, the place and the (perhaps unrealistic) idealism of tourism and gastro-tourism.

The challenges and practicality of planning and providing authentic food tourism 'experiences' have not received sufficient attention from academia.

The growth in gastronomy tourism research has led to the publication of review articles examining the relationship between gastronomy and tourism within specific theoretical perspectives and specific themes (De Jong et al., 2018). De Jong et al. (2018) contends that little attention is given to food tourism as an interdisciplinary area of research. The focus of the research done on gastronomy tourism thus far has been hospitality management, tourism and leisure, including the geographical aspects of planning and development. There is a greater need for research across subject areas, more focused development of theoretical and critical approaches, and a greater emphasis on sustainability. Ellis et al. (2018) reviewed and evaluated this growing area of research and found that the focus was on the identification of core concepts, perspectives, and specific disciplinary approaches. Cultural anthropology was an important perspective as much of the literature defines cuisine as place, and establishes the interactions this creates with tourists (Ellis et al., 2018).

As food is an important element in a tourist's selection of a destination and the anticipated experience they envisage, it is imperative to not only focus on research from a theoretical point of view but to include expertise from practitioners. This collaboration is essential when investigating food tourism experiences and determining more focused destination strategies incorporating both theory and practice. Gastronomy is indispensable to a deeper understanding of the culture, the lifestyle of the people and the destination itself. Therefore, tourists selecting a travel destination expect authentic tourism products that represent value and quality, and must be supported by well researched facts (Gheorghe et al., 2014). Contemporary tourists are more informed and experienced; they are looking for the origin of gastronomic experiences, they want an authentic culinary heritage experience based on researched, factual historic knowledge that is applied innovatively (Gheorghe et al., 2014; Richards, 2012).

To help practitioners to meet the practical challenges of planning and providing authentic food tourism experiences, it is essential that academia should pay more attention to this area. It is imperative that practitioners should embrace the research done by academics and apply the principles and relevant data to meet the gastro–tourist's expectation of a memorable food experience. The OECD report (Richards, 2012) is an example where good practices from industry are used to give policy direction to develop a collaborative approach to food tourism research.

Industry/Practitioners and Gastro-Tourism

The food and culinary culture of a society has become a means to convey its cultural assets and elements to others, such as gastro-tourists (Pekersen, 2020). Countries such as South Africa progressively assign greater importance to innovative food and beverage offerings, to promote them as desirable destinations to tourists, tour operators and the food service industry. Several empirical findings have shown that innovation is a tool to increase competitiveness, which means that food innovation in the gastro-tourism world can be usefully harnessed to increase food tourism (Suryani & Claudya, 2021).

Tour operators and other tourism practitioners operate to show a profit. Their business is about making money and contributing to the economy. This focus on profit may cause authenticity to be sacrificed to practicality, or culinary innovation to be disconnected from the gastro-tourist, its intended audience.

Specific intellectual culinary and cultural knowledge is required to present authentic food tourism experiences linked to a specific destination. This knowledge could be obtained through collaborations with research institutions, such as universities. However, consumer research currently appears to take place without real input from the food tourism industry as a whole.

Close relationships between food and gastro-tourism operators (whose *raison d'être* is local food) have developed over the past number of years (Ellis et al., 2018). Although food tourism is an ever-expanding scholarly research area (Andersson et al., 2017), it appears that academia and industry continue to operate individually and there is considerable scope for collaborative research.

Culinary Innovation

For the food industry, innovation (sometimes referred to as Open Innovation or IO) (Braun & Bockelmann, 2016) is undoubtedly one of the most important aspects to enhance organizational performance, and ensure success and long-term survival. In food or restaurant businesses, a company-centred, product-focused, and causational approach appears to be taken towards innovation. It appears that many food businesses follow this 'evolutionary-economical view of innovation' (Feuls, 2018), which implies that innovation may not be a specific practice in the food industry or restaurant context, but rather that it unfolds through everyday practices. A sadly under-researched area, many unanswered questions about the underlying dynamic and ongoing social processes of innovation remain (Feuls, 2018; Gherardi & Perrotta, 2014).

Albors-Garrigos et al. (2013) define the culinary innovation process as an experimental process consisting of two stages: The first stage is the conceptualization of a new idea, while the second stage is where value is added through teamwork and dissemination. On the other hand, Feuls (2018) states that organic innovation takes place in the culinary environment through three processes: Innovating through repeating, innovating through adapting, and innovation by differentiating. Harrington, Baggs and Ottenbacher (2009) describe an 'organic' process in high-end restaurant settings as a seven-step process which incorporates idea generation, screening, trial and error, concept development, final testing, training and, finally, commercialization.

According to Feuls (2018), innovation by repetition happens when kitchens continuously repeat the same practice with small, constant variations that could, if positively evaluated, lead to a change in practice. Hence, chefs and restaurant kitchens imitate, adapt, refine and/or renew classical recipes, ultimately presenting their own version of the dish, translating their experiences into creative food items (Horng & Hu, 2008). Feuls' (2018) conceptualization of innovation as adaption seems to be the exclusive preserve of high-end restaurants which have the staff and financial resources to afford the space and time to 'play' and create. Such environments in which play can lead to innovation may well be a chef's own home kitchen, test kitchen or laboratory (Svejenova et al., 2010). "Within these spaces, chefs consciously change tradition or well-known dishes by recreating, sampling, blending, reinventing, reinterpreting, interpreting, or deconstructing their cuisine" (Feuls, 2018).

Finally, innovation through differentiating is like the trend-mapping process, where high-end development and innovation eventually trickle down to the supermarket on the corner. From the high-end restaurant or food establishment with a dedicated innovation laboratory, new ideas will be assimilated into those of others through collaboration, consulting and possibly teaching (Feuls, 2018).

Innovation in a culinary environment involves creativity that is often based on the chef's artistic aspirations. Such aspirations or commitment to creativity is what initiates innovation and change in an industry through acceptance of the chef's reputation and leadership. Acceptance of such changes and innovations is distributed to the public through the media and other marketing tools.

In the food service industry, development is less formal and more organic. Development is less about market and financial cost analyses, but rather based on networking with colleagues and suppliers of raw materials and ingredients. Innovation thus becomes an iterative, natural process, where the success of the innovation outcomes are based on the chef's tacit skills and knowledge (Harrington, 2005). Other authors have followed the knowledge evolution approach and considered the tacit-explicit as well as the synthetic-to-analytic evolution models in culinary innovation (Albors-Garrigos et al., 2013). Harrington (2005) considered culinary innovation as an impulse that involves tacit knowledge, allowing chefs and food innovators to develop competitive advantages. Ottenbacher and Gnoth (2005) later applied a new service development approach to innovation in hospitality and found that market analysis and human resource management were critical to success. These are both areas where academia could greatly assist the food service industry to bring about innovation (Albors-Garrigos et al., 2013).

South African Gastro-Cultural Heritage Informing Tourism Development

Much like the NNC (New Nordic Cuisine) is, at the time of writing of this chapter, considered to be one of the most prominent global 'cuisines' and "branded as the world's new culinary Mecca" (Byrkjeflot et al., 2013), food service establishments in South Africa are also slowly coming to understand and to celebrate their own gastro-nationalism. Researchers examine the construction of meaning and value in identities (Khaire & Wadhwani, 2010), as well as

218 *Hennie Fisher and Gerrie du Rand*

how food service personnel adopt new identities when they innovate through the migration from classical dishes to new innovative food dishes (Rao et al., 2003). Furthermore, scholars have provided theoretical insights into "nascent identity legitimation by delving into the mediating role of cultural entrepreneurship" (Byrkjeflot et al., 2013), which, in the food service industry milieu, could allow control and coordinate expansion through identity and growth stories (Wry et al., 2011). Gastro-nationalism is used to address the use and influence of nationalist sentiments in the production and marketing of food (DeSoucey, 2012), such as in innovation, where food service establishments re-invent or adapt classics that may appeal to the gastro-tourist. Gastro-nationalism is therefore a tool to understand food and politics in an increasingly globalizing world (Ichijo, 2020). An example of this relationship between food and politics is the pre-apartheid 1929 Crayfish Agreement between the French and South African governments, which allowed South Africa to sell Crayfish (Spiny lobster, not real lobster – *Palinuridae*), and which further specified that wines produced in South Africa in French styles – such as sparkling wines produced in the Champagne style, later called MCC or Method Cap Classique (Coetzee, 2015) – would not be sold as Champagne.

However, it appears that the concept of gastro-nationalism may also have changed. There are now new types of gastro-nationalism, "one where a patriotic discourse is highlighted as means to achieve national pride and economic competitiveness at the same time" (Jönsson, 2020). Or perhaps in more simplistic words, a phenomenon that "supports the preservation of traditional culinary cultures of societies, revealing the level of awareness and awareness about the national cuisine of the people and preserving these values" (Pekersen, 2020).

Methodology

In the chapter, the authors aimed to present a narrative overview of the double-edged development of gastro-tourism in South Africa – likely similar than in other countries, where there is a disharmony in what research believes to be gastro-tourism, and actual practice. Theoretical foundations were identified and exposed from a variety of published content, which assisted in understanding both academic and practitioner-orientated literature (Bortolini et al., 2021). This was done through snowball sampling of sources such as research and professional journals, tourism business, and entrepreneurial records. The contextual situation or disharmony existing between academic theory and industry is provided in this overview in a descriptive-informative format.

Results

In the food or culinary services environment, food innovation often takes place 'naturally', or organically. The model used by restaurant chefs in the food service industry is said to be more organic, less formal, and less dependent on financial analysis than more traditional new product settings. Additionally, much of the process integrates a tacit or learn-by-doing style of managing the process. In other food service settings, the culinary innovation process may be a separate function with its own R&D team, typically followed in chain restaurants in a variety of sectors (QSR, quick casual, etc.) (Harrington et al., 2009).

High-end or independent restaurants are under many pressures to constantly produce new innovative recipes and dishes, which may result in the development process not accommodating feedback from the customer to the food service establishment. Establishments rely on innovation to set them apart from competitors, to grow, to be noticed by food reviewers and restaurant guides, and to set trends. Comparisons have been made between this aspect in the restaurant industry and the couture clothing industry – where the fashion industry, similar to the food industry, sets trends, builds image and establishes quality standards for the industry as a whole (Albors-Garrigos et al., 2013; Surlemont & Johnson, 2005).

Albors-Garrigos et al. (2013) continue that because there appears to be some contestation whether culinary service is considered a craft or an industry, researching the culinary innovation process is complicated. The authors of this chapter suggest a further consideration following recent developments in the food service industries which saw the merging of culinary arts and food science into culinary sciences or Culinology ©, adding a further academic or research consideration to complicate the issue. Globally, a huge expansion has been noticed in the restaurant industry where restaurants spend enormous resources on research sections (Tan et al., 2019). Even though the outputs of such research are offered on the establishment's tables as innovative new dishes, the work done there has much academic research potential.

It is suggested that for culinary innovation, people with personalities and abilities that combine personal predisposition, deep knowledge acquired through tough training and repetitive practice, practical knowledge of the rules integrated and internalized by kitchen personnel, as well as deep understanding and knowledge acquired through reflexive thinking about practice, are needed (Gomez et al., 2003). Chefs are therefore naturally talented organic innovators and are often sought out for such abilities.

Ideally, food service establishments would have the resources (manpower, finances, time, etc.) to conduct research into what consumers may wish for in terms of innovative new food items. But often food service establishments rather rely on a process where they present such innovations and then depend on sales and possibly criticism to guide them in terms of the feasibility of their innovations.

In South Africa, the restaurant industry probably follows historical timelines similar to many Westernized countries, and only recently came to apply the advantage of culinary innovation. The Cape Province, which comprise Cape Town and the Winelands, has for many years been considered the hotbed of gastro-tourism development in South Africa. Over the years, the *Eat Out*

Guide (an annual restaurant guide) received constant criticism from the rest of the country about the over-representation of Cape restaurants in the top restaurants listed. Examples of restaurants whose offerings often feature local heritage foods and who tap into the South African gastro-cultural heritage to offer a unique South African cuisine to the traveler are newly opened restaurant Klein Jan at Tswalu, Wolfgat in Paternoster, Foliage in Franschoek, and others (Unilever, 2021). Michelin-starred chef Jan Hendrik van der Westhuizen innovatively reinvents an éclair by filling it with one of South Africa's most iconic candies, Peppermint Crisp. He says: "If you've never had the pleasure, it's essentially luminous green, crunchy, mint-flavoured candy enrobed in milk chocolate – and is available at every corner shop, tuck shop and supermarket in the country" (Van der Westhuizen, 2022), and offers customers a glimpse of what is essentially a very South African taste or heritage food experience.

Other innovations using indigenous ingredients at the University of Pretoria include a beef stew served with Venda Kale dombolo (Figure 15.1), a wrap with Venda Kale filling (Figure 15.2), and a Caesar salad made from Venda Kale leaves (Figure 15.3). Venda Kale (part of the species of *Brassica rapa* L. subsp. *Chinensis*) originates in the Vhembe District of the Limpopo Province. It is primarily grown during the dry winter months and different landraces have been reported in South Africa, and locally known as *musharna, sepaile, dabadaba, lidzhainthi, tshikete* and *M'shai* or *mutshaina wa u navha* (Maseko et al., 2017; Oelofse & Van Averbeke, 2012). It is a mustard tasting green leafy

Figure 15.1 Beef stew with Venda Kale dombolo

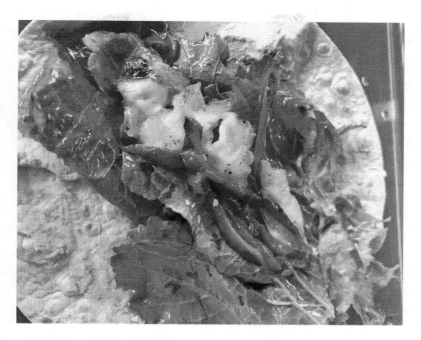

Figure 15.2 Wrap with Venda Kale leaves

Figure 15.3 Caesar salad with Venda Kale

222 *Hennie Fisher and Gerrie du Rand*

vegetable that is mostly gathered from the wild or cultivated at a few selected small farm plots and home gardens, and consequently not currently commercially available.

It appears that in the South African food service and restaurant industries, innovation follows similar patterns than in countries where culinary innovation is applied to gastro-tourism. We have seen an exponential growth in innovative offerings in the South African restaurant environment, celebrating gastronationalism and food heritage, utilizing indigenous ingredients, and applying rich food cultural practices.

Blogger Choplagos (2021) writes that food tourism is a growing industry in Africa, explaining that it is a type of tourism that focuses on the local food, culture and history of a certain place and aimed at travelers who want to experience local cuisine and food culture. In Africa and South Africa, we have many cuisines to celebrate the African continent's diversity.

Conclusion

The significant role of culinary innovation within the food service and the food manufacturing industries is becoming increasingly important (Harrington et al., 2009). It is understood that culinary innovation in the food service environment, and particularly the restaurant industry, happens 'organically' or naturally, by chance.

Various authors (Harrington, 2005; Ottenbacher & Gnoth, 2005), however, discuss the problems associated with new product innovation, such as high failure rates. Even though innovation is understood to be a critical aspect in terms of the long-term success of any food service establishment, high failure rates may occur as a result of a poorly executed product line, or perhaps because the new innovation was not correctly introduced to the consumer, or because consumers may harbour negative customer perceptions about new, innovative items on menus. (Harrington et al., 2009).

Such failures are at the core of this chapter, illustrating a possible disassociation between innovations and areas of research, the 'double edge of cuisine' in both research and practice. It is further possible that the 'unstructured' innovation happening in the restaurant environment occurs mostly without proper empirical evidence from research.

Braun and Bockelmann (2016) explains that those who innovate in the food service industry used absorptive and desorptive capacities to generate and market culinary innovations. Desorptive capacity is understood to be the safe transfer of knowledge from the sender, while absorptive capacity enables the acquisition and assimilation of external knowledge by the recipient (Roldán Bravo et al., 2020). Given this understanding, even high-end food service establishments would be influenced by what goes on around them, reflecting their absorptive capacities. It is in this regard that the authors of this chapter are postulating that such absorption should not only happen 'organically', but that such leaders or trend setters in the food service industries should be engaged in research, which should not happen in isolation.

Much like the NNC, South Africa could also use food heritage and gastro-nationalism as a drawcard for gastro-tourists, enticing them to come and experience the innovative use of local produce and heritage recipes (Byrkjeflot et al., 2013). South African examples include *Mondia Whitei* steamed idombolo in the shape of Huā juǎn (Mandarin twisted roll), Spekboom (*Portulacaria afra*) "Caesar" salad, Carob (*Ceratonia siliqua*) macaroon with melktert filling served with marula (*Sclerocarya birrea*) ice cream, African horned cucumber (*Cucumis metuliferus*) sauce and wild sage (*Salvia dolomitica*) crumble (see Figure 15.4). Others innovations include Madumbe (*Colocasia esculenta*) gnocchi, cassava (*Manihot esculenta*) mash, cowpea (*Vigna unguiculate*) vetkoek/Amagwinya, stamvrug/Transvaal milkplum (*Englerophytum magalismontanum*) jus, and many others.

The authors of this chapter suggest much deeper collaboration between industry and the food research environment, culminating in an environment where gastro-tourism can benefit from research that feeds back into industry. Such collaboration would contribute to a research strategy where a culinary tourism product would be delivered based on actual underlying and supportive

Figure 15.4 Carob macaroon with melktert filling and marula ice cream

research. Research into the culinary heritage, authenticity, and the art and science of product development should form the basis for developing well-informed, innovative culinary products. With such an approach and collaboration, the impact of what tourists eat and the resulting environmental issues indicated by Hall (2020) could be determined.

Therefore, it is imperative that practitioners embrace the research done by academics and apply the principles and applicable data to provide memorable food experiences. Meeting the experience needs of the contemporary gastro-tourist, providing sustainable culinary tourism products and protecting the environment will thus become an achievable goal. This is much more than the industrialization of the food, hospitality and tourism industries, where initiatives have been invented as a tool to be used in culinary tourism as indicated by Hall (2020).

Food for Thought

- Do you consider the double-edged role of cuisine between the food industry and academia to be real?
- What are the similarities of cuisine innovation between industry and academia?
- How can the potential of common ground between industry and academia become a win–win situation for all?

References

Albors-Garrigos, J., Barreto, V., García-Segovia, P., Martínez-Monzó, J. & Hervás-Oliver, J. L. (2013). Creativity and innovation patterns of haute cuisine chefs. *Journal of Culinary Science & Technology, 11*(1): 19–35.

Andersson, T. D., Mossberg, L. & Therkelsen, A. (2017). *Food and tourism synergies: perspectives on consumption, production and destination development.* 17(1): 1–8.

Bortolini, R. F., Nogueira Cortimiglia, M., Danilevicz, A. de M. F. & Ghezzi, A. (2021). Lean Startup: a comprehensive historical review. *Management Decision, 59*(8), 1765–1783.

Braun, A. & Bockelmann, L. (2016). An individual perspective on open innovation capabilities in the context of haute cuisine. *International Journal of Innovation Management, 20*(01): 1650002.

Byrkjeflot, H., Pedersen, J. S. & Svejenova, S. (2013). From label to practice: The process of creating new Nordic cuisine. *Journal of Culinary Science & Technology, 11*(1): 36–55.

Choplagos. (2021). Travel to Africa for the culinary experience of a lifetime. 2022(June) [Online] Available from: https://choplagos.com/travel-to-africa-for-the-culinary-experience-of-a-lifetime/#:~:text=culinary%20tourism%20in%20Africa%20is,for%20a%20day%20or%20two.

Cleave, P. (2013). The evolving relationship between food and tourism: A case study of Devon in the twentieth century. In C. M. Hall & S. Gössling (Eds.), *Sustainable Culinary Systems: Local foods, innovation, tourism and hospitality* (pp. 156–168). Routledge.

The Double-Edged Role of Cuisine in Both Research and Practice   225

Coetzee, F. (2015). Trade marks and Geographical Indications. Budapest [Online] Available from: www.wipo.int/edocs/mdocs/geoind/en/wipo_geo_bud_15/wipo_geo_bud_15_4.pdf.

De Jong, A., Palladino, M., Puig, R. G., Romeo, G., Fava, N., Cafiero, C., Skoglund, W., Varley, P., Marcianò, C. & Laven, D. (2018). Gastronomy tourism: An interdisciplinary literature review of research areas, disciplines, and dynamics. *Journal of Gastronomy and Tourism*, *3*(2): 131–146.

DeSoucey, M. (2012). Gastronationalism. In G. Ritzer (Ed.), *The Wiley-Blackwell Encyclopedia of Globalization*. John Wiley & Sons.

Ellis, A., Park, E., Kim, S. & Yeoman, I. (2018). What is food tourism? *Tourism Management*, *68*: 250–263.

Feuls, M. (2018). Understanding culinary innovation as relational: Insights from Tarde's relational sociology. *Creativity and Innovation Management*, *27*(2): 161–168.

Gajic, M. (2015). Gastronomic tourism – a way of tourism in growth. Quaestus (6):155–166.

Getz, D., Robinson, R. & Vujicic, S. (2014). Demographic history of food travellers. In E. Wolf, J. Bussell & C. Campbell (Eds.), *Have fork will travel: A practical handbook for food and drink tourism professionals* (pp. 63–69). World Food Travel Association.

Gheorghe, G., Tudorache, P. & Nistoreanu, P. 2014. Gastronomic tourism, a new trend for contemporary tourism. *Cactus Tourism Journal*, *9*(1): 12–21.

Gherardi, S. & Perrotta, M. (2014). Between the hand and the head: How things get done, and how in doing the ways of doing are discovered. *Qualitative Research in Organizations and Management: An International Journal*, *9*(2), 134–150.

Gomez, M.-L., Bouty, I. & Drucker-Godard, C. (2003). Developing knowing in practice: behind the scenes of haute cuisine. *Knowing in organizations: a practice-based approach*: 100–125.

Gyimóthy, S. & Mykletun, R. J. (2009). Scary food: Commodifying culinary heritage as meal adventures in tourism. *Journal of vacation marketing*, *15*(3): 259–273.

Hall, C. M. (2020). Improving the recipe for culinary and food tourism? The need for a new menu. *Tourism Recreation Research*, *45*(2): 284–287.

Hall, C. M. & Mitchell, R. (2006). Gastronomy, food and wine tourism. In D. Buhalis, C. Costa & F. Ford (Eds.), *Tourism business frontiers* (pp. 159–169). Routledge.

Hall, C. M. & Sharples, L. (2003). The consumption of experiences or the experience of consumption? An introduction to the tourism of taste. In C. M. Hall, L. Sharples, R. Mitchell, N. Macionis, & B. Cambourne (Eds.), *Food tourism around the world* (pp. 1–24). Butterworth-Heinemann.

Harrington, R. J. (2005). Part I: the culinary innovation process—a barrier to imitation. *Journal of Foodservice Business Research*, *7*(3): 35–57.

Harrington, R. J., Baggs, C. & Ottenbacher, M. C. (2009). Moving from a tacit to a structured culinary innovation process: A case for the BASICS and Just-Right Plots in evaluation. *Journal of Culinary Science & Technology*, *7*(1): 73–88.

Hegarty, J. A. & O'Mahony, G. B. (2001). Gastronomy: A phenomenon of cultural expressionism and an aesthetic for living. *International Journal of Hospitality Management*, *20*(1): 3–13.

Henderson, J. C. (2009). Food tourism reviewed. *British Food Journal*, *111*(4), 317–326.

Hjalager, A.-M. & Richards, G. (2002). *Tourism and gastronomy*. London: Routledge.

Horng, J.-S. & Hu, M.-L. (2008). The mystery in the kitchen: Culinary creativity. *Creativity Research Journal*, *20*(2): 221–230.

226 Hennie Fisher and Gerrie du Rand

Ichijo, A. (2020). Food and nationalism: gastronationalism revisited. *Nationalities Papers,* 48(2): 215–223.

Jönsson, H. (2020). A food nation without culinary heritage? Gastronationalism in Sweden. *Journal of Gastronomy and Tourism,* 4(4): 223–237.

Khaire, M. & Wadhwani, R. D. (2010). Changing landscapes: The construction of meaning and value in a new market category—Modern Indian art. *Academy of Management Journal,* 53(6): 1281–1304.

Kivela, J. J. & Crotts, J. C. (2009). Understanding travelers' experiences of gastronomy through etymology and narration. *Journal of Hospitality & Tourism Research,* 33(2): 161–192.

Maseko, I., Mabhaudhi, T., Tesfay, S., Araya, H. T., Fezzehazion, M. & Plooy, C. P. D. (2017). African leafy vegetables: A review of status, production and utilization in South Africa. *Sustainability,* 10(1): 16.

Mulcahy, J. D. (2019). Historical evolution of gastronomic tourism. In S. K. Dixit (Ed.), *The Routledge handbook of gastronomic tourism* (pp. 24–31). Routledge.

Oelofse, A. & Van Averbeke, W. (2012). *Nutritional value and water use of African leafy vegetables for improved livelihoods.* Water Research Commission.

Ottenbacher, M. & Gnoth, J. (2005). How to develop successful hospitality innovation. *Cornell hotel and restaurant administration quarterly,* 46(2): 205–222.

Pekersen, Y. (2020). The Hotel Chefs Perception on Traditional Kitchen Culture and Gastronationalism. *Anais Brasileiros de Estudos Turísticos-ABET,* 10(1, 2 e 3).

Rao, H., Monin, P. & Durand, R. (2003). Institutional change in Toque Ville: Nouvelle cuisine as an identity movement in French gastronomy. *American Journal of Sociology,* 108(4): 795–843.

Richards, G. (2012). Food and the tourism experience: major findings and policy orientations. *Food and the Tourism Experience,* pp. 13–46. Paris: OECD Publishing.

Roldán Bravo, M. I., Stevenson, M., Moreno, A. R. & Lloréns Montes, F. J. (2020). Absorptive and desorptive capacity configurations in supply chains: An inverted U-shaped relationship. *International Journal of Production Research,* 58(7): 2036–2053.

Surlemont, B. & Johnson, C. (2005). The role of guides in artistic industries: The special case of the "star system" in the haute-cuisine sector. *Managing Service Quality: An International Journal,* 15(6), 577–590.

Suryani, W. & Claudya, M. (2021). Competitive advantage: Empirical evidence from the small business of culinary. *Jurnal Inovasi Ekonomi,* 6 (01): 1–8.

Svejenova, S., Planellas, M. & Vives, L. (2010). An individual business model in the making: A chef's quest for creative freedom. *Long Range Planning,* 43(2–3): 408–430.

Tan, B. L., Tan, C. L., Yeo, S. F. & Ching, S. L. (2019). Examining the business venture success of restaurants: The role of innovation capability as a mediator. *Jurnal Pengurusan,* 55: 179–192.

Unilever. (2021). *2 South African restaurants foraging their way to the top.* [Online] Available from: www.unileverfoodsolutions.co.za/chef-inspiration/all-themes/insp iration-from-our-brands/Robertsons/2-south-african-restaurants-foraging-their-way-to-the-top.html [Accessed: 14 March].

Van der Westhuizen, J. H. (2022). Peppermint crisp caramel éclairs. [Online] Available from: https://janonline.com/recipes/peppermint-crisp-caramel-eclairs/ [Accessed: June].

The Double-Edged Role of Cuisine in Both Research and Practice   227

Weinberger, J. (2020). Have our bellies become our tour guides? Exploring the growth of food tourism 2000–2020. [Online] Available from: https://storymaps.arcgis.com/stories/29c82642c3e44043a7d909f3a1bb75d2/print [Accessed: June].

Wolf, E. (2006). *Culinary tourism: the hidden harvest*. Kendall Hunt Publishing.

Wry, T., Lounsbury, M. & Glynn, M. A. (2011). Legitimating nascent collective identities: Coordinating cultural entrepreneurship. *Organization science, 22*(2): 449–463.

16 What's in Store for Food Tourism in the Coming 10 Years?

Bendegul Okumus

Introduction

In the last 20 years, food and beverage tourism has gained significant momentum and become a unique and fundamental business worldwide. Academic research and industry reports indicate that food and beverage tourism is still an effective marketing and promotional tool for destinations, providing an essential source of income and abundant business opportunities for local and national business entrepreneurs. In this sense, it is crucial to understand the meaning of *food and beverage tourism* regarding the existing conceptual confusion. The literature on this topic is already immense, but the definition of the food and beverage tourism concept remains unclear. While some literature prefer to use the term *food and beverage tourism*, the others use *culinary tourism* or *gastronomy tourism*.

These three terms are not entirely interchangeable. The World Food Travel Association has given accurate and precise definitions pointing out the minor variations. Whereas food tourism is defined as "The act of traveling for a taste of place in order to get a sense of place," culinary tourism includes "the professional culinary training and beverage culture" while gastronomy tourism adopts a more elite approach by "following an area's culinary culture" (World Food Travel Association, 2022a). Although food and beverage-related activities offer tourists "new tastes, flavors, textures, cultures, heritage, local culinary cultures, customs and authentic food and beverage experiences" (Okumus, 2021a), resolving this conceptual confusion will open a clean path for scholars. Thus, scholars and industry experts can better analyze future trends by addressing tourist profiles, current demands, and rapidly changing business operations. However, it is difficult to predict the future of food and beverage tourism trends, especially after the crisis environment created by the COVID-19 pandemic.

Before the pandemic, the tourism industry witnessed the presence of many tourists who wanted to experience all food and beverage-related activities. Such travelers were ready to spend more money and time on these popular activities and food trends. This surge of demand prompted destinations to develop their food and beverage events and marketing efforts by leveraging

DOI: 10.4324/9781003282532-21

culinary resources, dining, farming, and food festivals, written or social media, TV programs, dramas, music videos, ads, websites, and other images (Chang et al., 2020; Okumus, Xiang, & Hutchinson, 2018). However, since late 2019, the COVID-19 crisis has drastically changed people's lifestyles and adversely affected tourism and travel activities. Governments, business operators, and stakeholders continue to face strict health guidelines and a new era of disconnection (Sariisik et al., 2022). The pandemic also put at risk the jobs of 100 million people in micro, small, and medium-sized businesses (Behsudi, 2020). Still, that does not seem to be the biggest problem for the future of food and beverage tourism.

While it is early to predict whether COVID-19 has permanently impacted food tourism, it is clear that the crisis has triggered some difficulties related to farming and food distribution channels. Global crises from the past to the present have had serious adverse effects on the economy. Similarly, the current pandemic severely affected the food supply chain, which is one of the most critical sectors of the economy. The entire process, from farm to consumer, has revealed significant concerns regarding food production, processing, distribution, and demand. Because of global changes in consumer demands, many food production facilities have closed and financial pressures have mounted in the food supply chain (Aday & Aday, 2020). Therefore, food production and supply chains should be discussed toward forecasting the future of food tourism.

COVID-19, Food Production, and Supply Chains

The USDA Economic Research Service reported that one of the most significant impacts of the pandemic has been on the agricultural sector. Like many economies, the US economy has been hit hard by the pandemic; farming has been disrupted by reductions in farm labor and other inputs, while output prices have been impacted by changes in product demand in certain market segments. In quick response, the US Congress passed six economic aid and stimulus bills in 2020 to provide financial aid to farm businesses and homesteads to mitigate some of the economic turmoil from COVID-19. The USDA and the other government agencies worked to implement authorized programs and make payments in 2020–22 (USDA Economic Research Service, 2022). Studies and reports from Asian countries enacted similar measures. Restricted quarantine practices of the pandemic, locust attacks, heavy rains, unsold crops, and the global financial crisis have disrupted agricultural activities by reducing food quality and increasing the costs of food production (Timilsina et al., 2020). The situation in South American countries is nearly identical. From institutional agricultural production systems to small and medium-sized businesses, the pandemic has harmed farming and food production severely.

The closure of public and private venues and pandemic restrictions at countries' borders have only exacerbated such damages (Lopez-Ridaura et al., 2021). However, data from Europe have shown different results reflective of the continent's robust food production and distribution systems. Many related issues before the pandemic have continued in Europe: labor problems, migrant workers, and short-term plans and programs. The pandemic did not affect food systems in that region as much as in the other continents (Meuwissen et al., 2021). On the other hand, unlike Europe, negative outcomes on food production and distribution came from Africa and Asia. The World Economic Forum reported that COVID-19 reduced Africa's food security and weakened its internal food supply chains because of the quarantine measures. In addition, locust swarms destroyed most of the crops in East Africa, thus straining the African continent as a whole. The World Food Program reported similarly adverse effects of the pandemic on agriculture and the family farming, mining, and tourism industries in West, East, and Central Africa (Ojokoh et al., 2022).

The growing global population struggles to access affordable, safe, and nutritious food for a healthy diet. The damage people cause to the planet for food production increases the need for sustainable and permanent solutions in such systems. The destructive factors mentioned above may lead to food shortages or scarcity, adversely affecting food tourism. Some countries are already experiencing food shortages due to climate change and war zones. According to United Nations Humanitarian Aid (2022), millions of locals may face severe food insecurity and shortages due to the ongoing conflicts in war zones. Approximately 49 million people have already begun to suffer from poverty, 820 million have experienced hunger, and more than 130 million have fallen into the extreme hunger category (Pereira & Oliveira, 2020). Individuals experiencing hunger have various physical and psychological problems, such as risks of weight abnormalities, anemia, growth issues, diabetes, hypertension, asthma, and cancer. Individuals experiencing hunger also face psychological distresses, including anxiety and depression, due to their inability to feed themselves and their families (Pourmotabbed et al., 2020).

The effects of the labor and immigration policy on the food supply chain have also been discussed by governments and primary agricultural and food manufacturing, distribution, and retail industries (Luckstead et al., 2021). However, it should not be forgotten that despite the strict food regulations and inspections of developed countries, food safety and security problems continue because of shortcomings in food policies and regulations (Okumus, 2021b; Okumus et al., 2019). Table 16.1 summarizes the current policies, gaps, and shortcomings of food policies and government regulations.

In addition to the above issues, COVID-19 adversely affected many low- and middle-income national economies, especially at the level of food supply chains. The data suggest that these impacts will be felt widely and unevenly in those low- and middle-income countries. Many small and medium-sized businesses and farms in urban areas faced food production, supply chain, labor, and taxation issues during the pandemic. Therefore, governments must develop new policies to respond to issues related to the pandemic that will impact all

What's in Store for Food Tourism in the Coming 10 Years? 231

Table 16.1 Policy-related food production and supply chain issues that may affect the future of food tourism

The aim of the food policies and regulations	Issues
Regulate farm activities, food distribution, FSCs, environmental practices, and sustainable food production	Complexity of the food system Focus on narrow objectives over larger systemic goals Lack of frameworks for policies and programs at the governmental level Growing populations, urbanization, and industrialization Rising food prices, declining agricultural productivity, food insecurity in rural areas, over-exploited natural resources, high oil and energy prices, and ineffective policy responses
Nutrition-related challenges	Economic costs of healthy eating Obesity Hunger Dramatic shifts in food consumption and dietary habits
State- and district-level food and beverage marketing practices, school nutrition programs	Lack of engagement with public health and food systems
Adequate food inspections in foodservice settings	Food poisonings, foodborne illnesses, recalls, food waste, risk-based inspections
Food supply management	Climate change, limited land and water, overpopulation, greenhouse gas emissions, increased organic and inorganic waste
Food security/scarcity	Populism and politicization of agro-food policies, lack of marine and aquaculture support for farmers, production of genetically modified foods, lack of information about novel food technologies Increased risk of undernourishment in low economic populations Poverty
Consumer welfare	Lack of knowledge among consumers Antitrust issues, product prices, market competition Unemployment rates
Food aid programs	Program budgets do not increase equally with inflation
Ecologically sustainable farming practices	Toxic chemicals, alteration of wildlife habitats, invasive species
Climate-friendly activities, soil preservation, prevention of land deprivation, creation of biodiversity, increase in socioeconomic equality	Land erosion, climate change, resource and energy shortages, sustainability, price instability, chemical usage Lack of animal welfare, environmental protection, food workers' rights, low-quality food imports

(continued)

232 *Bendegul Okumus*

Table 16.1 Cont.

The aim of the food policies and regulations	Issues
Economic freedom for food actors and citizens	Volatility in world food prices Increased job losses, oil prices State taxation of farmers Food price instability

Source: Developed from Caraher et al. (2013), Okumus (2021b), Prosekov & Ivanova (2018) and Thow et al. (2018)

aspects of the economy and prevent farmers, supply chain actors, and consumers from being affected too much by high food prices and the serious economic collapse of millions of workers (Reardon et al., 2020).

Future Trends of Food and Beverage Tourism

Previous studies show that food tourism has made significant progress in the last two decades, both in academia and the hospitality and tourism industry. The main research themes in food tourism include tourists' perceptions, unique dining experiences, authenticity through food and beverages, culinary and gastronomy destinations, wine tourism, marketing, sustainability, food festivals, culinary activities, and hygiene and safety issues (Okumus, 2021a). In terms of food and beverage tourism, destinations witnessed a very rich portfolio of food and beverage-oriented travelers before the pandemic. Those tourist groups had unique food and beverage experiences by participating in food and wine tours and culinary events organized by various destinations worldwide. Many tourists were willing to spend more time and money to experience the latest food and beverage trends. If the normalization efforts work well after the pandemic, food tourism will continue to create employment and economic activity through technological transformations, unique culinary and cultural identities, and hedonistic experiences.

Although it is difficult to predict the future of food tourism after the pandemic, destinations will continue their marketing efforts and try to attract more tourists to their regions. However, as discussed above, increased organic and inorganic food waste volumes (Goh et al., 2022; Gretzel et al., 2019), sustainability, environmental issues (Testa et al., 2019), lack of movement of policy adaptations, food scarcity, increased poverty, and global inflation will continue to cause severe issues for food and beverage tourism. Therefore, from an academic and industry perspective, food tourism research for the future should aspire to advance scientific progress in tourism. The following themes should receive further scholarly and industry attention to improve the future of food tourism:

What's in Store for Food Tourism in the Coming 10 Years?   233

- Disconnections between theory and application of economic food policies.
- Technological opportunities and social dining platforms: virtual (ghost) kitchens, online cooking classes, remote social eating and drinking, live guided tastings, virtual reality tours, and social media marketing.
- New cooking techniques, traditional and local cooking, culinary fusions, new ingredients, and recipes.
- Food waste, food insecurity during production, service, and storage.
- PsychoCulinary profiling (World Food Travel Association, 2022a), market forecasts, and preferences of demographic groups (generation Y, Z, and alpha segments).
- Agricultural and aquatic production issues: water, land, and marine ecosystems.
- Impact of climate change.
- Ecosystem management, education, and training of foodservice workers for sustainable food production.
- Food supply chain issues: traceability of shipping, poor communication process between partners, food frauds, and food safety issues during transportation.
- "Food is medicine" concept: culinary medicine, food and wellness, spirituality and food, and molecular gastronomy.

In addition to the above themes, Yeoman and McMahon-Beatte (2016) discussed the trends and future of food tourism through several driving forces. They emphasized the role of food tourism as a form of political capital, a symbol of ritual and identity, and a vision of political, scientific, and cultural aspects. They also discussed the characteristics of future food tourists through the lenses of affluence and exclusivity, personal identity, income, and wealth accumulation. Besides the food tourism themes, new research methodologies should be introduced to the field. For food tourism research, traditional data collection methods such as surveys, interviews, experiments, and content analysis have been widely utilized by scholars. However, there is an urgent need for more mixed-methods approaches in the field (Okumus, 2021a). If multidisciplinary collaboration and advanced research methods are developed by researchers and global food tourism events and conferences are held by food tourism industry partners, the identified themes, issues, and critical elements of food tourism promise to enliven the future of food tourism.

Transformations of Technology in Food and the Food Tourism Industry

Recent studies show that traceability plays a vital role in food quality and safety management. Traditional food supply chains (FSCs) aim for solid integration and coordination to improve food quality while reducing marketing costs. Thus, FSC's exchange partners have found themselves under increasing pressure to improve the transparency, exchange of reliable information, and tracking and tracing capacity of food and beverages from farms to consumers (Rejeb et al., 2020). For example, while traditional Internet of Things traceability systems provide practical solutions for quality monitoring, the system hinders consumers from obtaining transaction information. Radio-frequency identification technology has been applied for visibility and traceability (Hsu & Liao, 2019), and cloud computing platforms enable the storing of information and short messaging services for FSCs (Srivastava & Wood, 2015). However, blockchain promises to bring together multiple technologies, tools, and methods to enhance food safety and provide nutritional information through various digital platforms, including product information, batch numbers, expiration dates, farm details, manufacturing details, storage temperatures, and shipping details (Rejeb et al., 2020)—all while promising transparent traceability performance (Feng et al., 2020).

According to Willie (2019), blockchain technology offers valuable opportunities to the hospitality, tourism, and foodservice industries in the field of food safety, contamination and spoilage, waste, customer payments, and theft. Blockchain technology allows for more careful monitoring of restaurant records and reports while ensuring the accuracy of product labels and accountability among restaurateurs. In addition, payments using blockchain may offer cheaper options for restaurateurs since there is no need for client support from a credit card service provider and no time lag (typically three to five business days) in payment transactions. Smart business contracts can be held via blockchains, allowing all parties to see the most correct and up-to-date information and transactions. Because of the complete transparency and trust, the rules, procedures, and penalties could be clearly defined in contracts so that third-party service providers (lawyers, brokers, agents) would no longer be required. Also, inventory management such as orders, kitchen maintenance, and equipment purchases/leases could be handled via blockchain technology (Willie, 2019).

Previous studies and industry reports have also emphasized the rapid change in the agri-food ecosystem in recent years and the necessity of investments in digital technologies to help companies achieve efficient and better responses to changing customer demands. Food and beverage companies have started to invest in artificial intelligence platforms, bioinformatics, ingredient informatics, and alternative protein technologies to improve textures and better forecast consumer responses to new products, flavors, and contents (Danley, 2021).

Besides manufacturing and retailing, tourism in food and wine benefits from digitalization. Because food and beverage are vital factors in destination selection, culinary and gastronomy resources are becoming increasingly crucial for tourism researchers and stakeholders in the tourism sector. The number of digital platforms and apps where we can get information about food and beverage promotion, activities, festivals, bazaars, tours, and products is increasing exponentially. Accompanied by traditional marketing tools (e.g., texts, images,

What's in Store for Food Tourism in the Coming 10 Years?   235

videos, brochures, booklets, and websites), those digital platforms have become the most prevalent marketing tools used by local DMOs (Destination Management Organizations) to attract more tourists (Kim et al., 2009; Okumus & Bilgihan, 2014; Okumus, Xiang, & Hutchinson, 2018; Zhou et al., 2021). Psychological factors such as performance expectancy, effort expectancy, social influence, facilitating conditions, and personal innovativeness influence consumers' intentions to use such apps and digital platforms when ordering food (Okumus, Ali, Bilgihan, & Ozturk, 2018).

Word of mouth (WOM) is another essential marketing tool for linking local farmers and restaurateurs. Because WOM spreads organically, destinations should leverage this direct and informal communication system to strengthen the ties between hubs and other food tourism networks (Dougherty & Green, 2011) in conjunction with electronic word of mouth (e-WOM) communication through digital platforms. While developing these platforms, especially for e-WOM, destinations should focus on positive associations, such as content entertainment, social interaction, informational social impact, and self-expression, that influence e-WOM (Bu et al., 2021). The use of technology and digital platforms is increasing rapidly not only in farming, food and beverage manufacturing, food tourism, and marketing but also in the field of e-commerce applications. The unique benefits offered by the Internet have changed the sales and competition styles of businesses, and various sectors have developed e-commerce business models in their respective fields (Huang et al., 2009). Prior studies show that technology delineates both a creative focal point and destructive potential in tourism (Stipanuk, 1993). Research has started to discuss the creative and beneficial roles of technology (e.g., service robots) in gastronomy and dining experiences, especially after the pandemic. Since travel bans, curfews, and health-related rules that emerged with COVID-19 have significantly affected daily life, the use of advanced technology, artificial intelligence, and robots in tourism and the foodservice industry will transform food experiences and the sustainable development of communities and destinations (Fusté-Forné & Ivanov, 2021).

Hygiene and safety will continue to be perennial issues. Moreover, other crises that we may experience in the future related to wars, undocumented immigration, increased poverty, soil erosion, water scarcity, climate change, and the resulting food insecurity will only increase our need for technology. Yet, many sectors, including companies, governments, national and local organizations, consumers, and tech leaders, have witnessed the (intended and unintended) destructive consequences of technologies. Fake news, misinformation, breaches of privacy and personal information, increasing inequality in the workforce, reduced access to essential goods and services, alienation or social isolation, and damage to the environment are just some of the unintended consequences (Nohria &Taneja, 2021). For example, advances in 5G (fifth generation) technology have been used to connect all terminals, networks, and multiple wireless technologies even as its harmful effects on human health, the environment, and animals continue to be reported (Deivakani et al., 2021).

Conclusion

This chapter aimed to briefly analyze future trends and issues in food tourism and propose possible solutions for its development over the next decade from the perspectives of supply and demand in anticipation of the role of food in tourism futures. Although it is difficult to predict the future of food tourism and answer the question posed in this chapter's title in light of the factors listed above, wise planning and innovative actions can open new doors to destinations, food tourism ambassadors, and foodies in the future. In the end, people must physiologically eat every day. Eating is also a psychological need and a profoundly rewarding behavior intrinsically linked to emotions and mood (Meule & Vögele, 2013; Vögele & Gibson, 2010). Since eating will continue, new topics and themes related eating behavior and human psychology should be added to food tourism. Exploring these different themes is vital. Examples include food physiology, molecular gastronomy, food interactions, wellness and food tourism, safety concerns and issues, genders and generational cohorts regarding avoidance of new foods (food neophobia) and overt willingness to try novel foods (food neophilia), diet and food apps, and sustainable food tourism. According to the World Food Travel Association, it is essential to attract more visitors and make more sales with "knowledge about food traveler behaviors, attitudes, preferences, motivators, and spending." Thus, "businesses can more strategically target this general market and now, sub-markets of specific food lover types" (World Food Travel Association, 2022b).

Foodies and travelers could be categorized according to income levels and demographics by destinations to determine the strongest culinary supporters and the culinary sources, food, and beverages with which they are obsessed. A robust culinary brand should be developed as part of all destinations to promote unique traditional dishes. This will help foodies and other travelers understand the culture and traditions and open new doors to culinary fandom. Back et al. (2020) stated that culinary fans "tend to be emotion-based decision-makers, thus their decisions are more likely to be based on 'gut-feel' rather than rationality and logic." In light of this view, DMOs could improve their promotional materials and marketing strategies by focusing on emotional values using digital mechanisms efficiently. In this way, culinary products can be a core rather than a peripheral tourism product to attract tourists, culinary fans, and critics.

Food for Thought

- How can food tourism and health and wellness tourism be utilized together by destinations?
- How can destinations develop adaptive strategies to be more proactive to attract foodies?
- How can destinations use digital platforms to attract tech-savvy travelers and different generational cohorts to attract more foodies?

References

Aday, S., & Aday, M. S. (2020). Impact of COVID-19 on the food supply chain. *Food Quality and Safety*, *4*(4), 167–180.

Back, R. M., Okumus, B., & Tasci, A. D. (2020). Culinary fans vs culinary critics: Characteristics and behavior. *International Hospitality Review*, *34*(1), 41–60.

Behsudi, A. (2020). Wish you were here. *International Monetary Fund*. Retrieved from www.imf.org/external/pubs/ft/fandd/2020/12/impact-of-the-pandemic-on-tour ism-behsudi.htm

Bu, Y., Parkinson, J., & Thaichon, P. (2021). Digital content marketing as a catalyst for e-WOM in food tourism. *Australasian Marketing Journal*, *29*(2), 142–154.

Caraher, M., Carey, R., McConell, K., & Lawrence, M. (2013). Food policy development in the Australian state of Victoria: A case study of the Food Alliance. *International Planning Studies*, *18*(1), 78–95.

Chang, J., Okumus, B., Wang, C. H., & Chiu, C.Y. (2020). Food tourism: cooking holiday experiences in East Asia. *Tourism Review*, *76*(5), 1067–1083.

Danley, S (2021). Three technologies transforming the food industry. *Food Business News*. Retrieved from www.foodbusinessnews.net/articles/18000-three-technolog ies-transforming-the-food-industry

Deivakani, M., Neeraja, B., Reddy, K. S., Sharma, H., & Aparna, G. (2021). Core technologies and harmful effects of 5G wireless technology. *Journal of Physics: Conference Series*, *1817*(1), 012006). IOP Publishing.

Dougherty, M. L., & Green, G. P. (2011). Local food tourism networks and word of mouth. *Journal of Extension*, *49*(2), 1–8.

Feng, H., Wang, X., Duan, Y., Zhang, J., & Zhang, X. (2020). Applying blockchain technology to improve agri-food traceability: A review of development methods, benefits and challenges. *Journal of Cleaner Production*, *260*, 121031.

Fusté-Forné, F., & Ivanov, S. (2021). Robots in service experiences: Negotiating food tourism in pandemic futures. *Journal of Tourism Futures*, *7*(3), 303–310.

Gretzel, U., Murphy, J., Pesonen, J., & Blanton, C. (2019). Food waste in tourist households: A perspective article. *Tourism Review*, *75*(1): 235–238.

Goh, E., Okumus, B., Jie, F., Djajadikerta, H. G., & Lemy, D. M. (2022). Managing food wastage in hotels: discrepancies between injunctive and descriptive norms amongst hotel food and beverage managers. *British Food Journal*, 1–20.

Hsu, C.-L.; Liao, Y.-C. (2019). Bridging user perception and stickiness in business microblog contexts: A moderated mediation model. *Future Internet*, *11*, 134.

Huang, T. C., Lee, T. J., & Lee, K. H. (2009). Innovative e-commerce model for food tourism products. *International Journal of Tourism Research*, *11*(6), 595–600.

Kim, Y. H., Yuan, J., Goh, B. K., & Antun, J. M. (2009). Web marketing in food tourism: A content analysis of web sites in West Texas. *Journal of Culinary Science & Technology*, *7*(1), 52–64.

Lopez-Ridaura, S., Sanders, A., Barba-Escoto, L., Wiegel, J., Mayorga-Cortes, M., Gonzalez-Esquivel, C., ... & García-Barcena, T. S. (2021). Immediate impact of COVID-19 pandemic on farming systems in Central America and Mexico. *Agricultural Systems, 192*, 103178.

Luckstead, J., Nayga Jr, R. M., & Snell, H. A. (2021). Labor issues in the food supply chain amid the COVID-19 pandemic. *Applied Economic Perspectives and Policy*, *43*(1), 382–400.

Meule, A., & Vögele, C. (2013). The psychology of eating. *Frontiers in Psychology, 4*, 215.

Meuwissen, M. P., Feindt, P. H., Slijper, T., Spiegel, A., Finger, R., de Mey, Y., ... & Reidsma, P. (2021). Impact of COVID-19 on farming systems in Europe through the lens of resilience thinking. *Agricultural Systems, 191*, 103152.

Nohria, N. & Taneja, H. (2021). Managing the unintended consequences of your innovations. *Harvard Business Review*. Retrieved from https://hbr.org/2021/01/managing-the-unintended-consequences-of-your-innovations

Ojokoh, B. A., Makinde, O. S., Fayeun, L. S., Babalola, O. T., Salako, K. V., & Adzitey, F. (2022). Impact of COVID-19 and lockdown policies on farming, food security, and agribusiness in West Africa. In U. Kose, D. Gupta, V. H. C. de Albuquerque, & A. Khanna (Eds.), *Data Science for COVID-19*, pp. 209–223. Academic Press.

Okumus, B. (2021a). Food tourism research: A perspective article, *Tourism Review, 76*(1), 38–42.

Okumus, B. (2021b). Food Policies and Issues in the United States, Europe, and Asia. *Journal of Hospitality Financial Management, 29*(1), 4.

Okumus, B., & Bilgihan, A. (2014). Proposing a model to test smartphone users' intention to use smart applications when ordering food in restaurants. *Journal of Hospitality and Tourism Technology, 5*(1), 31–49.

Okumus, B., Ali, F., Bilgihan, A., & Ozturk, A. B. (2018). Psychological factors influencing customers' acceptance of smartphone diet apps when ordering food at restaurants. *International Journal of Hospitality Management, 72*, 67–77.

Okumus, B., Xiang, Y., & Hutchinson, J. (2018). Local cuisines and destination marketing: Cases of three cities in Shandong, China. *Asia Pacific Journal of Tourism Research, 23*(6), 584–599.

Okumus, B., Sönmez, S., Moore, S., Auvil, D. P., & Parks, G. D. (2019). Exploring safety of food truck products in a developed country. *International Journal of Hospitality Management, 81*, 150–158.

Pereira, M., & Oliveira, A. M. (2020). Poverty and food insecurity may increase as the threat of COVID-19 spreads. *Public Health Nutrition, 23*(17), 3236–3240.

Pourmotabbed, A., Moradi, S., Babaei, A., Ghavami, A., Mohammadi, H., Jalili, C., Symonds, M. E., & Miraghajani, M. (2020). Food insecurity and mental health: A systematic review and meta-analysis. *Public Health Nutrition, 23*(10), 1778–1790.

Prosekov, A. Y., & Ivanova, S. A. (2018). Food security: The challenge of the present. *Geoforum, 91*, 73–77.

Reardon, T., Bellemare, M. F., & Zilberman, D. (2020). How COVID-19 may disrupt food supply chains in developing countries. In J. Swinnen & J. McDermott (Eds.), *COVID-19 and global food security* (pp. 78–80). International Food Policy Research Institute.

Rejeb, A., Keogh, J. G., Zailani, S., Treiblmaier, H., & Rejeb, K. (2020). Blockchain technology in the food industry: A review of potentials, challenges and future research directions. *Logistics, 4*(4), 27.

Sariisik, M., Sengul, S., Okumus, B., Ceylan, V., Kurnaz, A., & Kapucuoglu, M. I. (2022). In-house responses and anxiety levels of commercial kitchen employees towards new COVID 19 food safety regulations. *Journal of Foodservice Business Research*, 1–28.

Srivastava, H. S., & Wood, L. C. (2015). Cloud computing to improve agri-supply chains in developing countries. In M. Khosrow-Pour (Ed.), *Encyclopedia of Information Science and Technology*, 3rd Ed, pp. 1059–1069. Hershey, PA: IGI Global.

Stipanuk, D. M. (1993). Tourism and technology: Interactions and implications. *Tourism Management, 14*(4), 267–278.

What's in Store for Food Tourism in the Coming 10 Years? 239

Testa, R., Galati, A., Schifani, G., Di Trapani, A. M., & Migliore, G. (2019). Culinary tourism experiences in Agri-tourism destinations and sustainable consumption – understanding Italian tourists' motivations, *Sustainability*, *11*(17), 4588.

Thow, A. M., Greenberg, S., Hara, M., Friel, S., duToit, A., & Sanders, D. (2018). Improving policy coherence for food security and nutrition in South Africa: a qualitative policy analysis. *Food Security*, *10*(4), 1105–1130.

Timilsina, B., Adhikari, N., Kafle, S., Paudel, S., Poudel, S., & Gautam, D. (2020). Addressing impact of COVID-19 post pandemic on farming and agricultural deeds. *Asian Journal of Advanced Research and Reports*, *11*(4), 28–35.

United Nations Humanitarian Aid (2022). Ukraine war could create widespread food insecurity, warns FAO. Retrieved from https://news.un.org/en/story/2022/03/1114962

USDA Economic Research Service (2022). Farms and farm households during the COVID-19 pandemic. Retrieved from www.ers.usda.gov/covid-19/farms-and-farm-households#:~:text=The%20coronavirus%20(COVID%2D19),commodities%20in%20certain%20market%20segments.

Vögele, C., & Gibson, L. (2010). Mood, emotions and eating disorders. In W. S. Agras (Ed.). *Oxford Handbook of Eating Disorders. Series: Oxford Library of Psychology*, pp. 180–205. New York: Oxford University Press.

Willie, P. (2019). Can all sectors of the hospitality and tourism industry be influenced by the innovation of Blockchain technology? *Worldwide Hospitality and Tourism Themes*, *11*(2), 112–120.

World Food Travel Association (2022a). What is food tourism? Retrieved from https://worldfoodtravel.org/what-is-food-tourism/

World Food Travel Association (2022b). State of the food travel industry. Retrieved from https://worldfoodtravel.org/annual-food-travel-industry-report/

Yeoman, I., & McMahon-Beatte, U. (2016). The future of food tourism. *Journal of Tourism Futures*, *2*(1), 95–98.

Zhou, Y., Kim, W. G., Okumus, B., & Cobanoglu, C. (2021). Understanding online travel communities: A literature review and future research directions in hospitality and tourism. *Journal of Travel & Tourism Marketing*, *38*(2), 194–212.

Conclusion

Francesc Fusté-Forné and Erik Wolf

In recent years, while different volumes have brought together the relationships among food, beverages and tourism, there is not a single comprehensive book that covers the most pressing current topics within food tourism practice and research, elaborated by the leading researchers and practitioners in the field. In particular, the book you have in your hands offers a balance between the contributions from academia and the industry, and provides a point of difference which will serve as an academic and industry reference to food and beverage tourism. Based on local and global examples from all over the world, the book is a diverse and rich approach to the relationships between food and tourism in contemporary times.

As a departing point, the book is an avenue to expand the bridges between academia and the industry, and it examines the future challenges of food tourism management and marketing. In this sense, the book also acknowledges the complexities of the relationships between food and tourism, which connect people, places and practices through one of the most representative elements of culture and nature. Food is a symbol of place. Food is a matter of business. Food is also a political representation. The main contribution of the book is the dialogue it offers between academics and practitioners, as a pathway to recognize the relevance of food for tourism theory and practice in a current moment where there is an impressive number of academic articles and industry reports that illustrate the golden age of *food and beverage tourism*.

Each chapter has offered a unique approach to a dimension of food tourism systems. There are topics which have been largely analyzed in the context of food tourism management and marketing during the last couple of decades, but now have gained new attention due to the challenges of the pandemic and climate change. Food is not static. Food changes. Food has large local and global influences which help to shape it. A technological development, a migration movement or even a military conflict, can all change food. This book is not only a source of updated knowledge about food and beverage tourism, but also a 'food for thought' monograph which aims to understand the contemporary advances in food tourism management and marketing. To achieve it, the chapters have contributed to the critical analysis of a diverse range of topics like food makers, food diversity, commensality, automation, media, responsibility,

DOI: 10.4324/9781003282532-22

Conclusion   241

food safety, the sharing economy, or gastrodiplomacy, which are expressions of the food and tourism relationships.

The meanings attached to food and beverage tourism are also relevant to the understanding of tourism systems which will continue to have a large impact on local and global scale issues and drive the environmental, economic and sociocultural wellbeing of communities all over the world. While the book extension is limited, the endeavor for food tourism academics and practitioners to expand the boundaries of food tourism management and marketing is endless. This book is a call to further collaborate in projects that focus not just on its academic impact, but also on the never-ending learning process we all are immersed in, as part of a system, tourism, through food, an ingredient with a power to change, challenge and improve the planet.

Index

Note: References in *italics* are to figures, those in **bold** to tables.

Abarca, M. 10
academia and gastro-tourism/food tourism
    214–215
Acuria, Gaston 203
Adema, P. 9
Africa and COVID-19 230
Ahmed, Sara 97
Aitchison, C. 134
Albors-Garrigos, J. et al. 216, 219
Algeria 202–203
apps 116
archipelago destinations 50–51
artisan is the hero 20–21
Atsiz, O. et al. 150, 155, 157, 158
Augmented Reality 119
Australia 86, 200
authenticity 37, *38*, 153, 186
avocado 142
Azhar, Rosyid 57

Back, R. M. et al. 236
backstage passes 28–29
Bae, S.Y. 164
Baker, B. 193
Barr, A. 100
Barrère, C. et al. 187–188
Barthes, R. 8
Batat, W. 186
Baumann, S. 97–98
Beers, S. J. 59
Berno, T. et al. 7, 11, 14
Bessière, J. 9
Bloch, M. 68
blockchain technology 234
Blomstervik, I. H. et al. 69, 70
Bockelmann, L. 222
borsch 203

Botsman, R. 153
Bourdain, Anthony 199
Bourdieu, P. 101
branding 117, 204–206
Braun, L. 222
Brillat-Savarin, J. A. 197
Bucher, E. et al. 153
Buhalis, D. 89
business image 116–117
Byrkjeflot, H. et al. 217, 218

Campos, A. C. et al. 70
Canada: indigenous communities 143
Capcut 116
Carvalho, M. et al. 156
celebrity chefs 53, 96, 98–100
challenging consumer culinary expectations
    see Indonesia
Chang, David 192
change agents 128
changing consumer culinary expectations:
    literature review 36–39; main conclusions
    in wider context 43–45; methodology
    39–41, **40**; results and discussion **41–42**,
    41–43; food for thought questions 45
changing face of gourmet tourism 183,
    185–186, 193–195; attributes of travelers
    187–189; case study: Houston (Texas)
    190–193; fine-dining restaurants
    186–187; "gourmet" defined 184,
    193–194; "gourmet" food travelers **185**,
    185–186; other food and drink activities
    189–190; Psychoculinary®profiles **185**,
    185–186, 187; conclusion and strategic
    implications 193–195; food for thought
    questions 195
Chassagne, N. 127

Index   243

chefs 44, 98–100
China: TikTok 112–113; *Ultraviolet* restaurant, Shanghai 85
Choi, M. 192
Choplagos 222
Cifci, I. et al. 155
circular 139–140
citizen food ambassadors 198–200
Clapham-Rosenow, Holly 193
CNN Indonesia 51
CNN Travel 53
coconut culture 57–58
co-creation of culinary tourism 37, *38*; gastronomy tourist experiences 154–155; in meal-sharing economy *156*, 156–158
Colby, J. 10
Collinson, P. 69, 74
Colombia 203, 204
commensality 68–70, 74, 76
complaints 118
connoisseurs 186
conscious travel 127–128
Cook, A. 193
cooking methods 58–59
Copenhagen 85, 95, 101, 104, *104*
Costa, A. 149
couscous 202–203
COVID-19 pandemic: effects of 2, 31, 32, 36, 37, 44, 45, 99, 205–206, 208; feeding centres 207–208; food production and supply chains 229–232, **231–232**; food safety measures 164, 166–171, *170*, 174, 204; food waste and shortage 144–145; school closures 208; travel anxiety 166
creators, makers and other entrepreneurs: artisan is the hero 20–21; effective culinary stories 27; local is how you win culinary tourists 21–26; local treasures 32; options for deeper experience 28–31; conclusion 32–33; food for thought questions 33
Criswell, A. 191
Crowther, g. 204
Cuellar, Alejandro 204
cuisine, defined 8
cuisine as a manifestation of culture 7; food, culture, cuisine and place 9–11; food, culture and tourism 11; food and identity 7–9; of rice, culture and tourism 7, 11–16; food for thought questions 16
culinary culture 149–150; co-creation 154–158; sharing economy 150–154; conclusion 158–159; food for thought questions 159

culinary diplomacy, defined 198
culinary innovation 216–217
culinary stories 25–26, 27
culinary storytelling 22, 35, 37, *38*
culinary tourism, defined 1, 183, 228
Culinology© 219
cultural anthropology 215
cultural heritage 67
cultural identity 8
cultural intermediaries 101
cultural omnivores 190
culture 10–11

Daily Meal, The 205
Daries, N. et al. 187
Datau Messakh, Vita 53
David, Elizabeth 97
De Guzman, C. C. 53
De Jong, A. et al. 215
Del Grande, Robert 191
Delphi technique 39
Denmark 85, 95, 101, 104, *104*, 200
De Solier, I. 100
Destination Management Organizations (DMOs) 235
digitalization *38*, 39
digital marketing in the future of food tourism 108, 234–235; apps 116; branding 117; business image 116–117; complaints 118; content easy to find with SEO 115–116; dialogue with consumers 117–118; future of digital marketing? 119–120; hashtags 108, 111, 115–116; platform for each purpose 109–115; receiving feedback 118; risks of giveaways and influencer marketing 118–119; social media usage in travel by the numbers 108–109; what value are you providing? 109; conclusion 120; food for thought questions 120
digital media and democratization of food authorities 100–102
DMOs *see* Destination Management Organizations
double-edged role of cuisine 212; academia and gastro-tourism/food tourism 214–215; culinary innovation 216–217; food as specialty offering to gastro-tourist 212–214; food tourism, underdog niche of tourism 214; industry/practitioners and gastro-tourism 215–216; methodology 218; results 218–222; South African gastro-cultural heritage 215–216, 217–218, 219, *223*,

244 *Index*

223–224; conclusion 222–224; food for thought questions 224

Dredge, D. 154

EatWith 154–155

eclecticism 186

Economist, The 207

Ellen McArthur Foundation 146

Ellis, A. et al. 215

email 114–115

emotional intelligence 200

entrepreneurs 20

environment 9, 10, 50; *see also* sustainability issues at local level

Espeitx, E. 74

Estiasih, T. 57

Euromonitor 149

European Travel Commission 108

European Union: Ecolabel 129; Regulation EU 1169/2011 165

Everett, S. 70, 134

Everyingham, P. 127

e-word of mouth (e-WOM) 235

experts 186

Facebook 108, 109, 110, 114, 116

facilitation 68

fans 29

FAO *see* Food and Agriculture Organization

farming: crop diversification 141; regenerative farming 140; vertical farming 141

Ferjanic, D. 73–74, 75–76

festivals 30–32, *31*

Feuls, M. 216–217

fine dining, defined 184

fine-dining restaurants 186–187

fine-dining travelers: attributes of 187–188, **188**; defined 187; other food and drink activities **189**, 189–190

Fischler, C. 68

Floyd, Keith 97

Food and Agriculture Organization (FAO) 168–169, 171

food and beverage tourism: defined 228; future of 228–236; conclusion 240–241

food and identity 7–9, 70–71

food and wine tourism: particularities and… benefits? 71–74

food as high tech 81; evolution of food tourism experience 81–83; technology applications to food tourism experience

81, 83–86, 223–225; technology for a never-ending food tourism? 86–89, *87*; conclusion 89–90

food as high touch 67; gastronomy 70–76; sharing food 68–70; conclusion 76–77; food for thought questions 77

food heritage 74

foodies 100–102, 200

foodie traveller activity profiles 37–38

food miles 141

food safety *see* health and safety issues

food shortage 144–145

food supply chains 229–232, *231–232*, 233–234

food tourism, defined 1, 36, 49, 127, 214

food-washing 203–204

food waste 144–145, 146

Formaloo 118

Fountain, J. 128

France: Crayfish Agreement (1929) 218; *La Cité du Vin* 85; *Visit French Wine* 83–84

Future Food Institute 49–50

future of food tourism 37–39, *38*, 228–229; COVID-19, food production, supply chains 229–232, **231–232**; future trends 232–233; transformations of technology 233–235; conclusion 236; food for thought questions 236

Gajic, M. 214

Garine, Igor de 71

Garjito, Mudjiati 56

Gascón, J. 72, 75

gastrodiplomacy's role in marketing identity 197–198; can a nation be a brand? 204–206; food-washing 203–204; future of gastrodiplomacy 207–208; middle power food diplomacy 200–202; multilateral institutions and branding 202–204; power of citizen food ambassadors 198–200; food for thought questions 208

gastroecology 207

gastro-nationalism 218

gastronomy: on food, cuisines, identities, and heritages 70–71; food and wine tourism: particularities and… benefits? 71–74; food as local heritage… and tourism experience 74–75; local food culture, local heritage, local development 75–76, 215; trendsetting, image building, quality 35–36; conclusion 76–77

gastronomy tourism 1, 74–75, 154–155, 183, 212–214, 228
Gault & Millau 96
genetically modified organisms (GMO) 142
"geographies of taste" 9
GetFeedback 118
giveaways 118–119
Global Brooklyn 102–104, *104*
Global Gastros 199–200
glocalization 128
Gnoth, J. 217
Gomez, K. 12
Gonzalez, A. 192–193
González Turmo, I. 69
Goode, Jim 191
Google Business 109, 115
Google Forms 118
Gourmet (magazine) 184
gourmet, defined 184, 193–194
"gourmet" food travelers **185**, 185–186
gourmet restaurants 186–187
gourmet tourism, defined 36, 183; *see also* changing face of gourmet tourism
Gozzoli, C. 183
guidebooks 95–97
Guzman, Anibal 203
Gyimóthy, S. 154, 214

Halawa, Mateusz 102–103
Hall, C. M. 36, 183, 213–214, 224
Harrington, R. J. 216, 217
Haryadi, Irma 59
hashtags 108, 111, 115–116
health and safety issues 164–165, 235; COVID-19 food safety measures 164, 166–167, *170*, 174, 204; food consumers' approach 165–166
health and safety issues: methodology 167–168
health and safety issues: results 168; allergens and cross-contamination protocols 171–174; COVID-19 protocols and food safety 168–171, *175*
health and safety issues: conclusion 174–176
healthy foods 37, *38*
Heldke, Lisa 97
Hendijani, R. B. 49
herbs and spices 51–52, 53–55, 59
heritage 35, 74, 75
Hinduism 50
Hollows, J. 98
Hong King Tourism Board 111
Houston (Texas) 190–193

Houston Chronicle 192
Hynes, C. 50

identity 7–9, 70–71
image building 35–36
India 86, 146
Indonesia 49–50; ancient ritual cooking methods 58–59; archipelago destinations 50–51; Bali 56–57; coconut culture 57–58; ethnic foods and drinks 51–53; Gadjah Mada University 55–56; Gorontalo, Sulawesi 57–58; herbs 51–52, 53, 59; history, culture and food 53; hot food and honesty 56; plant-based delicacies 56–57; poisonous tubers 57; popularizing strange foods 60–61; pungent foods and condiments 55–56; Satan food 55; signature dishes 52; Sobat Budaya Foundation 51–52; Sobat Kuliner Foundation 52; spices 52, 53–55; "storynomics tourism" 51; super-priority destinations 51; taste & story 70–71; tourist attractions 51; travel destinations 51; Ubud Food Festival (UFF), Bali 61; West Papua 58; food for thought questions 61
Indonesia Gastronomy Network 53
influencers 102, 119, 120, 200
innovation 186, 216–217
Instagram 99, 109, 110–111, 113, 116, 117
interaction 68
Inter-American Development Bank 169
International Academy of Gastronomy 60
International Association of Culinary Professionals 60
Internet of Things 234
Inuit food system 143
Ireland 69
Islam 50
ISO 22000 Food Safety System 165
Italy 85

James Beard Awards (1992) 191, 192
Japan 57, 85–86, 200, 201, 202
Johnston, J. 97–98
Jones, S. 98
Jönsson, H. et al. 68, 69, 70, 218

Karaty, N. 89
Kesar, O. 73–74, 75–76
Ketter, E. 154
Kimchi Diplomacy 199, 201
Kim Su Tran La 191

246 *Index*

Kittler, P.G. et al. 8
Kjær, K. M. 97
Klosse, P. R. 49
Kobez, M. 101
KOKS, Faroe Islands 102

Laubreaux, Alin 11
Laurenzo, "Mama" Ninfa 191
Law, M. 50
Lawrence, B. 8
Lee, Nancy 98–99
Leer, J. 97
LeJeune, K. 204–205
Levy, P. 100
Lin, P. et al. 150, 155, 157–158
literature review 36–39, 82–83
local heritage 74–75
local is how you win culinary tourists 21;
  and COVID-19 208; effective culinary
  story 27; if you don't tell us … 25; local
  dishes 23, 23–24, 24, 25; local growers
  and producers 21–22; local ingredients
  21; tell your story 25–26
local treasures 32
London: *Inamo Restuarant* 85
Lonely Planet 104
looking towards the future 2–3

McMahon-Beatte, U. 233
McNeill, F. M. 10
Maffesoli, M. 68
Maghreb countries 202–203
Malaysia 200, 201
Marago, G. 193
Market Line 205–206
Mauritania 202–203
Mausbach, V. 149
meal-sharing economy 153–154, 156,
  156–158
media influence on food travel 94–95;
  digital media and democratization
  of food authorities 100–102; from
  guidebooks to influencers 95–97; is social
  media homogenizing food destinations?
  102–104; mediatized celebrity chefs as
  reason to go 98–100, 100; search for
  authenticity 97–98; conclusion 105;
  food for thought questions 105
Merriam-Webster 184
Messenger 114, 116
metaverse, defined 89
Mexico: *Ven a Comer* 203–204
Michelin guide 96

Montaigne 96
Morocco 202–203
Morris, J. 191, 192
Muryanto, P. 57
Mykletun, R. J. 214

Napu, Arifasno 56
National Restaurant Association 20,
  186–187
nation-branding 198, 200–202, 204–206
Negeri Rempah Foundation 53
Netflix - *Chef's Table* 98
Neubauer, I.L. 59
New York Times 192
New Zealand: *Cloudy Bay* winery 84
Niaga, Ipong 57
NNC (New Nordic Cuisine) 217
NOMA 96, 98–100, 100
Nordic Food Diplomacy 202
Nordic Food Movement 202
North America 142
Norway 200

Okumus, B. 165, 228
Oliver, Jamie 53, 97
Omar Niode Foundation 60
Open Innovation 216
options for deeper experience 28; backstage
  pass 28–29; visitors and tours 28
Ortega Hugo 192
Ottenbacher, M. 217
outdoor food spaces 37, 38

packaging 141
Parasecoli, Fabio 102–103
Parasuraman, A. et al. 109–110
peer-to-peer (P2P) dining 150, 155
Pekerson, Y. 218
personalization of experiences 37, 38
Peru 200, 203
Pesonen, J. 153
Peterson, J. E. 200
Peterson, R. A. 190
Pham, M. J. 201
Pinterest 109, 112
place 9–10
planet conscious 139, 144
plant-based delicacies 56–57
plastic 145–146
poisonous tubers 57
Pollock, A. 126, 127, 128
Prats, L. 71
Psychoculinary® profiles **185**, 185–186, 187

Index   247

public diplomacy 198, 209n1
Punyaratabandhu, L. 12–13

Rachão, S. et al. 157
Rakowitz, M.: Enemy Kitchen 198
Ramsay, Gordon 53, 97
Redzepi, René 98, 99–100
refugee kitchens 206
regenerative tourism 125–127, 130,
    131–132
regional gastronomy 44
regional specialities 9
Reisinger, Y. 128
re-ruralization of gastronomy 44
responsibility and sustainability 138–139;
    food waste and food shortage 144–145;
    is plastic the real enemy? 145–146;
    planet conscious 144; rethink the circular
    model 142–144; what's new? 139–142;
    conclusion: how do we make the change
    146–147; food for thought questions
    147–148; see also sustainability issues at
    local level
restaurant food kits 205–206
rice, culture and tourism in Thailand 7, 11;
    rice for life 12–13, 13; rice in tourism
    14–16, 15; rice is everywhere 13–14
Richards, G. 155, 158, 215
Robersi, Sara 49–50
Robertson Smith, W. 68
Rockower, P. S. 198, 200, 201
Rogers, R. 153
Rowe, G. 39
Russia 203
Rwanda 203, 204

Sakarya, Umut 102
Samuelson, Marcus 192
Santich, B. 10–11, 72
Scarpato, R. 72
scent marketing 119–120
Scoville Heat Units (SHU) 55
seals 143
Search Engine Optimization (SEO) 113,
    115–116
seasonal events 29–30
seaweed 142
sensory experiences 37, 38, 119–120
serious leisure 100–101
Seubsman, S. A. et al. 12
sharing economy 68–70, 150–151;
    meal-sharing initiatives 153–154, 156,
    156–158; psychological motives 152;

social appeal 152–154; sustainability
    concerns 151–152; utilitarian motives 152
Sharples, L. 53, 183
Sheldon, P.J. 128, 129
Shepherd, Chris 192
Siemonsma, J.S. 53
Simkus, A. 190
Siriwan, S. 12
Slow Food International 60
Snapchat 116
Sobal, J. 68
social gastronomy 207
social interaction 37, 38, 152–154
social media 102–104, 108–109, 118, 200
Soulard, J. et al. 128
South Africa 212; Cape Province 219–220;
    Crayfish Agreement (1929) 218; Eat Out
    Guide 219–220; gastro-cultural heritage
    215–216, 217–218, 219, 223, 223–224;
    University of Pretoria 220; Vend Kale
    220, 220–222, 221; conclusion 222–224
South America 229
South Korea 199, 200, 201
soybeans 140–141, 142
Spain: Bodegas Ramòn Bilbao 85; ecological
    hotels in Catalonia 125–126, 129–134,
    131, 133
special events 29; festivals 30–32; seasonal
    events 29–30
spices 53–55
Spotify 116
Stone, M. J. et al. 183, 187
Stories 117
"storynomics tourism" 51
Suciu, A. 75–76
Sugar, R. 192
Sumunar, S. R. 57
Suri, Reno Andam 54
SurveyMonkey 118
sustainability issues at local level 38, 39,
    125–126; community collaboration
    126–127; hosts lead conscious changes
    127–128; methodology 129–130;
    regenerative tourism 125–127, 130,
    131–132; results 130–134, 131, 133;
    sharing economy 151–154; taste of place
    130; theoretical background 126–129;
    transformative food experiences
    128–129; discussion and conclusion
    134–135; food for thought questions 135;
    see also responsibility and sustainability
Sutomo, Popie 59
Sweden 200

248 *Index*

Taiwan 200, 201
taste of place 130
technology applications to food tourism experience 81, 83; pre-travel stage 83–84; during the travel 84–86; post-travel stage 86; transformations of technology 233–235
technology for a never-ending food tourism? 86, *87*; pre-travel: deciding to buy the experience 86, *87*, 88; during the travel: having a memorable experience *87*, 88; post-travel: recalling and sharing memories *87*, 88–89
Telegram 116
telling your story 25–27
terroir 9–10
Thailand 200; food tours 155; gastrodiplomacy 207; Global Thai Campaign 200–201; restaurants 199; rice, culture and tourism 7, 11–16
Thompson, D. 12
Thulin, Sten Gustaf 145–146
TikTok 112–113, 116
TIME magazine 59, 98
Timothy, D.J. 7, 8, 9
tofu 140–141, 142
Too Good To Go 116
Toto, Charles 58
tours 28, 155
transformative tourism 128
travelogue food shows 96
trendsetting 35–36
Tresserras, J. et al. 74
TripAdvisor 110, 111, 113
Tucci, Stanley 199
Tunisia 202–203
Turkey: Syrian refugees 206
Turner, Sylvester 192–193
Tushman, M. 8
Tussyadiah, I. 153
Twitter 99, 111–112, 117, 118
Typeform 118

Ugly Food Movement 37
Ukraine 203, 208
UNEP (United Nations Environment Programme) food waste index 145
UNESCO 143, 200; Convention on Intangible Cultural Heritage 202–203
United Nations: Humanitarian Aid 230; Sustainable Development 145, 208;

World Tourism Organization (UNWTO) 11, 149, 154, 168, 169
United States: *Castello di Amorosa* winery 84; COVID-19 229; University of Southern California 200; USC Center on Public Diplomacy 201; USDA Economic Research Service 229; *Visit Napa Valley* 84
Universal Studios 117

value 109
Van der Westhuizen, J. H. 220
Vertices Food Service 205–206
Virtual Reality 119
visitors and tours 28, 155
von Braun, J. et al 50
Vongvisitsin, T. 14

W50 list 96, 99
websites 113–114
WhatsApp 116
Wijaya, S. et al 49
wild yam 57
Willie, P. 234
wine enthusiasts 101
wine museums 85
wine tourism 71–74, 83–84
Wisansing, J. 14
Withlocals 154, 155
Wolf, E. 213
word of mouth (WOM) 235
World Association of Chefs' Societies 60
World Economic Forum 207, 230
World Food Program 230
World Food Travel Association (WFTA) 36, 49, 183, 207, 213, 228, 236; Psychoculinary® profiles **185**, 185–186
World Health Organization (WHO) 165, 168–169, 171
Wright, G. 39

Yahoo 108
Yeoman, I. 233
Yu, Justin 192

Zaiem, I. 70
Zgolli, S. 70
Zhang, J. 207
Zoho Survey 118
Zoom 84, 116

Printed in the United States
by Baker & Taylor Publisher Services